Contents at a Glance

Table of Contents

THE ULTIMATE PLAYER'S GUIDE TO MINECRAFT®

PLAYSTATION™ EDITION

Stephen O'Brien

800 East 96th Street,
Indianapolis, Indiana 46240 USA

The Ultimate Player's Guide to Minecraft: PlayStation Edition

Copyright © 2015 by Que Publishing

ISBN-13: 978-0-7897-5358-8
ISBN-10: 0-7897-5358-8

Library of Congress Control Number: 2014956781

First Printing January 2015

Trademarks

All terms mentioned in this book that are known to be trademarks or service marks have been appropriately capitalized. Que Publishing cannot attest to the accuracy of this information. Use of a term in this book should not be regarded as affecting the validity of any trademark or service mark.

Minecraft is a trademark of Mojang Synergies / Notch Development AB. PlayStation is a registered trademark of Sony Computer Entertainment.

This book is not affiliated with or sponsored by Mojang Synergies / Notch Development AB or Sony Computer Entertainment.

Warning and Disclaimer

Special Sales

For information about buying this title in bulk quantities, or for special sales opportunities (which may include electronic versions; custom cover designs; and content particular to your business, training goals, marketing focus, or branding interests), please contact our corporate sales department at corpsales@pearsoned.com or (800) 382-3419.

For government sales inquiries, please contact governmentsales@pearsoned.com.

For questions about sales outside the U.S., please contact international@pearsoned.com.

U.S. Corporate and Government Sales
1-800-382-3419
corpsales@pearsontechgroup.com

For sales outside of the U.S., please contact

International Sales
international@pearsoned.com

Editor-in-Chief
Greg Wiegand

Executive Editor
Rick Kughen

Development Editor
Rick Kughen

Technical Editor and Contributor
Alex Barry

Managing Editor
Sandra Schroeder

Project Editor
Seth Kerney

Copy Editor
Megan Wade-Taxter

Indexer
Tim Wright

Proofreader
The Word Smithery LLC

Publishing Coordinator
Kristen Watterson

Book Designer
Mark Shirar

Compositor
Bronkella Publishing

About the Author

Stephen O'Brien is an Australian-born writer and entrepreneur currently residing in Sydney after too many years in Silicon Valley. He has written more than 30 books across multiple editions with publishers such as Prentice Hall and Que, including several best-selling titles. He also founded Typefi, the world's leading automated publishing system, and in his spare time he invented a new type of espresso machine called mypressi. He has been using Minecraft since its early betas and remains astounded at the unparalleled creativity it engenders. Stephen is also the author of *The Advanced Minecraft Strategy Guide*, published by Que.

Dedication

To Mika, who with every new title turns first to the dedication page, and remains ever thrilled. Here's another my darling boy, and I hope many more to come.

Acknowledgments

Thank you to everyone at Que for working so hard to get this book out on time: Rick Kughen, as always, for not just moving mountains, but also ensuring no mole-hills grew to unconscionable size. Sandra Schroeder and Seth Kerney for ensuring the wheels were well greased. And Megan Wade-Taxter, for keeping the copy on track. You are all quite the formidable team.

Many thanks are also due to Alex Barry for a copious technical edit and extensive contributions.

Finally, to Minecrafters everywhere who have taken to the PlayStation edition of this amazing sandbox in quite astonishing numbers.

We Want to Hear from You!

As the reader of this book, *you* are our most important critic and commentator. We value your opinion and want to know what we're doing right, what we could do better, what areas you'd like to see us publish in, and any other words of wisdom you're willing to pass our way.

We welcome your comments. You can email or write to let us know what you did or didn't like about this book—as well as what we can do to make our books better.

Please note that we cannot help you with technical problems related to the topic of this book.

When you write, please be sure to include this book's title and author as well as your name and email address. We will carefully review your comments and share them with the author and editors who worked on the book.

Email: feedback@quepublishing.com

Mail: Que Publishing
         ATTN: Reader Feedback
         800 East 96th Street
         Indianapolis, IN 46240 USA

Reader Services

Visit our website and register this book at quepublishing.com/register for convenient access to any updates, downloads, or errata that might be available for this book.

Introduction

When Minecraft launched as a downloadable on the PlayStation, it broke all kinds of records. For very good reason.

Having already become gaming's largest indie success on the PC and Mac, there was something, to say the least, of a pent-up demand to see it on console.

We saw something similar with the release of *The Ultimate Player's Guide to Minecraft*. There are numerous subtle and not-so-subtle differences between the game in its Java form on PC and Mac and the edition released for the PlayStation, and many readers clamored for more specific guidance.

With that in mind, we completely overhauled the book from top to tail, producing the first PlayStation-specific Minecraft title, with in-depth tutorials and detailed information on every mob, crop, enchantment, and potion.

If you've played through the in-game tutorial, you'll have learned some of the game's basic mechanics, but this book goes far beyond. From survival tips and tricks to the best places to find key resources. From redstone to railways, combat and defense, automated farming, brewing potions, casting enchantments, and a lot more besides, you'll find yourself getting more out of Minecraft than you ever thought possible.

Use this book to guide you through your own generated world, or create one with the included seed to play alongside me as we find villages and natural resources, create a crop farm, travel far to the North to gather cocoa beans, build up our armory, then go to The Nether and back again, find a stronghold, enter The End region, and defeat its formidable boss: the Ender Dragon.

It's going to be quite a journey, and one that's perfect for all ages.

What's In This Book

Survive and thrive in Minecraft with 12 chapters of detailed step-by-step guides, tips, tricks, and strategies. Each chapter in this book focuses on a key aspect of the game, from initial survival to building an empire. Make the most of your Minecraft world today:

- Chapter 1, "Getting Started," walks you through the various new game settings and options including texture packs and multiplayer. You also learn how seeds control world generation, including the one used throughout this book, so you can learn Minecraft in the same environment.

- Chapter 2, "First-Night Survival," is an essential strategy guide to one of the most challenging times in Minecraft. You learn to craft essential tools, create torches, build your first mob-proof shelter, and reset your spawn point, all in less than 10 minutes of gameplay.

- Chapter 3, "Gathering Resources," teaches you everything you need to know about the heads-up display and how to fill out the skills you need to build a permanent base of operations, craft better tools, store resources, and find food to stave off hunger. I also show you how to use the built-in GPS so you can always find your way home, even after extended forays into the wilds, and I give you a complete guide to the Creative inventory.

- Chapter 4, "Mining," unlocks some of Minecraft's deepest secrets. I show you the best tunneling plan to uncover the most resources in the shortest possible time, the essential tools required, and the layers you should dig to uncover everything from basic iron ore to diamonds.

- Chapter 5, "Combat School," gets you ready to tackle any mob, including the creeper. From sword-fighting techniques to armor, this chapter has you covered. Slice and dice your way through Minecraft. You also learn essential perimeter protection strategies for your home and how to build snow and iron golems for additional defense.

- Chapter 6, "Crop Farming," helps you become completely self-sufficient, ensuring the hunger bar stays full, constantly boosting your health. Learn to hydrate 80 blocks of farmland with a single water block and automate your harvests at the touch of a button.

- Chapter 7, "Farming and Taming Mobs," is all about Minecraft's passive animals: the chickens, pigs, cows, and more that populate its world and provide you with instant BBQ. Learn to breed animals, tame ocelots to scare off creepers, and get a wolf pack on your side.

- Chapter 8, "Creative Construction," helps you unleash your inner architect. From grand constructions to inventive interiors, learn about the decorative ways you can use Minecraft's blocks and items to build the perfect abode. Then knock it all down and build something better!

- Chapter 9, "Redstone, Rails, and More," empowers your world with a host of automated devices. Control redstone power and automated doors; send minecarts on missions; and build stations, stopovers, and more. Soon you'll be able to zoom across the plains, careen through underground tunnels, and scare the heck out of guests on a knife-edged rollercoaster ride.

- Chapter 10, "Enchanting, Anvils, and Brewing," gets you brewing up a storm. Cast spells, improve your weapons and armor, and fall from great heights with grace. Believe me, you'll need this in The End region.

- Chapter 11, "Villages and Other Structures," gets you rampaging around the nonplaying characters and introduces you to dungeons, strongholds, and nether fortresses.
- Chapter 12, "Playing Through: The Nether and The End," is the strategy guide you'll need to get through these tricky sections of the game. Find a fortress fast, get what you need, and then prepare for the Ender Dragon. It's easy when you know how.

How to Use This Book

Throughout this book, you'll see that I have called out some items as Notes, Tips, and Cautions—all of which are explained here.

NOTE

Notes point out ancillary bits of information that are helpful but not crucial. They often make for an interesting meander.

TIP

Tips point out a useful bit of information to help you solve a problem. They're useful in a tight spot.

CAUTION

Cautions alert you to potential disasters and pitfalls. Don't ignore these!

Crafting Recipes

You'll also see that I've included crafting recipes throughout this book. I've included the actual ingredients in the text, so you can ensure you have what you need before making a trip to the crafting table.

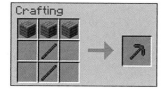

Getting Started

In This Chapter

- Select your gameplay style.
- Like your monsters plentiful and deadly, or do you prefer a more peaceful existence?
- Become a terraforming titan! Control your world generation with seeds and other options.
- Confused by the controls? See the complete list.
- Become a Minecraft maestro by hosting and controlling multiplayer games.

Minecraft is an amazing place. Far more than just a game, it's a world filled with pixelated possibility: an incredible 3D grid of blocks, resources, creatures, monsters, and pitfalls. It features multiple gameplay styles including the safe, free-soaring Creative mode; the challenging Survival mode with four levels of difficulty; and two multiplayer modes available either via local split-screen for up to four players or with a party of as many as eight friends on the PlayStation Network (PSN). As always, all players will need a subscription to PSN to join a multiplayer session online, but this isn't required for split-screen play.

The PlayStation Network Store and retail disc versions are identical, including their price point. Updates via PSN also come free of charge, and these go far beyond the usual bug fixes seen in most other game titles, adding new features several times per year. This is good news: while Minecraft: PS3 and PS4 Editions do lag behind the latest developments on Minecraft for PCs, you can expect to see continuous improvements that bring with them new creatures, blocks, tools, and other types of functionality, completely free of charge.

Speaking of the PS4 Edition, if you've upgraded your console from a PS3 to a PS4, you'll see a few—but not too many—changes. I'll take you through them:

1 World size has seen a significant increase. In fact, worlds have expanded a whopping 33 times to 5,000 blocks per side, as compared to 864 per side on the 360. This is great news as it allows worlds to generate in ways that are far more varied. They also provide plenty of room for up to eight online players to pillage their way across and under the landscape and not run out of resources.

2 View distance has increased by a factor of two. You'll appreciate this as you traverse the landscape. Increasing the distance by two times might not seem like a lot, but it makes a huge difference in gameplay.

3 You can take your worlds with you, transferring them from the PS3 to the PS4. There's a new option in the Play Game screen for the PS3 called **Upload Save for PS4**. Select your world and hit ▲ to start the upload. Once complete, go into the Play Game screen on the PS4 and press ✕ to commence downloading and converting the new world. Unfortunately, you can only do this one world at a time, and the world will stay the same size as it was on the PS3, but it's certainly a nice feature to have.

4 When starting a game on the PS4, hit **More Options** and you'll see a very useful addition: Disable Autosave. This is the perfect way to avoid permanent damage if you are hosting an online game and your friends, or the friends of your friends, turn out to be griefers and destroy your hard work.

With that out of the way, let's start a new world and play.

In this chapter, you'll learn about the different gameplay modes and how to customize your game settings, determine the way the world generates, and how to control your Minecraft character.

TIP

Trying the Trial

If you haven't yet purchased Minecraft, download the trial via PSN. You'll be able to play for 100 minutes within the included tutorial world.

Starting a New Game

You're going to have a lot of fun with Minecraft, but before you jump right into punching wood, take a brief read through the rest of this chapter so you can set up your game the right way to play through the rest of this book. I'll also tell you about a game seed that creates a very awesome world we can share as you learn more about the game.

On starting Minecraft you'll see the title screen shown in Figure 1.1. Select **Play Game** and choose the storage device on which you'd like to save your Minecraft world. You'll then see the Start Game screen shown in Figure 1.2.

TIP

Moving Worlds

Select a flash drive (also known as a USB stick or thumb drive) as your storage device, and you'll be able to take your world with you so you can also play it on other PlayStation consoles. Press ✛ at the Start Game screen to change storage devices and to load worlds saved on other drives or sticks. You can also use your console's storage management to copy Minecraft worlds between different storage devices, so you can always play on the built in storage, then copy that world to a flash drive to use elsewhere, or to make a backup.

To copy the save on to your flash drive:

1 Press △ on one of the saves located in **Saved Data Utility**.

2 Select **Copy**.

3 Select **USB Device** for your flash drive.

To transfer the saved world out of the flash drive:

1 Navigate to your USB Device located in **Saved Data Utility**.

2 Press △.

3 Select **Copy** to move the game to the new console.

Alternatively, if you are a PlayStation Plus member (additional cost involved), you can save the game to your online storage located under **Game** and via **Saved Data Utility** and **Online Storage**. Once saved online, you can log in from a different PlayStation and transfer the save back into the local storage.

You can also rename any saved games, but only through Minecraft's Play Game screen. Once there, press **R1** to view the Save Options screen where you can rename and delete previous saved games.

FIGURE 1.1   Welcome to Minecraft!

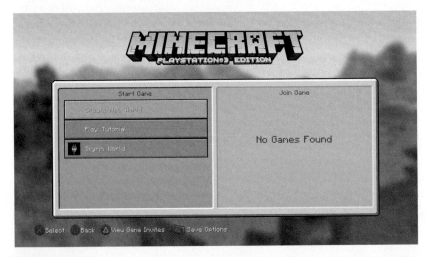

FIGURE 1.2   The Start Game screen shows all your current worlds as well as the Tutorial and any downloaded mash-up packs such as the Skyrim World shown here.

The Tutorial is a neat way to learn the basic game mechanics (see Figure 1.3). Time is frozen while you're in the first part of the Tutorial, saving you from the sudden onset of night, so it's a good place to practice and build up your mastery of the essential controls. It is, however, just an introduction, and I'll walk you through everything covered by the Tutorial and a whole lot more throughout the rest of this book. If you're feeling fearless, feel free to skip the tutorial; you can always go back and launch it at any time if you want to get more used to the controls away from the usual risk posed by Minecraft's many creepy critters.

FIGURE 1.3   The built-in Tutorial walks you through Minecraft's essential elements and has a lot of interesting places to explore, including a hidden path over a lava lake, a ship, a castle, a minecart system, and more, but feel free to skip it if you'd prefer the challenge of learning the basics out in the woolly wilds of a new world.

CAUTION

Worlds are Linked to Profiles

World's created under one profile are not directly accessible under another. The only way to get to them is via multiplayer.

When you're ready, click **Create New World**. This screen starts out with some basic defaults, but we'll change it to the one shown in Figure 1.4. You could leave them all as they are and just click the new **Create New World** button that appears at the bottom of this window to start a random new world, but let's take a quick look at some of the options and set up a custom world. Use ✤ to move up and down the window:

■ **World Name**—Press ⊗ and type in any name you like. You can leave it as New World and create any number of saved worlds with the same default name, but this can become a little confusing over time. (Which world is which?) I've called this one *Elysium*, but the actual name doesn't have any effect on the world generation. The next option does!

■ **Seed for the World Generator**—The seed controls almost every aspect of the world's generation—its terrain, structures, and dungeons; the locations of diamonds and other minable objects, trees, animals; and so on. (See the section "Understanding World Seeds", later in this chapter, if you want to know more.) In this case, press 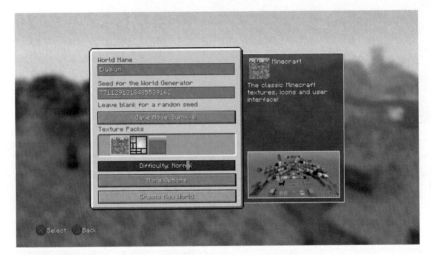 and type in the number **7711291318485539162**. That's a long number, I know...it was generated by a random world, but it is the world I'll be using almost exclusively throughout this book, so if you type it in and check it twice, you'll find yourself in the exact same world. And you'll appear right next to a village, which is kind of nice.

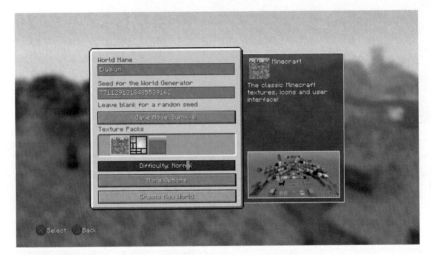

FIGURE 1.4   Setting up a custom world.

NOTE

Changing Generations

From time to time, the actual program code underlying the world generation goes through an update, and this can change the world that results from any particular seed. The seed provided above was generated under Minecraft: PS3 edition and is confirmed to work at least through to TU18 (otherwise known as Title Update 18). I can't promise it will generate the same world as Minecraft moves through future title updates, but changes to world generation tend to be quite rare. The seed doesn't deliver the same results on the PS4 edition, but if you have a PS3, you can use it to generate the world, then transfer it to the PS4 so that you can play in the same arena in which this book was written. (Sometimes I give hints for resource locations, but otherwise, playing in the same world as used in this book isn't absolutely necessary.)

■ **Game Mode**—Click the **Game Mode** selector to choose between Survival and Creative modes. (See "Single-player Game Modes" later in the chapter for more information.)

For now, leave it on **Survival**. You can switch game modes whenever you load a saved game, so even though the initial mode is Survival, you can always jump into the fun-flying action of Creative later.

■ **Texture Packs**—Use texture packs to change the look of all the blocks and items in your world. They're optional paid content, costing a few dollars each, but you can use the free trial versions to see how they look with the limitation that you won't be able to save your game without unlocking the full pack. So, for now, leave the first one selected.

■ **Difficulty**—The four difficulty levels are explained more fully in the section "Single-player Game Modes" later in this chapter. Leave **Normal** selected for the full Minecraft experience. It's the one I'll also use in almost all the examples throughout this book. Keep in mind that you can also change difficulty levels at any time just by saving your game and reloading it, so if the going gets tough, switching to **Peaceful** or **Easy** might not be a bad option. You'll still be able to play on **Survival** mode, just without worrying as much about hostile mobs.

When you're ready, click **Create New World** and turn to Chapter 2, "First-Night Survival." You can also read on to learn more about the other settings.

NOTE

How Big Is Your World?

Each block in Minecraft measures 1m per side, or one cubic meter. Each world in the PS3 edition measures 864 × 864 blocks on the surface, or a total of 746,496 square meters. On the PS4, there are 5,000 x 5,000 blocks, although when creating a new world, you can choose one of four sizes, from the classic 864 blocks up to the current 5,000 maximum. Although these worlds are much smaller than those created on the PC edition (they're a huge, never-ending 64,000 kilometers long by 64,000 kilometers wide), it'll still take you quite a while to explore the entire aboveground world, not to mention everything below ground, as well as the dimensions of The Nether and The End. By the way, to see someone traversing a world created in the PC edition, see *Far Lands or Bust* at http://farlandsorbust.com. You can track Kurt and Wolfie's daily journey to the fabled Far Lands. Kurt is journeying to raise money for a children's charity and has been trekking since March 2011. He and his canine companion probably have quite a few more years to go.

More Options

A host of different settings are available, all under the **More Options** button. Note that these options are found on the second tab in the **More Options** window on the PS4.

■ **Online Game**—Allow this world to appear in your friends' list of games so that they can join. (See "Hosting and Controlling Multiplayer Games" later in this chapter for more information.) By the way, this option is only selectable if your PlayStation profile is associated with a PSN subscription. Also, any games played with this option selected will continue to run with the in-game menu open, leaving you vulnerable even if you are the only one playing at the time. Deselect this when in single-player mode so that opening the in-game menu (via the ▶ button) actually pauses the game, allowing you to take a break when needed.

- **Invite Only**—Show the world to your friends only if you've sent them an invitation. Send invitations by entering the world and pressing ▬. Press ◉ to send an invitation and then ⊗ to select from **Friends**. A list will come up of your online friends; press ⊗ to send the invite. Alternatively, you can select **Enter an Online ID** to send a personal message and invite to a new friend. If you're feeling extra sociable, you can choose **Select from Chat Rooms**, which allows you to choose all players in a chat room as recipients by selecting a chat room that you have previously joined on PSN.

- **Allow friends of friends**—Select this option to allow friends of any friend of yours to also join the world, after your direct friend has joined.

- **Players vs. Player**—In Survival mode this option allows players to attack other players. If you're playing cooperatively, turn this off so when you and your friends are battling monsters at close quarters, you don't accidentally also hit each other.

- **Trust Players**—Disable this option to prevent certain actions being performed until those players have been authorized. Press ▬ while in game to select the player from the list of current players, then ⊗ to view their authorized actions. You can then allow him to do any or all of the following: build and mine, use doors and switches, open containers (such as chests), attack players, attack animals, become a moderator and, once that is selected, assign the ability to teleport and also become invisible (see Figure 1.5).

- **Fire Spreads**—Want to stop fire from completely destroying your perfect wood cabin? Disable this option to prevent it from spreading. This, along with the next option, is a good way to prevent *griefing*, also known as players destroying other people's creations faster than a posse of creepers.

- **TNT Explodes**—Disable to prevent TNT blocks from causing wanton damage and destruction.

- **Host Privileges**—Turn on a range of special abilities including gaining the ability to fly, not suffer exhaustion (running out of hunger points), become invisible to other players, and teleportation, as well assigning those same abilities to other players. Note, however, that any world where Host Privileges have been enabled even just once will have Achievements and Leaderboard updates permanently disabled.

- **Reset Nether**—Select this to generate a new Nether region. This may be useful if you are playing a game from an older world (created with an earlier version of Minecraft where the world generation method may have been different), and can't find the Nether Fortress. It will also wipe out any changes you've made to the Nether region, returning it to a pristine state. Use this option extremely carefully as it doesn't actually change the layout of the Nether region if the world generation algorithm hasn't changed; the Nether generated for any particular seed in the same version of Minecraft will always stay the same.

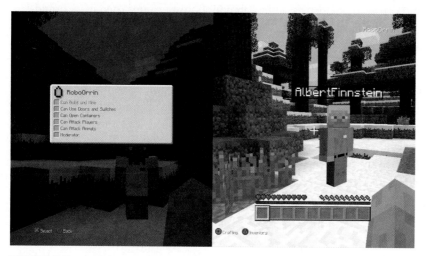

FIGURE 1.5   Disabling Trust Players lets you selectively enable the actions of other players in split-screen or online multiplayer.

There are three more options related directly to the way the world generates. Leave **Generate Structures** turned on so you see villages, dungeons, and other good stuff, and turn off the other two. A **Superflat World** is one that is flat as a pancake with the exception of any generated structures. This type of world is handy for testing things such as redstone circuits and transport systems in creative mode. The **Bonus Chest** creates a chest near your starting location, your *spawn point*, containing a random selection of items. Let's go a little hardcore, though, and leave that turned off. It's easy enough to create everything you need as you go.

Single-Player Game Modes

Minecraft on the PS3 provides two gameplay modes:

- **Survival**—This is the default mode for all new games and is the one I'll mostly focus on throughout the book. Survival mode is made up of two phases: day and night. During the day, you have a 10-minute window to gather resources, mine, build, farm—do whatever you need to do. During the first few days, this is usually made up of a few key activities, but after you've established your base, be it underground, in a walled fortress, in a building, or even in a tree house, you can rest a little easier. If you spawn near sheep, you can also kill a few to quickly build a bed, even out in the open, and blissfully slumber the night away as long as no hostile mobs are present. I'll show you how in Chapter 2. Daylight is followed by 1½ minutes of dusk—time to get back to your base. The nighttime phase lasts 7 minutes and is a time you definitely don't want to be outside protected by nothing but your stumpy fists. They might be able to beat chunks out of trees, but they won't help you in a deadly scrap. Sunrise and dawn last another 1½ minutes and cause some hostiles, although not all, to burn up. Then it's a brand-new day. Death in this mode is only temporary. You'll respawn within 20 blocks of your original spawn point and live to fight another day.

- **Creative**—I love Creative mode. This is where Minecraft really shines after you get through the core challenge of Survival mode. Think of it as flying, not dying. At least, that's the way my 9-year-old describes it. Just press ⊗ twice to jump and enter free-flight. (Sometimes it does require several presses in quick succession.) Hold ⊗ again to gain more height, or tap it twice to quickly descend to ground level. Once you are flying, push 🄻 forward twice, as if to enter sprint mode, and you'll move into a type of very fast flight where you can quickly soar around in any direction the crosshairs are pointed. It's a neat way to quickly explore a world. Creative mode is also a great way to build absolutely enormous structures, intricate redstone circuits, and fantastic rail systems.

CAUTION

Switching From Survival to Creative Mode

One caution: if you do switch a Survival mode game to Creative, you'll lose the opportunity to book Achievements and advance on the game's Leaderboard—at least within that world.

Survival mode offers four levels of difficulty, and you can switch between them any time you load a saved game:

- **Peaceful**—All hostile mobs disappear instantly and permanently until the difficulty setting is switched to any of the other three mentioned next. Your hunger bar also remains at maximum, or the level it was when you switched to peaceful. You can still die, and therefore respawn, so you should be wary of long falls, lava pits, and other threats. However, it is, eponymously, a peaceful existence.

- **Easy**—You see hostiles, but they deliver less damage than normal. Your hunger bar does deplete, but it still leaves you with 10 health points at a minimum, or 5 hearts in the HUD. Some other mob effects, such as poison, are minimized.

- **Normal**—As the name suggests, this is the default mode. Hostile mobs deliver normal damage (which, when without armor, can quickly kill you), and running out of food reduces your health to just half a point, making you particularly vulnerable.

- **Hard**—Hostile mobs cause more damage, and running out of food kills you...eventually.

NOTE

Mobs, Spawning, and Respawning

In Minecraft, any other creature besides your player and villagers (known as NPCs, or non-player characters) is called a *mob*. The term originated from "mobile entity." You'll meet three kinds of mobs in future chapters: peaceful, neutral, and hostile. The sudden appearance of any entity in the game world is called a *spawn*. Your own character will probably also die at some point. It's practically unavoidable. In any difficulty level except hardcore you'll "respawn" shortly after death. There is no limit to the number of times you can do so.

Hosting and Controlling Multiplayer Games

Minecraft takes on a new dimension when you play with friends. Tasks that can feel a little repetitive such as digging out a new mine, and searching for those elusive diamonds, become a lot faster and a lot more fun when you're playing with friends. Even a trek across the Overworld, battling enemies together, becomes that much more interesting. There will be laughs a plenty, guaranteed.

It lends itself rather nicely to cooperative play, but that's not to say that you can't also play a competitive, or PvP (player versus player) game. With up to 4 players on split-screen, or up to 8 online, there's something to be said for everyone spawning into the same, new world and then battling it out for resources. And you can make your own rules and conditions for winning. Ban griefing (destroying each other's structures), but allow player battles and your spoils will be the loot dropped by the defeated. Become the first to collect 24 diamonds, or make it a race to the end portal, it doesn't really matter what—just set a goal and go for it!

Minecraft's multiplayer mode operates via split-screen play, online, or both.

With PSN you can also use the standard PlayStation multiplayer management system to create a party of players, or invite individual friends.

Let's take a look at how it all works.

First, if you plan to use start a multiplayer game, ensure you select **Online Game** in the **Options** settings when starting or loading a world. For splitscreen play, just press the ▶ button on a second, third, or fourth controller. Games launched with this setting open show the connect controller screen shown in Figure 1.6. Games launched without this setting open straight into Minecraft, however you can connect new controllers for split-screen play at any time as long as all the players who log in also have PSN accounts. Keep in mind that online games keep running even when you've paused your own version. Mobs can still get to you.

Want players to connect split-screen even if not all have PSN accounts? Just start or open a game without **Online Game** selected and any controller can connect at any time just by pressing any button and then ▶.

FIGURE 1.6 Start with *Online Game* selected and you'll see the standard connect controller screen.

Once loaded, access the multiplayer menu from within a game world by pressing ▬. You'll see the window shown in Figure 1.7.

TIP

Helping Your Screen Do The Splits

Switch the split-screen orientation for two players in local multi-player between horizontal and vertical by pressing ▶ to open the in-game menu. Then select **Help & Options**, **Settings**, **User Interface**. You'll see the option to switch the orientation, as well as a slider that adjusts the size of the split-screen HUD.

If you are playing an online game, you can press ⬛, then ⬤ to invite online friends. From here you can add friends, view your online friends, and create a gaming party.

FIGURE 1.7   Use the controller's ⬛ button to open the multiplayer menu.

There are two parts to the multiplayer menu.

Click **Host Options** to open the window shown in Figure 1.8.

There are two option settings:

- **Fire Spreads**—Deselect to prevent fire spreading from one block to another—a useful way to stop your magnificent wooden country mansion going up in smoke.

- **TNT Explodes**—Deselect to prevent TNT from exploding. This can also help destroy other structures and cause other general mayhem with a few strategically placed TNT blocks.

If you did start the world with **Host Privileges** enabled you'll also see two buttons:

- **Teleport To Player**—Click to open a list of all currently connected players, besides yourself. Select another player, and press ⊗ to jump instantly to their location. You'll appear on their exact location and will actually see the inside of their head—don't worry, all Minecraft skins are empty-headed, not a brain in sight, which must disappoint the zombies—until one of you moves.

- **Teleport To Player**—Likewise, click this button to open the same list and select any other player to make them immediately jump to your location.

FIGURE 1.8 Use the Host Options window to change the way fire and TNT behave, and also to magically teleport players around.

Use the lower part of the multiplayer menu shown in Figure 1.7 to invite friends if playing an online game. Just press ⬛ to open the players/ invite window.

If you have also turned on Host Priviliges, select any player in the list, other than yourself, and press ⊗ to open the special abilities window shown in Figure 1.9.

There are quite a few options, so let's take a quick look at them all:

- **Moderator**—Assign another player the ability to also give capabilities to players besides the host. You must select this option before you can choose any of the remaining below.

- **Can Teleport**—Adds the teleport options described above.

- **Can Fly**—Let them take off into the wide blue yonder, even on Survival.

- **Can Disable Exhaustion**—Play on multiplayer Survival without worrying about hunger.

- **Can Become Invisible**—I call this the Herobrine option. Become invisible to all other players, although you can still teleport players to you, or jump to their own. Donning the cloak of invisibility does not prevent other mobs from knowing you are there, or from them coming after you. Even Endermen will react if you glance their way.

By the way, if you are playing on Creative, you'll only see options for **Moderator**, **Teleport**, and **Invisibility** as the ability to fly and not suffer hunger pangs is already baked in.

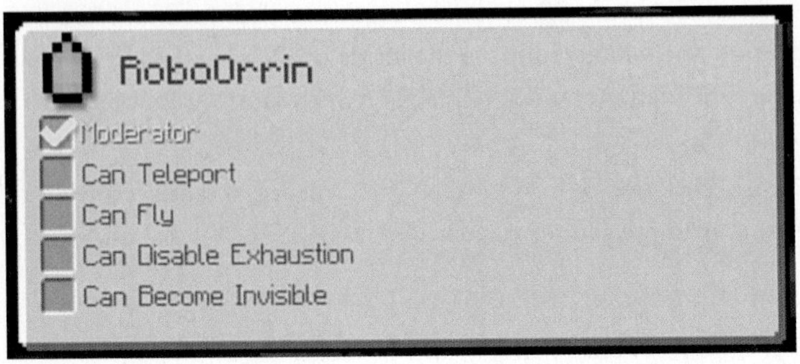

RoboOrrin

☑ Moderator
☐ Can Teleport
☐ Can Fly
☐ Can Disable Exhaustion
☐ Can Become Invisible

FIGURE 1.9 Want to gain and give special powers? They're all here.

Select yourself in the menu, either as a host, or as a player who has been granted moderator status, to toggle the actual powers available. Obviously there are three in all as the teleport option comes via the **Host Options** menu but any not assigned to you are disabled:

- **Can Fly**—Select to turn on your own flying capability.
- **Disable Exhaustion**—Become immune to hunger.
- **Invisible**—Turn on your own invisibility.

Minecraft's multiplayer options provide a wide range of variations on the standard game. Explore them when you can. They add new dimensions to the game and, while not as comprehensive as the PC edition's multiplayer server options, are very much worthwhile.

Understanding World Seeds

Minecraft worlds are randomly generated using an algorithm that takes a number, or *seed*, as its starting point. This seed comes from the clock that keeps track of the date and time in your console. As time marches on the clock provides the seed for trillions of worlds, each one unique. However, you can also override this and provide your own seed as I also did earlier. Each world created with that seed will be identical in terrain, including the location of mining resources, and will generally have the same mob spawn locations. You can use just about anything for the seed, including a random set of numbers or letters, such as a phrase ("Minecraft rocks!") or even your birth date. Actually, something quite fun to do is to create a Minecraft world seeded with your own real name or your profile name on the PS3. It is, essentially, a world created just for you. Try it and explore your new domain.

TIP

Sharing Seeds

Share the seed you used with a friend, and your friend can play in Single-player mode in a similar world to your own. Some worlds happen to be more interesting than others, so this makes for an easy way to share the better ones. If you don't know it already, you can discover any seed by saving and then reopening the game. Text seeds are converted to numerals and they all appear in the window shown when you open an existing world. Some websites also provide lists of seeds that create unusual worlds. Keep in mind that the world generation algorithm changes now and then, which in turn changes the world that results from any particular seed.

Controls

You don't need to memorize too many button and trigger combinations to start playing Minecraft. Table 1.1 lists the full set available. You can reassign all the controls through the Options window (accessed by pressing ▶ while in game or from the main title screen), using any of three layouts, but I recommend leaving them as they are for now to avoid confusion. Figure 1.10 shows the standard layout.

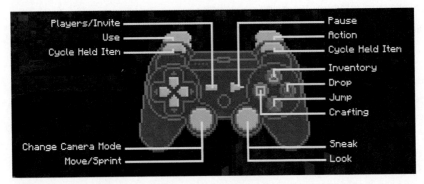

FIGURE 1.10 Minecraft's controls. Up to three layouts are available, along with options for look inversion and a left/right flip for southpaws.

TABLE 1.1 Minecraft's Default Controls

Control	Action
L2	Use items, place items and blocks, and hold to block attacks.
R2	Mine and attack. In Creative mode, destroy blocks.
L1 R1	Cycle the held item by changing the active Hotbar slot.
⬅L➡	Move, or push forward twice, quickly, to sprint.
⬇L⬆	Click to change the camera mode between first-person and forward and backward-facing external views.
⬅R➡	Look around: that is, change your viewing direction.
⬇R⬆	Click to enter Sneak mode (click again to exit), and when flying, click and hold to drop down fast.
▶	Go to the pause menu.
▬	Invite other players to join your game.
✕	Jump, or in Creative mode, double-tap and hold to start flying.
◉	Drop the held item.
▢	Open the crafting interface, or the Creative mode inventory.
△	Open your character's inventory.

The Bottom Line

It's difficult to decide whether to call Minecraft a game or a creative sandbox. It straddles both in a way that has rarely been achieved before. Best of all, it also gets continually updated, so there'll always be additional surprises in store. You can always expect something new, whether you play on your own or with friends, online buddies, frenemies or what have you on multiplayer.

Minecraft world seeds also provide some useful opportunities. Not happy with how your gaming is working out? Copy your old one from its launch window and create a new world using the same seed to generate the same terrain and spawn at or close to the same point. There will be some differences, but not too many.

Finally, don't feel daunted by the control list. It will all fall quite naturally to hand after a remarkably short while, and there are always prompts onscreen to help you get by.

First-Night Survival

In This Chapter

- Welcome to your new world.
- Harvest your first resources and start crafting essential tools.
- Head for the hills and build a fast shelter in style.
- Cut your clicks with Inventory shortcuts.
- Bring some light into the night.
- Skip the night in seconds.

When you start a Minecraft world, your in-game character arrives with nothing but the shirt on his back, some dodgy-looking pants, and fists of fury. You've got work to do! There are many ways to end up suddenly demised in Minecraft, and you're bound to discover quite a few of them in time. But it's actually quite easy to survive your first night and get enough done to set you up for a great next day. There's no need to become spider bait, zombie fodder, or a handy target for skeleton archery practice when darkness falls and the mobs come out to play.

This chapter shows you how to pull through that first night and come out in better shape than ever.

Surviving and Thriving

Your first day in Minecraft is an important one because you need to accomplish a few things quickly to prepare for the dangerous night ahead. As soon as you spawn into a new Minecraft world, take a quick look around. Just move 🎮. Your first targets are trees for their wood because they provide the starting point you need for crafting tools and, frankly, it's difficult to get anywhere without them.

NOTE

Welcome to The Overworld

The Minecraft world is comprised of three dimensions. You arrive in The Overworld, the largest dimension. Over time, you'll make your way through a portal into The Nether, Minecraft's very Dante-esque "hellish" dimension, and then finally into The End, a small dimension where you'll fight the Enderdragon. However, most of your time will be spent in The Overworld. Chapter 12, "Playing Through: The Nether and The End," will help you move back and forth between all three, but don't worry too much about that for now. There's a lot to do between now and then.

Your second main task is to scout for a handy cliff or mound into which you can dig your first shelter or, failing that, a little bit of level ground so you can build the Minecraft equivalent of a shepherd's hut, even if it's just made from some dirt blocks.

Here, then, is a brief list of your first-day tasks:

- Find a few trees and punch their trunks to obtain wood.
- Turn the wood into planks and build a crafting bench.
- Turn some of those planks into sticks.
- Craft a wooden axe out of planks and sticks to speed up the collection of more wood.
- Craft a wooden pick to dig up stone, turning it into the cobblestone required to build a furnace.
- Craft a wooden sword, just in case.
- Dig out a basic shelter.
- Build a wooden door for your shelter, but you can also just block it off with some of the materials you've dug up if you run out of time.
- Build a furnace and smelt some wood to make charcoal.
- Use the charcoal and sticks to create torches.
- Optionally, find three sheep so you can build a bed.

That's quite a list, but it won't take you long. Think of it as survival of the quickest.

TIP

Pause for Thought

Minecraft days are short, so feel free to press your controller's ▶ button any time you need to pause the game. Just keep in mind that online games never actually pause.

Heading for the Trees

Start by heading toward the trees. You'll need a few, so look for a group. Use your  to set your direction and the to move. Most biomes contain trees, so they shouldn't be too far away, and if you spawned into a jungle, forest, or taiga biome, trees are all around you. Figure 2.1 shows a spawn point by a village. In the interests of making the most of what you're given, I'll use the world created with the seed in Chapter 1, "Getting Started," for the remainder of the book. If you prefer to start your own world, there is a chance you might not be so lucky. Some biomes such as the desert simply don't have trees. If you don't see any wood nearby, head straight for the nearest hill and jump to the top to get a good view. Press to jump up each block while you move forward. If you spot any trees in the distance, make haste—the countdown to nighttime has already begun!

FIGURE 2.1   The initial view of Elysium, created by the seed from Chapter 1.

When you reach those woody perennials, start swinging by holding down **R2**. That fleshy appendage you can see to the right of the HUD is your arm. Hold the trigger down while pointing the crosshairs at the trunk to chip away at the tree, as shown in Figure 2.2. It slowly develops a spidering of cracks as you wear it down, and it will take only a few seconds to punch out the first block of wood. You'll see a smaller representation of the block fall toward the ground and float, bobbing gently up and down. Congratulations on your first harvested resource. Well done!

If you are close enough, the block is scooped up into your inventory automatically. If not, just move closer until it jumps in. Now take out the rest of the blocks, or as many as you can reach, and do the same to another two or three trees. You'll need about 15 blocks to get off to a good start. Don't worry about that mass of foliage remaining behind. It fades away, although if you do hack away at some of it, you have a good chance of getting a few saplings that you can replant in the interests of sustainability. You might also score an apple or two that you should save for later.

Lumberjacking Tips

There's an easy way to get most of the blocks from the trunk. Start by taking out the two blocks just above the one that is on the ground. Then jump onto that block and look straight up. Finish punching blocks out of the rest of the trunk above you. They'll fall on you and go straight into your inventory. When you've gone as high as you can go, look straight down and take out the block on which you are standing. You can take out most tree trunks this way. If for some reason you can't jump onto the block after you remove the two above it, you might need to clear out some foliage directly above you.

FIGURE 2.2 Punching out wood takes a little patience, but you'll build some tools shortly that speed that up quite significantly.

Now you've harvested your first resources, it's time to get familiar with your inventory and crafting.

Using Your Inventory

The inventory screen is central to your management of resources as you start collecting and crafting various materials and items.

You've already seen part of it: those nine slots showing at the bottom of the screen are known as the Hotbar. They'll show items you've already collected, such as the wood blocks from the trees, and perhaps a sapling or two. However, this is only one-quarter of your total inventory.

Press ⓐ to open the inventory screen. You'll see the window shown in Figure 2.3 with at least the blocks of wood showing.

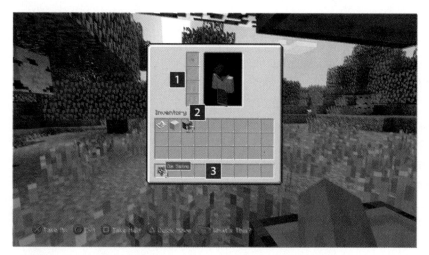

FIGURE 2.3 The inventory screen has three sections.

1. Armor

2. Inventory

3. Hotbar

Let's take a closer look:

- **Armor slots**—These four slots allow you to don armor. From the top down, they represent your helmet, chestplate, leggings, and boots, and each can be made from five materials. Initially, you'll probably start with materials made from leather or iron because they are relatively easy to obtain. I'll show you how to craft them in Chapter 5, "Combat School." When you have armor, you can just select it in the inventory and press ⓐ to automatically place it into the correct slot.

- **Inventory slots**—These slots represent your full inventory. The top three rows provide storage space for items you don't immediately need but want to carry with you. This might include items you've picked up on your travels and intend to carry back to your shelter for longer-term storage or to use for construction and further crafting. Typically, you should store weapons and tools, some food to quickly rebuild your health, and other vital items as you see fit in the Hotbar slots. Keep the rest upstairs.

- **Hotbar area**—The bottom row provides quick access to items, changing the one you are currently holding. Use 🄻🄳 and 🅁🄳 to move between slots. You can use any selected item in this row with 🄻🄳 as the action key or discard it with a quick press of ⊙.

Minecraft has some neat tricks up its blocky sleeve that make it easier to move items between the slots in your inventory. Here's what you really need to know:

- **Pick up items—** △ to pick up a full stack of items or ▣ to take just half. Use ⊕ to shift the pointer around.

- **Place items—**Press ✕ to place all items or ▣ to place just one. If the slot is occupied, the items are swapped so that you end up holding the item or stack of items that was there initially.

- **Move items between the main storage and the quick access grids—**Press △ to move an item between the inventory area and the Hotbar. Items of the same type are automatically stacked in the target grid until they reach their stack limit.

- **Learn about items—**Press R2 to pull up some helpful information on any selected item.

Now that you are familiar with the inventory, let's get on to crafting.

Building a Crafting Table

 Crafting allows you to build tools and other items. There are two stages, with the first providing a range of simple crafting recipes based on a 2×2 grid. The fun really starts when you build a crafting table because its 3×3 grid provides the space to create more complex items. However, you can't build a crafting table without first using the basic crafting grid. Follow these steps to knock together your own crafting table:

1 Open the crafting interface by pressing ▣. Use R1 and L1 to shift through the tabs at the top of the window, and use ⊕ to move from one recipe to the next. Some recipes are collected under the one entry. In that case, push ⊕ up and down to scroll through them. You'll be able to activate only recipes for which you have all the necessary ingredients.

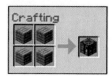

2 Remember those wood blocks you punched out of the tree? You need to turn those blocks into planks. Scroll through the recipes listed under the leftmost tab until you find an available plank recipe, as shown in Figure 2.4. Then press ⊗ to create a stack of planks. Do this four times so you build 16 planks.

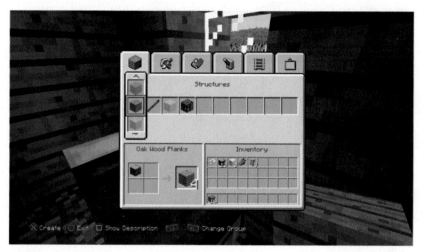

FIGURE 2.4 Crafting may seem complicated, but it has a beautiful simplicity on the console editions compared to the PC.

3 Now use ⊕ to move across to the crafting table, and press ⊗ to create your first table.

4 Finally, ensure the crafting table is located in one of the Hotbar slots so you can place it.

CAUTION

Mobs Can Strike Even with Inventory Open

Don't walk away with your inventory or crafting screen open, thinking you've paused the game. Time still passes, night still falls, and you're still just as vulnerable to hostile mobs. You can easily come back to find that your character has keeled over after an attack right there in the window. Remember to use ▶ to properly pause the game if you need to duck away for a while.

Okay, now the fun really begins. Let's place the crafting table and build some tools!

Use **L1** and **R1** to scroll through the Hotbar slots until you have the crafting table selected. Now look for a clear space to put the table, point your crosshairs down, and pull **L2** to place it on the ground.

Let's Build Some Tools

Our initial crafting list requires an axe, a pickaxe, and a sword. Building tools takes no time at all and will give your fists a bit of a break from punching.

Point your crosshairs at the table and use **L2** to open the crafting window. You'll notice many more possible recipes because the 3×3 grid provides more room to place crafting ingredients. We're going to use all of it!

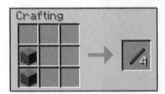

First, craft some sticks to form the handles for your tools. Create four in all.

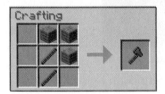

Now craft an axe using two sticks and three wooden plank blocks. This will make it faster for you to collect more wood. Finally, create your first pickaxe, a sword, and a shovel.

That's all there is to it. Easy, right? There are hundreds of crafting recipes in Minecraft, but fortunately unlike the Minecraft edition for PCs, you don't need to worry about remembering the recipes when playing on PS3.

You can use the shovel to quickly dig through softer blocks such as dirt, sand, and gravel, although your bare hands are also quite effective for this. The pickaxe is useful for harder blocks such as the ever-prevalent stone. Create more sticks and planks if you need to, but don't go overboard. Just make what you need. The inventory looks like it has plenty of space right now, but it fills fast, and while you can stack most items in piles of 64 in each inventory slot, it's more efficient to store wood in its most efficient form. You see, if 1 wooden block can create 4 planks of wood, then converting 64 wooden blocks to planks creates 256 planks, and they completely fill another 4 slots. Converting all those blocks to sticks fills 8 slots! So just craft what you need when you need it.

When you've finished, your inventory should look something like the one shown in Figure 2.5. One last thing: you'll see any missing ingredients highlighted in red. For example, the pickaxe shown in Figure 2.5 is missing one of the sticks required for the handle.

FIGURE 2.5 Your first set of tools, but they definitely won't be your last.

You're done for now, so switch to an empty slot in the Hotbar and break down the crafting table with your fists. Walk over to it to scoop it up into your inventory so you can use it again.

Creating a Shelter

Now that you have some basic tools, it's time to prepare for the night. By far the quickest way to do this is to dig a little hideout into the side of a hill. Don't just duck into a cave because you might get a nasty surprise.

NOTE

Building an Aboveground Shelter

If you have spawned into a flat area, see "Finding a Building Site" on page 58 to build an aboveground shelter, or just dig a few blocks down into the ground.

Head toward any convenient hill, cliff, or mound and select your pickaxe. You'll be digging a space that's two blocks high, but because you also need a roof over your head, the target area should be at least three blocks high. Use ▣ to swing the shovel and quickly break up any dirt blocks in front of you at ground level and the next one above it that's at eye level. Switch to the pick when you reach stone. If you are facing a terraced hill (and Minecraft doesn't have any that aren't), just dig out a couple of blocks at ground level until you've created the path to a three-block-high space like in Figure 2.6.

FIGURE 2.6   Tunneling into a hill is as effective as using a cliff face for a shelter.

Move forward and keep swinging that pick because you need to carve out a little bit of room to fit your crafting table; a furnace; and, potentially, a bed. A space 4×4 should do for now, although you can certainly expand it later. As you move forward, you automatically collect the blocks you're breaking. If you break out into a cave or through the hill and outside again (see Figure 2.7), open your inventory and pull some of the blocks you've collected back down into your Hotbar, select them as your active tool, point your crosshairs at the top of the block beneath the gap, and use R2 to fill the gap with a new block.

FIGURE 2.7   Whoops! Better fill the gap.

Unfortunately, your shelter still lacks a door. In a pinch, you can just place a block in the gap and huddle in for the night, but doors are easy enough to create. You'll just need six wooden plank blocks.

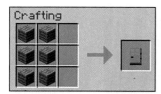

Place your crafting table in a corner of the room, open the crafting interface, and select the door from the recipe list. You might need to make more wood planks.

Now head outside your shelter, select the door (move it to a Hotbar slot first if you need to), and point your crosshairs at the ground block that is under the first section of your shelter where you have a true two-space high tunnel with a roof. Use **L2** to place the door. Figure 2.8 shows mine. You can then use **L2** again to open the door, step through, and click once more to close it. Now we're getting more homey, but we're still missing something vital—light! There are no energy-saving bulbs in Minecraft. For light, you need a torch fashioned from a stick and a lump of coal.

CAUTION

Close the Door While You're Gone!

Always remember to close the door when you leave your shelter. Leaving it open is like leaving out the welcome mat for mobs, and you don't want to find any lurking inside when you return.

TIP

Airlocks, Iron Doors, and More

In the Hard difficulty level, zombies can break through wooden doors. If you do decide to play on that level, give yourself a better chance of survival by building airlock structures using two doors instead of just one. If a zombie breaks through the first door, it will take him some time to break through the second. Hopefully, creepers aren't lined up behind. Iron doors are impervious to their attack but can be opened only with buttons or other redstone devices. Perimeter structures such as fences, moats, and lava pits also keep mobs away. See "Protecting Your Perimeter" on page 153 for a few examples.

FIGURE 2.8 Shelter secured! In the Easy and Normal difficulty levels, zombies still try to break down your door, and you will even see some worrying cracks appear. Don't panic! Zombies give up before they break through.

CAUTION

Install Doors Properly!

Facing a door the wrong way allows mobs to attack you. Skeletons are often deadly accurate and can actually fire their arrows through a door that's facing the wrong way. For this reason, always place doors while you are standing outside the area you want to protect.

 You can find coal in the ground here and there. The blocks are patterned with flecks of black and are often visible on the sides of cave walls. But you can't dig too far or venture too deep into a tunnel complex without the lack of light becoming a problem. Fortunately, there's an easier way to make torches, and that's by using charcoal instead of coal. To make charcoal, you need a furnace, and for that you need cobblestone.

NOTE

Emergency Shelters and Pillar Jumping

Caught out exploring as night falls? You can easily survive a night in the open if you can't get back to base. Here are a few techniques. First, find the most precarious ledge you can on a cliff. Switch to Sneak mode by clicking 🎮 as you approach cliff edges to avoid a potentially fatal fall. The cliff edge location doesn't guarantee survival, but mobs are less likely to find you, and you can improve the situation by digging into the cliff a little way, creating a corridor two blocks high. Go sideways at the end to create an L shape where you can hide out of sight. Block the lower half of the doorway with sand, dirt, or gravel—whatever you have that's handy, really—and wait out the night in your nook.

Another way to protect yourself fast is to dig down three blocks in anything other than sand or gravel. Just dig down the first two blocks; jump in the hole; and dig out the last one, hoping it doesn't drop you straight into a lava pit or into the top of a deep cave. Place one block of the material you removed above your head, ensuring first it isn't sand or gravel because if it is, you'll suffocate, somewhat defeating the purpose. Wait about eight minutes of real time, or knock out the block and replace it now and then check for daylight before you knock out a block in front of you to create a step so you can escape into the dawn.

A final trick, which can be quite handy if you spawn in the midst of a giant desert, is to dig up about 10 blocks of sand or other ground covering and then place the first block down, climb on top, and with some careful timing, jump while looking straight down to place another block directly beneath you (hold 🎮 while tapping ❌)—also known as *pillar jumping*. Repeat until you are perched on top of a pillar 10 blocks high. This keeps you well out of reach of hostile mobs. When sunrise hits, look down and dig out the blocks beneath you, easing yourself back down to the ground.

The Furnace Is Your Friend

Furnaces are crafted from eight blocks of cobblestone, and to get that you need to mine stone. But stone is everywhere. It's the second most common element in Minecraft besides air and is usually found just one or two blocks under a layer of dirt, if not just laying around in the open waiting for you to stub an inadvertent toe. One trick to stone, though, is that you can't render it into cobblestone with your fists. You'll just pulverize it to dust instead. You'll need at least a wooden pickaxe to do it properly.

Check your inventory and if you haven't yet found eight blocks of cobblestone, start expanding your shelter using the pickaxe to render any stone you find into cobblestone. Don't dig more than one block down at a time because you won't be able to jump back up. Use a shallow staircase effect if needed, but try to just stick to the horizontal plane for now, expanding the perimeter of each interior wall rather than plowing into a long tunnel.

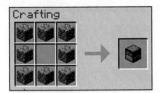

As soon as you have the blocks, head back to your crafting table. You'll find the furnace recipe sitting under the crafting table recipe.

Drag the completed furnace to one of your Hotbar slots, and then place it next to your crafting table. It's torch time!

Let There Be Light

Light is a great way to dispel fear of the dark—in any setting. In Minecraft, light keeps hostile mobs at bay. Or, more specifically, it prevents them from spawning nearby. Certain rules are built into the software that prevent mobs from springing into existence close to you, no matter the light level, but they also can't spawn anywhere near light. As you expand your shelter, mine, and explore, the judicious placement of torches keeps the coast somewhat clear. Besides that, torches add that much-needed ambient touch to any home.

Use ⒧2 to open the furnace. You'll see your inventory screen again, shown in Figure 2.9, but this time with a crafting grid containing just two slots. The lower slot holds the fuel to power the furnace, while the upper holds the object you are smelting. Place some blocks of wood in each of the lower and upper slots to start making charcoal, as shown. You'll soon see the charcoal pop into the output grid. Each chunk of charcoal, when combined with a stick, can make four torches.

TIP

Buckets of Lava Are the Best Fuel

You can use both coal and charcoal as sources of fuel in a furnace, and they are much more effective than most other materials, able to process 8 blocks apiece. But what's the best fuel possible? A bucket of lava. You'll be able to find these easily enough later. For now, just keep it in mind. One bucket equals 100 smelted blocks. It's like your own personal nuclear reactor.

The furnace can take a little time to do its thing, but it's also set and forget. Walk away, and the furnace keeps on burning while it has fuel and something to work on. When either runs out, the furnace just shuts down, and you can collect the results later. No need to worry about leaving the gas on or the pot boiling over.

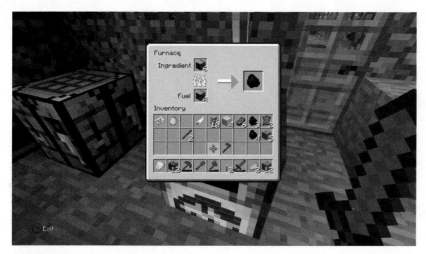

FIGURE 2.9 Burn, baby, burn. The furnace smelts objects into items more useful for crafting, building, decorating, and cooking. Keep one handy at all times.

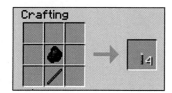

Now that you have some charcoal, open the crafting window (or use your crafting table if you prefer), move to the Tools and Weapons tab, and select the Torch from the list. Great work! You've just created four torches, and in Minecraft they're going to be some of your best friends.

Place the torches in the Hotbar and step back a moment. Find a nice position on a wall, select the torch, and use **L2** to attach it to a convenient wall. Torches never burn out, so you never need to replace them, although you can knock them down with **R2**, scoop them up, and place them elsewhere if your interior decorating instinct kicks in. Torches can also provide a useful homing beacon if you place a few outside your shelter. They'll create a nice pool of light you can spot from a distance, especially if you're making a last-minute dash for home at sunset.

Figure 2.10 shows the much-needed result in our first hidey-hole. Note that torches can be placed on most flat surfaces as well as against walls.

FIGURE 2.10 Cave, sweet cave. Safe for the night, and cozy enough to keep on crafting.

Slumbering with Lumber

Beds are great because they make a house a home. They lend an aesthetic a crafting table and furnace can't really provide. But more than that, they serve a purpose that gets right down to the underlying game mechanic. A bed protects you. It provides you with a timeout through the night so you can skip to sunrise and get on with your day.

Sleeping in a bed also resets your spawn point to its location so you can venture farther and farther out into the world, even covering vast distances, without starting at your point of origin should you—and by *should you* I mean *you will*—die. However, if the last bed you slept in is destroyed for any reason, your spawn point reverts back to your original point of origin, so it pays to keep your bed safe.

> ## NOTE
>
> **Time Is on Your Side**
>
> While you are sleeping, time doesn't really tick by. Sleeping is really just an instant adjustment in the game's clock that leaves everything else in the same state before you actually went to sleep.

Building a bed is easy, but you first need to find and kill three sheep to get their wool. Later you can build shears for a more sheep-friendly experience, but for now, lamb skewers are the only option.

If you've seen sheep nearby, take your sword in hand and have at them with a few clicks of
R2. Keep track of your bearings, though. The sheep make a dash for it on the first attack,
and you don't want to become lost as you give chase.

NOTE

Sleep Without Sheep

Sheep are the easiest way to harvest wool for a bed. If you can't find any, skip the
bed-building and start on Chapter 3, "Gathering Resources." Spend the night improving your tools at the crafting table. You can quietly dig up more cobblestone by
expanding your shelter. Just remember to place torches every nine or so spaces to
ensure you leave no dark places where a hostile mob can spawn. If there are simply
no sheep anywhere nearby, look for spiders. Each drops up to 2 pieces of string.
Collect 4 of those and you can make a block of wool; collect 12 and you'll have
enough for a bed. Fair warning, though: it can take a while for enough spiders to
come calling.

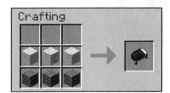

Each sheep drops one block of wool. Attack them with your sword—it should take just a few
blows. When you've collected three, head back to your crafting table, and select the bed
recipe in the Structures tab. Voilà! A bed is born.

You can place the bed anywhere there is space for two blocks. Stand facing the direction
you want the bed to face where the foot of the bed would be closest to you. Then click the
block where the foot should go, not the head. Figure 2.11 shows the placement, and Figure
2.12 shows the end result in a now very comfortable, if simple, shelter.

When it's night, point your crosshairs at the bed and press L2 to sleep. Unfortunately, sleep
won't come easy if there are monsters nearby, so at times you'll need to wait for them to
drift away first.

FIGURE 2.11   Bed placement can be a little tricky because a bed takes two blocks. Always aim for the space you plan to place the foot of the bed.

FIGURE 2.12   The bed is now tucked against the wall.

TIP

Take a Bed with You

Keep a bed in your inventory if you're trekking through the wilderness. You can place it down anywhere there's enough space, and, as long as no monsters are nearby, sleep cozily through the dark. If you don't want to dig a shelter, build a pillar four or five blocks up with a small platform on top and place the bed there. The bed is Minecraft's equivalent of a Get Out of Jail Free card because it skips to dawn, and at that point most skeletons and zombies burn up and spiders switch out of hostile mode and go back to their usual spidery business. But this technique does have its hazards, and it really takes little effort to build a quick shelter. In other words, use at your own risk.

The Bottom Line

Surviving your first night can seem tough at first—it's a bit of a learning curve. But get through it just once, and survival becomes much easier if you need to do it again. First-night survival entails just a few simple steps: harvest wood, create a crafting table, build tools, and hollow out a shelter. The rest are optional.

But remember, Minecraft days pass all too fast. Keep an eye out for the sun setting in the west, and make sure you can at least create a small cave in a cliff or hillside so that you are out of harm's way when night falls. When you head out again in the morning, check for hostile mobs. Their sound gives them away. Some lurk all day while others burn up in the sunlight, but be especially careful if it's an overcast day or raining because the lower light level makes it easier for them to survive.

Now that you've had an initial taste of Minecraft, I bet you're hungry for more. At this point we've only scratched the surface of the crafting table, and while the shelter serves its purpose, Minecraft provides unlimited real estate and resources—enough to create any architectural dream. In the next chapter, you learn some essential survival tricks, including how to stave off hunger, deal with mobs, and build a few more useful tools.

Gathering Resources

In This Chapter

- Learn the secrets of the HUD.
- Improve your tools with more durable materials.
- Safely store your hard-earned resources.
- Learn the easy way to manage hunger.
- Build your first outdoor shelter and enjoy the view.
- Access the full Creative mode inventory.

Minecraft is filled to the brim with all manner of resources, and gathering them is the first step toward getting the most out of the game. In Chapter 2, "First-Night Survival," you put together a pack of essentials sufficient to last the first night, but this is really just the smallest prequel to the real game, and describing how to find, create, and use other types of resources forms much of this book. This chapter is about building the foundation you can use to launch into the rest of the game. Your focus is on a few key points: build an outdoor shelter, find food to stave off hunger, improve your collection of tools, and build a chest to safely store items. This solidifies your position (making your base more impervious to attack), allows you to do all sorts of Minecrafty things more efficiently, and sets you up for longer excursions both above and below ground.

The good news is that you already have a base, so you can explore during the day, try not to lose your way, and head back at night. However, you still need to avoid at least some of the hostile mobs that persist during the day.

Introducing the HUD

Before we start, let's take a look at the Heads-Up Display (HUD)—that collection of icons and status bars at the bottom of the screen. Figure 3.1 shows the HUD as it appears in Survival mode with all possible indicators displayed. (The Creative mode HUD shows only the Inventory bar.)

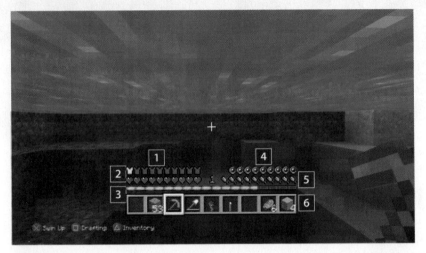

FIGURE 3.1 The HUD provides key status indications. Health is all important, but low hunger also leads to low health, so keep a close eye on both.

1. Armor bar

2. Health bar

3. Experience bar

4. Oxygen bar

5. Hunger bar

6. Hotbar

Each section of the HUD provides a key nugget of information about the health or status of your avatar:

- **Armor bar**—The armor bar appears when you've equipped your avatar with any type of armor and shows the current damage absorption level. Each armor icon represents an 8% reduction in the damage you'll take, so a 10/10 suit of armor reduces the damage you take by 80%, whereas a 1/10 suit absorbs only 8%. Armor becomes less effective the more damage it has taken, although the rate at which it deteriorates also depends on its material—leather being the weakest and diamond the strongest. In the case shown in Figure 3.1, a set of leather boots really doesn't provide much protection.

- **Health bar**—You have up to 20 points of health available, represented by the 10 hearts shown. Each heart disappears in two ticks. Health and hunger have a complicated relationship. You can read more about them starting in the section "Hunger Management."

- **Experience bar**—The experience bar increases the more you mine, smelt, cook, kill, and fish. Your current level is shown in the middle of the bar. When it's full, you move to the next experience level. Experience isn't generally important until you start enchanting and giving additional powers to items such as swords (see Chapter 10, "Enchanting, Anvils, and Brewing"). Unlike other roleplaying games, experience in Minecraft is more like a currency that you spend on enchantments, so it waxes and wanes. But all experience gained counts toward the final score shown on the screen when you die. Killing a mob drops experience orbs that either fly directly toward you or float to the ground waiting to be collected. You can also gain experience by smelting certain items in the furnace and carrying out other activities such as finding rare ores. Dying causes a substantial drop in your current experience level, so if you start to gain substantial experience points (for example, a level that's up in the 20s), it might be time to think about spending them on an enchantment or two.

- **Oxygen bar**—The oxygen bar appears whenever you go underwater, and it quickly starts to drop. You can probably hold your own breath for longer! As soon as your oxygen level hits zero, your health starts taking a two-point hit every second, but it resets if you resurface for just an instant. You can do this by holding down the ⊗ button until you breach the water. Diving isn't that big of a deal in Minecraft, at least not for completing the core game, but you can use the ability to do interesting things like building an underwater base. An example is shown in Figure 3.2, and I'll show you how to build your own in Chapter 8, "Creative Construction," as well as sharing with you some other underwater breathing techniques.

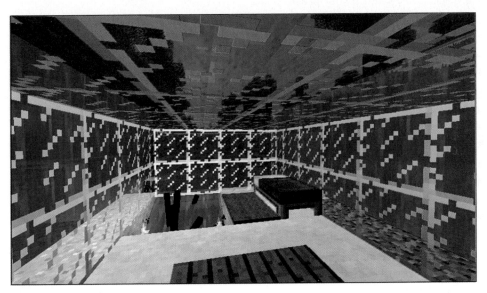

FIGURE 3.2 Underwater bases are impervious to mob attacks, even when built from glass, but you'll need to watch your oxygen bar carefully to ensure you don't run out of air while building this type of structure. By the way, the only mob that spawns underwater is the friendly, curious squid. Can you make out the one shown here? Say hello to Ceph.

- **Hunger bar**—You also have 20 points of hunger available, as well as a hidden value called Saturation. Like health, each hunger bar icon holds 2 points and can reduce by half an icon (that icon is, incidentally, a "shank," or the lower part of a leg of meat) at a time.

■ **Hotbar**—These nine slots represent items you can select and use. Press ⒶTo access your full inventory and to change the items in these slots. The white number next to some shows that slot's count of stacked identical items. A durability bar also appears under each tool's icon in green, gradually reducing as you use the tool until the tool breaks and disappears from your inventory. You'll have some warning of this because the bar turns red when it's close to zero. See "Improving Your Tools" later in the chapter to learn more about the durability of various materials.

NOTE

Hiding the HUD

If you want to hide the HUD, press ▶ to open the **Help & Options** menu. Scroll down to **Settings→User Interface** and deselect **Display HUD**. Unfortunately, there isn't a quicker way to do this at present.

Avoiding Getting Lost

It's easy to become lost in Minecraft. Run helter-skelter from your base, chase a herd of livestock, discover a natural cave system, or take a shot across the sea like that famed Norseman Leif Eriksson. It's all part of the Minecraft charm. But don't become Columbus in the process.

You'll find a map in your inventory that can help you return to your home base or other locations in the world (see Figure 3.3). The map can display the entire world on the PS3 edition (it takes more than one on the PS4 edition) but only updates while you have it active in the Hotbar, so it will take some time for it to build up the big picture. However, it does provide coordinates. Take note of those displayed for your home base.

The coordinates are based on the world's center where X and Z equal 0. (Y shows your current level above bedrock.) Jot down the current values. If you become lost, you can always find your way back to your original spawn and, presumably, your first shelter by traveling in a direction that will bring both X and Z back to those noted values.

When you need to return—and I should warn you that this *can* take some experimentation and a little practice—turn and take a few steps while tracking the change in your current coordinates. Your goal is to shift those X and Z values back toward those you originally recorded. You'll probably wander around a bit, but eventually you'll get there and the map will help you get your orientation and head off in the right general direction.

When you are able, craft a compass. It takes some redstone and iron, and both are relatively easy to obtain with some assiduous mining. The only problem with a compass is that it always points to your original world spawn point. Think of that point as the magnetic north pole—it's not a GPS. Sleeping in a bed resets your spawn point but not your compass, so this method falls out of date as soon as you move to new dwellings and update your spawn point.

A compass is actually more useful when transformed into a map, see "Mapping, or There and Back Again" on page 217. You might need to do that if you lose the original map.

FIGURE 3.3 Point your ⊕ down to view the map. In this screenshot I've also turned off the HUD for a better view.

Improving Your Tools

Wooden tools wear out fast, so it's best to upgrade your kit as quickly as possible.

Each type of material has a different level of *durability*. Think of durability as the number of useful actions the tool can perform before it wears out completely, disappearing in a sudden splintering of wood. I've included the durability in parentheses after each material's description:

- **Gold (33)**—Although this is the least durable material, a gold pickaxe can break blocks out of most softer materials in the blink of an eye, and it happens to be the most enchantable material, so you can imbue it with superpowers (see Chapter 10). But given that gold is about five times as rare as iron, and gold can be used to craft many other useful items, I wouldn't recommend using it for tools.

- **Wood (60)**—It's easy to obtain, especially in an emergency aboveground, but think of wood as just a means of getting to cobblestone because, unlike the latter, wooden tools can't mine the more valuable ores such as iron, gold, diamond, and redstone. You will at least need a wooden pickaxe to mine stone because doing so with your bare hands will just break the stone into unusable dust, but after that, swap it out for something tougher.

- **Stone (132)**—With just a touch over twice the longevity of wood, stone makes a great starting point for more serious mining and other activities such as slaying mobs. Stone tools are built from cobblestone blocks, which in turn come from stone. That might seem a little confusing, but it will seem natural enough after a while.

- **Iron (251)**—Iron will become your go-to material. It is found most commonly all the way from bedrock, the lowest layer of the Minecraft world, up to about 20 levels below sea level. Iron is used for building all kinds of tools, implements, and devices including armor, buckets (for carrying water, lava, and milk), compasses, minecarts, and minecart tracks. All these require at least iron ingots obtained by smelting the ore in a furnace, with each block of ore producing one ingot. Ingots and many other items are found scattered throughout the world in village chests, mine shafts, dungeons, and strong-holds. You might also find them as drops from slain zombies and iron golems—although I definitely don't recommend tackling the latter.

- **Diamond (1562)**—It's the strongest material of all but also the most expensive given that diamonds are relatively rare. (You will enjoy the moment you do find your first diamond, but it's found only in the first 16 layers above bedrock, the lowest layer in the Minecraft world, and even then it's about 25 times as scarce as iron.) A diamond pickaxe is the only material that can successfully mine obsidian, a material required for creating the portal to reach The Nether region. Given that diamond is much scarcer than iron but only six times as durable, you should use iron pickaxes as much as possible and only switch to diamond when you need to mine obsidian to reach The Nether. You're better off saving any diamonds you find for weapons (a diamond sword does more damage, and that combined with its increased durability will ensure it lasts much longer than any other material while doing more damage where it counts), armor, and enchantment tables.

NOTE

Different Materials for Different Items

Durability applies to all tools, weapons, and armor, although there are differences in the materials that can be used in each case. For example, you can craft leather armor and make stone tools, but not vice versa.

The recipes for crafting tools from all materials are identical, save for the replacement of the head of the implement with the material of choice. As long as you have the right materials, that version of the tool appears selectable in the crafting interface:

- To make a stone pick, you need two wooden sticks for the handle and three cobblestone blocks.

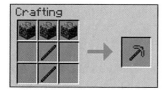

- Replace in the same way for the axe and the sword.

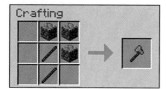 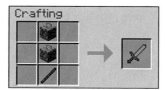

- You might also want to add a shovel to your collection because it's about four times faster than using hands to harvest softer materials such as dirt, gravel, sand, clay, and snow, and it helps some of those blocks deliver resources rather than just breaking down. For example, only a shovel can gather snow balls from snow.

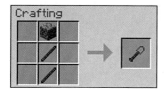

As you craft more items, you need to find somewhere to store those you don't need to use right away. You should also store other resources and food you find on your travels so they're not lost if you come to an unfortunate end. That comes next.

Chests: Safely Stashing Your Stuff

Whenever you head away from your secure shelter, there is always a reasonably high risk of death. Creepers, lava pits, long falls—they can all do you in. Respawning is only a moment away, but the real danger here is that any items you've collected and carry in your character's inventory drop at the location of your untimely death and may prove impossible to retrieve in the 5 minutes you have to get back to them before they disappear forever.

Chests act as an insurance policy. Put everything you don't need in a chest before you embark on a mission, and those things will be there when you get back or after you respawn.

The natural place to leave chests is in your shelter, but you can also leave them elsewhere, perhaps at a staging point as you work away in a mine or even outside. Mobs will leave them alone, and the only real risk you face is leaving them out in the open in a multiplayer game or getting blown up from behind by a creeper in Single-player mode while you're rummaging around inside.

Chests come in two sizes: single and double. A single chest can store 27 stacks of items. Create a double chest by placing two single chests side by side. The double chest stores up to 54 stacks of items. Given that a stack can be up to 64 items high, that's an astonishing potential total of 3,510 blocks in a crate that takes just 2×1 blocks of floor space. If you've ever followed the *Dr. Who* TV series, consider chests the Tardis of storage!

Create a chest at your crafting table with eight blocks of wooden planks.

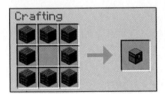

Place and then use to open it. You can then move items back and forth between your inventory and the chest. In Figure 3.4, I've transferred all the items I don't need for the next expedition.

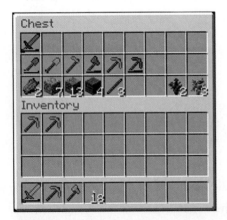

FIGURE 3.4 Chests act as an insurance policy for your items so they aren't lost if you die. Use the inventory shortcuts you learned earlier to quickly move items between your active inventory and the chest's storage slots.

Before you head out, there are two other things you should know: how to avoid monsters and how to deal with hunger. Read on.

Avoiding Monsters

There's a key difference between the Minecraft world on the first and second days. In a word, *mobs*: hostile ones to be specific. Mobs spawn only in dark areas, and some only during the night, so if you are outside during your first day and stay in well-lit areas, you'll be reasonably—although not entirely—safe. By the second day, however, mobs have had a chance to build their numbers and wander about. It's not that likely you'll encounter them on day 2, but it's best to be prepared.

There are 14 types of hostile mobs. These are the ones you might meet on your second day outside:

- **Zombies**—Zombies burn up in sunlight but can still survive in shadows or rain, when wearing a helmet, and of course in caves all hours of the day or night. They are relatively easy to defeat, and if too many come after you from out of the shadows, just head to a well-lit area and keep your distance while they burn up in the sun.

- **Skeletons**—Skeletons also burn up in sunlight unless they are wearing a helmet, and they can survive at any time in lower light conditions. They're quite deadly with a bow and arrow and best avoided for now.

- **Spiders**—Spiders come in two variants: large or blue. You'll probably only see the larger spiders at this stage. They are passive during the day but become hostile in shadow and can attack at any time if provoked. They'll climb, they'll jump, and they are pretty darn fast. Fortunately, they're also easy to kill with some swift sword attacks. The blue spiders are a smaller, poisonous variant called cave spiders. They live only in abandoned mine shafts underground, but in substantial numbers. If you suffer from arachnophobia, I don't have much good news for you, except that with a little time you'll get used to them and they won't seem quite so nasty.

- **Creepers**—Creepers have a well-earned reputation as the Minecraft bad guys. They are packed to their green gills with gunpowder, and they'll start their very short 1.5-second fuse as soon as they are within three blocks of you. Their explosions can cause a lot of real damage to you, nearby structures, and the environment in general. If you hear a creeper's fuse—a soft hissing noise—but can't see it, run like heck in the direction you're facing. Remember to sprint by pushing your 🎮 forward twice in quick succession. With a little luck, you'll get three blocks away and the creeper's fuse will reset. Creepers are usually best dealt with using a ranged attack from a bow and arrow, but if you sprint at them with an iron or diamond sword and take a swipe at just the right moment, mid-leap, when you're past the apex of the arc and descending in a wild fury, you can send them flying back out of their suicidal detonation range, causing the fuse to reset. Most creepers despawn (that is, disappear) around noon, leaving the afternoon generally free of their particular brand of terror.

■ **Slimes**—Slimes spawn in the swamp biome and in some places underground. Their initial appearance is that of a quite large Jello-like green block, but they won't sit there gently shaking: they are more than capable of causing real damage. Attacking eventually breaks them up into 2–4 new medium-sized slimes. These can still attack but are relatively easily killed, only to spawn a further 2–4 tiny slimes each! These last kind don't cause any attack damage, but they can still push you into peril if you're unlucky.

If you come across a lone spider, a zombie, or even a slime, now is as good a time as any to get in some sword practice. Just point your crosshairs at the creature and strike repeatedly with R2. Timed well, you can also block their attacks with L2. Keep clicking as fast as you can, and you have a very good chance of killing the mob and picking up any items it drops before it lands too many blows. Try to avoid the other mobs for now.

TIP

Switch to Peaceful Mode to Get a Break

Getting mobbed by mobs? Remember that you can always exit the game and reenter it, changing the Difficulty setting to Peaceful as you open the game once more. Peaceful mode despawns all hostile mobs and allows your health to regenerate. But do try to switch the level back to Normal as soon as you can.

So how do you avoid mobs? Use these tips to survive:

■ Stay in the open as much as you can, avoiding heavily wooded areas if possible.

■ Most mobs have a 16-block detection radar. If they can also draw a line of sight to your position, they will enter *pursuit* mode. (Spiders can always detect you, even through other blocks.) At that point they'll relentlessly plot and follow a path to your position, tracking you through other blocks without requiring a line of sight. Pursuit mode stays engaged much farther than 16 blocks.

■ Keep your sound turned up because you'll also hear mobs within 16 blocks, although creepers, befitting their name, are creepily quiet.

■ Avoid skirting along the edges of hilly terrain. Creepers can drop on you from above with their fuses already ticking. Try to head directly up and down hills so you have a good view of the terrain ahead.

- Mobs are quite slow, so you can easily put some distance between them and yourself by keeping up a steady pace and circling around to get back to your shelter. Sprint mode will leave them far behind.

CAUTION

Sprinting Makes You Hungry

Sprint mode burns up hunger points, so try to use it only in emergencies. Unfortunately, in a real emergency, if you make a dash from a creeper when your health is low, you'll find it impossible to sprint. Remember, always keep your hunger topped up so your health continually regenerates and you'll avoid getting caught in this leaden-footed nightmare.

Hunger Management

Hunger plays a permanent role in Minecraft, much as in real life. While it's possible to starve to death only on Hard difficulty, hunger does affect your character in other ways, so it's always important to ensure you have the equivalent of a couple of sandwiches packed before heading deep into a mine or on a long trek.

Hunger is a combination of two values: the one shown in the HUD's hunger bar, as well as a hidden value called *saturation*. The latter provides a buffer to the hunger bar, decreasing first. In fact, your hunger bar doesn't decrease at all until saturation reaches 0. At that point, you see the hunger bar start to jitter, and after a short while it takes its first hit. Saturation cannot exceed the value of the hunger bar, so with a fully satiated bar of 20 points, it's possible to have up to 20 points of saturation. However, a hunger level of 6 points also only provides a maximum of 6 points of saturation, and that makes you vulnerable.

You'll find some key information about the hunger system here:

- On Easy and Normal Survival modes, your character won't drop dead from hunger, although it can still pose a danger because your health won't regenerate if hunger has dropped more than 2 points from its maximum. If you're close to home and pottering around in your farm or constructing some building extensions, you're fairly safe, but your health *will* start to drop. Eat something as soon as you can to rebuild your hunger bar and therefore your health.

- Sprinting and jumping up blocks both cost hunger points. Also, sprinting becomes impossible when the hunger bar drops below six hunger points, or three shanks, as shown in the HUD.

- Keeping a relatively full stomach at 18 hunger points (9 shanks in the HUD) allows health to regenerate at 1 point (half a heart) every 4 seconds.

- Health depletes if the hunger bar drops to zero, increasing the risk of dying from one of the many imaginative ways on offer in Minecraft's deadly smorgasbord (see Figure 3.5).

FIGURE 3.5   The effects of extreme hunger on Normal difficulty: health depletes to just one point, or half a heart.

- There are some limits to the amount health can drop that vary according to the difficulty level. On Easy, health cannot deplete from hunger further than 10 points, or half the full quotient. On Normal, it can drop to 1 point, which is an extreme level of vulnerability. On Hard, there are no limits; don't ignore the hunger bar, or death from starvation could be just moments away. See "Food on the Run" later in this chapter to avoid this unfortunate fate.

Your Mission: Food, Resources, and Reconnaissance

Your second day is the perfect opportunity to gather food and other resources and to take a quick survey of the landscape surrounding your first shelter, in particular to find somewhere suitable for your first outdoor abode. Keep an eye out for any of the following:

- **Passive mobs**—Chickens, pigs, and cows all provide a ready source of food, or at least raw protein that can be cooked on the furnace and made more nutritious. Cows also drop leather that you can use for your first armor and can be milked, giving you an instant cure for food poisoning. Chickens also lay eggs, which are used to make cake, so gather any that you find. You can also obtain feathers from killed chickens—useful for later crafting arrows.

- **Natural harvest**—The harvest includes cocoa pods, apples, sugar cane, carrots, potatoes, and seeds. Knock down tall grass to find seeds; then use a hoe to till some ground next to water. Seeds mature into wheat within 5–8 day/night cycles, although wheat, potatoes, and carrots are also grown by villagers, as you can see with the wheat crop shown in Figure 3.6. From wheat, it's easy to bake bread, one of the simplest but most effective sources of food, especially if there are no passive mobs nearby. When combined with cocoa pods, bread will make cookies, which are always useful for a quick hunger bar top-up. See Chapter 6, "Crop Farming," for more on agricultural techniques.

- **Construction resources**—You can mine plenty of cobblestone quite safely by expanding your original shelter, digging into the terrain. But some other resources will definitely come in handy. Wood is always useful. If you see any sand, mine it so you can smelt it into glass blocks to let light into your shelter and provide a view. (There's no point moving from your first cave into the outdoor equivalent of another!) Also keep an eye out for coal. You can often see it in veins on the surface of the walls of small caves or on the sides of cliffs. If you can safely get to it, make like a miner and dig it out. Use the coal to make torches and to smelt other ores.

FIGURE 3.6   Wheat is an easy crop to farm and then to turn into bread—a handy food if you're stuck with no other options.

TIP

Making Use of Bones

The morning sun burns up skeletons, leaving behind bones that you can craft into bone meal. Bone meal acts as a fertilizer, helping your crops grow faster. You can also use bone to tame wolves, providing you with an extra level of protection. Chapter 7, "Farming and Taming Mobs," has a lot more information on breeding and taming mobs in Minecraft.

Start early, heading out with a stone sword at the ready, just in case. If you are low on wood, swing an axe at a few nearby trees.

Move carefully so you don't lose your bearings. The sun rises in the east and sets in the west, and the clouds also travel from east to west, so you can always at least get a sense of direction. Following a compass cardinal point (north, south, east, or west) and using the sun and clouds as a reference can lead you away and reasonably accurately back home again, and keeping your map active in a Hotbar slot will also fill it in as you travel.

Food on the Run

If you are getting dangerously hungry, head to the nearest equivalent of a fast food outlet—a passive mob—sword at the ready. Your best bet is to look for cows and pigs because they each can drop up to three pieces of raw meat, with each restoring 3 hunger units and 1.8 in saturation. They're an excellent target of opportunity. You can also eat raw chicken, although with a 30% chance of developing food poisoning, or you can try rotten meat harvested from zombies, which is guaranteed to give you a taste of the stomach aches. But after you have mined three pieces of iron and crafted a bucket, you can also cure any type of food poisoning by drinking milk obtained with that bucket from a cow. You can also eat any amount of poisoned meat, gaining the restorative benefits, and curing the whole lot with one serving of milk. So keep that rotten flesh the zombies drop around! And the bucket o' milk.

That said, unless you are desperate, it is actually much better to take the time to cook all your meat first. In fact, the secondary processing of foods makes them all healthier, restoring more hunger and saturation points. If you are far from home, you could choose to always carry a furnace in your inventory, along with fuel. Place it, cook, and break it up to use again. Or you could, if you don't mind seeming like a crazed pyromaniac, both kill and cook pigs, chickens, and cows in one blazing swoop by setting the ground beneath them on fire with a flint and steel (click on the ground next to the animal) or, a little more chaotically, by pouring lava from a bucket. Just take caution that you don't do this anywhere it could pose a risk such as near that fantastic wood cabin you just spent the last three weeks building; there's no undo in Minecraft.

NOTE

Fishing in the Sea of Plenty

Mobs such as chickens, cows, and pigs spawn quite rarely compared to hostile mobs, so consider them a nonrenewable resource if you kill them in the wild. You're better off breeding them in a farm so they can be readily replaced. Fish, on the other hand, are unlimited in quantity and very plentiful, and fishing from a boat works very well. Your hunger bar won't decrease, and you'll be relatively safe from hostile mobs. Even better, you can eat on-the-go because you won't ever get food poisoning from raw fish. Sushi anyone? See Chapter 7 for more information.

TIP

Let Them Eat Cake

What's the quickest way to fill your hunger bar? Eat cake. Unlike another well-known game, Minecraft's cake is not a lie. Cake has a quite complicated recipe, but each full cake provides up to 6 slices, each worth 1.5 hunger points, or 9 in total, and it's less resource intensive than creating golden apples. Minecraft rewards calories, so eat as much as you like without penalty, quickly building back your full hunger bar. However, as in the real world, the nutrients are lacking, so cake doesn't provide any saturation benefit. Make sure you eat some more nutritional foods such as protein as your hunger bar starts to top out to ensure you also get that extra boost. Personally speaking, if there was a choice between cake and pizza, I'm going for the former!

Finally, if you simply cannot find mobs, your hunger bar has dropped to starvation, and your health has plummeted to half a point, consider at least planting a wheat field and waiting it out in your shelter for a few days so that at least three blocks of wheat can grow and be baked into bread.

If all is lost, even then, consider one final alternative—a pretty neat if somewhat dramatic trick. Assuming you have reset your spawn point to a bed or are still near origin, head to your shelter, place everything you carry in a chest, and then head outside and either jump off a cliff, drown in a lake, or wait for a mob to kill you. You respawn back in your shelter with full health, a full hunger bar, and all your possessions waiting for you in the chest. The only downside is that you'll lose some experience points in the process, which impacts enchanting, but I'm sure you can build those up again quickly enough. It's a good last resort and will let you quickly head out again, fully equipped, to live another day.

Finding a Building Site

As you scout around, keep in mind that you are also looking for a new building site. This doesn't have to be fancy or even particularly large. A 6×5 space manages just fine, and even 6×4 can squeeze in the basics. You can also level ground and break down a few trees to clear space. I did this in Figure 3.7.

FIGURE 3.7   A nice, flat, elevated building site created on a nearby hill after filling out the platform with dirt.

I usually prefer space that's a little elevated because it provides a better view of the surroundings, but it's perfectly possible to create a protected space just about anywhere. You may even decide to go a little hybrid, building a house that's both tunneled into a hill and extending outside.

TIP

Light Those Caves

Check for any caves or tunnels close to your site's location. If they aren't too big, light them up with torches to prevent mobs spawning inside and wandering out during the day, or just block their entrances for now.

So what can we build on this site? Let me show you a basic structure. It takes 34 cobblestone blocks dug out of the first shelter and 12 wood blocks for the roof obtained by cutting down 3 trees. This is about as minimalistic as it gets (see Figure 3.8).

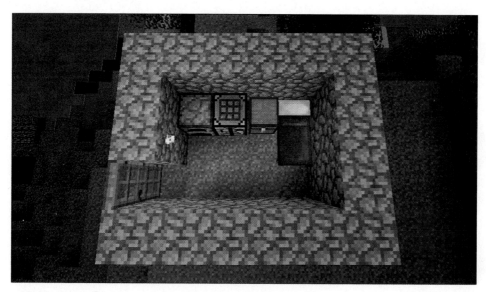

FIGURE 3.8   The layout for a small cobblestone cabin using a total of 46 blocks, roof not shown. The sharp-eyed will notice it can be reduced in width one space further, but for the sake of four blocks, that would feel just a little too claustrophobic.

You can build the roof from almost any handy material, including dirt, cobblestone, and wood. Avoid blocks that fall down, such as gravel and sand. A two-block-high wall keeps out all mobs except for spiders because they can climb walls. An overhang on the wall keeps spiders out because they can't climb upside-down, but it's easier to just add a roof, and this will protect you if there are any trees nearby the spiders can climb and use as an arachnid's springboard to jump straight into your dwelling. (Yes, it has happened to me. Sent shivers up my spine.) Figure 3.9 shows the finished hut with a few torches on the outside to keep things well lit.

TIP

No Housing Codes in Minecraft

The roof in Figure 3.9 rests right on the lip of the inner wall. You can't directly build a roof like this from scratch. First, place a block on top of the wall, and then attach the inner block for the roof. Remove the first block, and the inner block floats. Attach new blocks to that to build out the roof structure. It won't pass a building inspection, but it certainly works in Minecraft.

FIGURE 3.9 The finished hut—basic but serviceable. And it's spider proof. Although there is a large gap above the door, in Minecraft's geometry the door fills the entire space. Spiders are two blocks wide, so they can't fit through a one-block-wide gap. You could actually leave the door wide open, and spiders will just gather outside and make horrible noises, but don't do that because it's an invitation for other mobs to enter.

Building a wall even two blocks high can take a little bit of fancy footwork. Some basic techniques help:

- Place your walls one layer at time. Put down the first layer, and then jump on top to place the second.

- If you fall off, place a temporary block on the inside of your structure against the wall, and use this to climb back up. You can remove it when you're finished.

- Use pillar jumping if you need to go higher. While looking directly down, press ⊗ to jump and then use **L2** to place a block underneath you. You land on that block instead of the one below. Repeat as often as necessary. Dig the blocks out from directly underneath you to go back down.

- Click ⊛ to activate Sneak mode as you work around the top of tall walls so you don't fall off. You can even use this technique to place blocks on the side of your current layer that are normally beyond sight.

See Chapter 8 for more building techniques and ideas.

A Resourceful Guide to the Creative Mode Inventory

Minecraft resources fall into several primary categories. Some of them are a natural early focus as you improve your position from those gathered for first-night survival; others come into more focus as you get further through the game, gear up for your exploration of The Nether and The End regions, and start to become more creative with all that Minecraft has to offer. Here's a quick summary of the categories. You can view all the possible tools and resources by opening a game in Creative mode and pressing 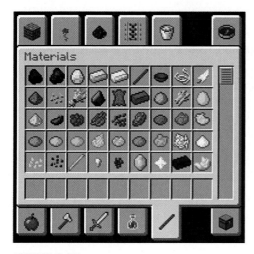, as shown in Figure 3.10. The categories that follow correspond to the tabs running across the upper and lower sections of the Creative mode inventory. Scroll the inventory with **L1** and **R1** for tabs, and then within the inventory using.

FIGURE 3.10   Creative mode inventory provides access to the full set of resources and tools.

- **Building Blocks**—Building blocks are used, as you might expect, for construction, including housing and almost anything else. Build a bridge for your redstone rail. Construct a dam. Elevate a farm above a level that won't get trampled by mobs, or put up a fence. Build a skyscraper or reconstruct a monument. Minecraft provides a large number of primary blocks—cobblestone, gravel, wood, dirt, and so on—that can be harvested directly, but things definitely become more interesting when you start creating secondary types of blocks from primary materials. You can store many items more efficiently (for example, by converting nine gold ingots into a single gold block) and climb more efficiently by crafting stairs instead of jumping up and down blocks on well-travelled routes. These blocks are, without being too punny, the building blocks of creativity.

- **Decorations**—Decorations are something of a catchall category. Generally, they are things you can use to make your constructions more interesting. Some of those are just visual, such as the various mob heads, whereas others such as item frames and book-cases also serve functional purposes.

- **Redstone and Transportation**—Redstone is an almost magical resource. You can use it to build powered circuits, quite complex ones, and then activate pistons to automati-cally harvest a farm plot, set up traps, open and close doors, and a huge amount more. The limits are set only by your imagination. Redstone is also used to craft powered rail tracks and a range of other useful items such as compasses and clocks. This category also includes other items used for transportation such as the various types of minecarts and boats. See Chapter 9, "Redstone, Rails, and More," for more information. There are enough options here to enable you to build everything from massive transportation systems to incredible rollercoasters.

- **Materials**—Materials is a catchall category, composed of items derived from another action. For example, killing a chicken can drop feathers, and you'll need those for the fletching on arrows unless you gather arrows directly from slain skeletons.

- **Food**—Food contains the full range of edibles, including the enchanted form of the golden apple, the rarest edible in the game. Take a few of these with you the next time you think you'll be in a tight spot, and you might just be able to make it through that moaning zombie horde.

- **Tools, Weapons, and Armor**—Tools can be wielded as weapons, but not very effec-tively. They are, however, great at digging, chopping, hoeing, and setting a Nether Portal on fire with the flint and steel. You'll also find shears for stripping the wool from sheep, a fishing rod, and the full set of armor and tools.

- **Brewing**—The Brewing tab contains all possible potions and a number of the rarer ingredients required that don't fit into other categories. Potions are incredibly handy, delivering such useful effects as protection from fire—something of an advantage when traveling to The Nether. You can learn more about brewing in Chapter 10. Use ⊕ in this tab to cycle through the potions of various strengths.

- **Miscellaneous**—Miscellaneous contains a range of useful and obscure items. You'll find the buckets quite handy for setting up new water and lava sources, and you can use the eggs to spawn most of the mobs, populating a farm and more.

Use ⊗ to take individual items or △ to take the full permissible stack. Get rid of a single stack from your Hotbar by picking it up, dragging it off the side of the inventory screen, and pressing ⊗ once more to drop it. You can also replace items by dropping the new one on top of the old.

The Bottom Line

Congratulations! You've now learned everything you need to know to understand how your character is doing, improve your tools for better longevity, hopefully not get lost on your travels, and create your first mob-proof outdoor shelter.

These are the keys to Minecraft. Just remember to head back to your chest often to store the valuables you've gathered or to build other chests further afield.

You might also want to consider building a pillar and platform on top of your new shelter. It can help you survey your terrain and act as an easy-to-see landmark when you're out and about. Put some torches on top because mobs can spawn on any platform, no matter how small, and you don't want to poke your head up through the platform only to discover a creeper on a short fuse. It will also help you spot home from a distance.

The next chapter is all downhill, but in a good way. You'll be delving deep into your first mine.

Mining

In This Chapter

- Learn the essentials you need for your first mining expedition.
- Head down to the most profitable mining layers.
- Avoid a speedy death with essential tips.
- Build an express elevator straight down to the diamond layer.
- Discover the most efficient mining techniques.

Mining is a core part of the Minecraft experience. Sooner or later you're going to need to take a few pickaxes in hand, supplies to satiate hunger, a bunch of torches, and a sword or two and start plumbing the depths. There be resources down there—iron, gold, diamonds, redstone, and more. You'll find all the things you need to progress in the game. This chapter helps you find specific ores and develop efficient mining patterns that leave no stone unturned. You'll also learn a few tips on how best to avoid an inadvertent respawn, or at least recover with most of your hard-won resources and dignity intact.

Dig Deep, My Friend

Most of the desirable ores in Minecraft are located deep, close to the bedrock. Getting down there is a challenge in itself. There are a couple of strategies you can take:

- Find an existing ravine, canyon, or cave complex. These can sometimes also lead to abandoned mine shafts. Some caves run on for hundreds of blocks, joining with the surface here and there and occasionally running very deep. You'll usually see a range of exposed ores on their walls that make for easy pickings. The danger is that they are dark places, so in the larger caves you'll also run into a range of mobs. For now, even though they'll give you a head start, I'd suggest you leave these alone until you have armor, ranged weapons, and some sharp swords.

- The second strategy is to create your own mine. Keeping it well lit ensures there are no dark places for mobs to spawn, and you can go quietly about your business. For maximum convenience, you can even start this within your own shelter so there's no need to go outside. I'll focus on this method first. It is also likely you will break out into cave complexes as you mine, so we'll take a look at that second.

Before you begin, ensure you have the right equipment for the job. At a minimum, you need the following:

- **Torches**—Take at least 20 torches, but bring more if you plan to go down for an extended period of time. Place a torch whenever it gets too dark to see properly, and then take a look around to ensure you haven't missed any ores. It's surprisingly easy to do when things start to get a little dim.

- **Wood blocks**—These can be turned into ladders, torches, tool handles, chests, and crafting tables. The only place you can find wood underground is in an abandoned mine shaft or a stronghold filled with all kinds of hostile mobs, so bring wood with you as often as you can. Fifteen or so blocks should do for now.

- **Pickaxes**—Take at least three stone pickaxes to dig out iron ore and a shovel for digging out dirt and gravel, although you can build more at a crafting table while you're down there—more on that later. When one breaks from overuse, just switch to the next and keep on digging! Bring some stone swords as well, just in case.

- **Food**—Nourishment is absolutely vital because a full hunger bar helps you heal from any damage you incur. Bring at least cooked meat, and bring bread if you've had the chance to build a wheat farm. In Chapter 6, "Crop Farming," and Chapter 7, "Farming and Taming Mobs," you'll learn how to ensure a consistent supply of food.

- **Map**—Finally, don't forget to bring your map so you can check the Y coordinate to confirm when you've tunneled all the way down to layer 11, the most profitable layer to mine.

This will get you started. When you have found enough iron ore, you'll also want to craft the following items:

- **Two buckets**—One for water and the other for lava. You can use the water bucket to create pathways across lava pools, to make obsidian, and even to create waterfalls that you can safely descend and ascend over otherwise lethal vertical distances. The bucket of lava makes a great source of energy for the furnace, for fighting off mobs in cave complexes, and for generating obsidian. (It's not a great strategy because items the mobs drop can be burned up in the lava, but it's a good emergency measure.)

- **An iron pickaxe**—This is for mining the more valuable ores such as gold, redstone, and diamonds.

- **An iron sword**—Take one for good measure. Polished to a gleam.

NOTE

You'll Need Obsidian

You might not be lucky enough to find diamonds on this first expedition, but when you do you also need to create a diamond pickaxe for mining obsidian—it's the only type of pickaxe that can do so. Obsidian is needed to build the portal to access The Nether region described in Chapter 12, "Playing Through: The Nether and The End."

The Mining Layer Cake Guide

Before you start digging, let's take a brief look at the ore layers in Minecraft. There are nine types of naturally occurring minable ore in the Overworld, as well as a lower layer of indestructible bedrock. (Obsidian isn't included because it only occurs due to a reaction between water and lava. I'll show you how to make it in Chapter 12.) Figure 4.1 shows all those you can swing a pickaxe at as you dig your way through the landscape.

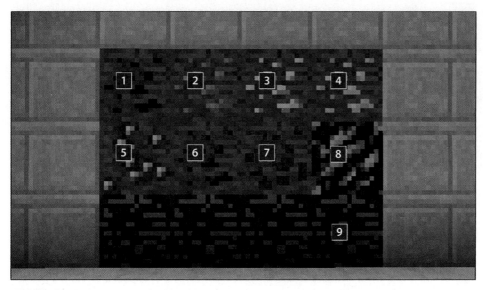

FIGURE 4.1   Each ore in the Minecraft world. Go get them all!

1. Coal

2. Iron

3. Gold

4. Diamond

5. Emerald

6. Redstone

7. Lapis Lazuli

8. Nether Quartz

9 Bedrock

World generation scatters various ores here and there in a statistical pattern that leads to a variety of striations. All the layers shown in Table 4.1 are counted from bedrock up. So layer 5, for example, is five layers above the lowest layer of bedrock, layer 0. (It might help if you think of layers as *altitude*.) Use your map to check your current altitude above Layer 0. It's the value shown next to the Y coordinate.

TABLE 4.1 Ore Layers

Appearance	Ore	Most Common Layers	Less Common Layers	Used for	Mined with
	Coal	5–52	Up to 128	Torches and a fuel source.	Any pickaxe
	Iron	5–54	Up to 64	Tools, weapons, armor, and other.	Stone, iron, or diamond pickaxe
	Gold	5–59	Up to 23	Tools, weapons, armor, and other.	Stone, iron, or diamond pickaxe
	Diamond	5–12	Up to 29	Tools, weapons, armor, and other.	Iron or diamond pickaxe
	Emerald	5–29	Up to 29	Villager trading. NOTE: Emeralds are only found in the extreme hills biome.	Iron or diamond pickaxe
	Redstone	5–12	Up to 12	Circuits and powered items, clock, and compass.	Iron or diamond pickaxe
	Lapis Lazuli	14–16	Up to 23	Dye for decorative items.	Stone, iron, or diamond pickaxe
	Nether Quartz	The Nether	The Nether	Creating quartz blocks.	Any pickaxe
	Bedrock	0–4	4	None.	None

The pattern of ore distribution in the table shows a few layers where every ore can be found: layers 5–12. Although you can hit lava just about anywhere, including on the surface, it pools primarily from layers 1 to 10. This makes layer 11 a good target for mining. On your way there, you will definitely see plenty of ore including coal and iron and cart loads of dirt, gravel, and stone.

Getting there is a matter of luck and skill, and that can make for an exciting journey!

Lava Lakes and Other Pitfalls

Mining has its share of pitfalls, in both the figurative and the literal sense. Before you don your virtual miner's hat, check through the following list of do's and don'ts:

- **Don't dig straight down**—It's tempting, certainly. You could potentially dig all the way to bedrock using just one iron pickaxe. The problem with that approach is that you never know what lies beneath. You could break through the top of a cave's roof and face a fatal drop, fall into a nest of hostile mobs, or splash down in a lava lake and lose not only your life, but also all your possessions.

- **Don't dig straight up**—It's easy to get lulled into a false sense of security after tunneling for a while, but you have no idea what may be on top of the block just above your head. You might spot some telltale drips of water or lava in time, but it's easy to become lost in the moment. Tapping an underground lake and flooding your mine isn't a complete disaster. Fight your way back against the current and plug the gap with another block. But that's not always possible. If you are mining higher levels, you could even tap straight into the bottom of the ocean. Punching into the bottom of a lava flow is far more dangerous, but very likely. Alternatively, you might just hit a bunch of loose gravel or sand waiting to suffocate you. Always mine up at least one block away from your current position so you have the chance to retreat and block off the tunnel if things go awry.

- **Do keep some blocks in your Hotbar**—Always have cobblestone or dirt at the ready to block off your tunnel in case you break through into a danger zone. Water probably won't kill you, but it can wash you back quite quickly, even back off a ledge, and it will leave you in the dark by extinguishing your torches. Lava oozes along much more slowly but is far more deadly. Be ready to block off any unexpected breakthroughs.

- **Do be careful, be prepared, and always know your way out**—It's easy to get lost down there, especially if you break into a cave complex and decide to explore. Use torches, signs, cobblestone arranged into arrows, blocks attached to a wall with a torch facing the way out, and so on—they can all act like a trail of bread crumbs to help you find your way home.

- **Do keep your mines well lit**—Any area you leave open and dark can spawn mobs that will come for you eventually.

- **Do block off any unlit areas**—These can include caves and fully explored tunnel branches. You can even knock your torches off the wall and collect them on your way out, as long as you remember to block off the entire branch when you get back to the main trunk so the mobs don't break through. If you do break into a cave, place a torch on the wall inside the cave and block it off, leaving no more than a one-block gap. (Okay, if you must, explore, but remember, you're on a mission!) You'll be able to see the torch or at least the light from the torch on the other side as an indication that you can come back and explore it later. Then head in a different direction.

- **Do improve your tools to mine more valuable ores**—Some ores can only be mined with the right tool. For example, mining iron, gold, and Lapis Lazuli (an ingredient for making blue dye) requires a stone pickaxe, whereas mining redstone, emeralds, and diamonds requires at least an iron pickaxe. And if you find obsidian (a type of block, rather than an ore, so it's not listed in Table 4.1), you'll need a diamond pickaxe. Building a base with a crafting table and furnace will ensure you can smelt down iron and use it to craft an upgraded pickaxe so you can then mine redstone and diamonds; from there, you can mine anything but bedrock. Tools made from better materials also get the mining (and other jobs) done much faster. Refer to Table 4.1 for the materials required to mine each type of ore. I tend to use stone pickaxes for removing material, gathering iron, and so on because they're so readily created, and I switch to more advanced tools only if required.

- **Don't push forward against the wall-face as you mine**—Try to mine blocks that are a few steps forward in front of you, moving ahead only after you're sure all is well. This will help you not stumble forward into a hazard you might have just uncovered.

Mining is composed of two parts: getting down and then cutting across to uncover as much valuable ore as possible. There are a few ways to do both.

Descending to Layer 11

Just the process of descending is also a process of discovery, and no two journeys will be the same. In all cases, follow any ore seams you find on the way down and then return to the plan. Check in with the layer level shown beside the Y coordinate on your map, or for a less accurate method, just dig all the way to the lowest layer of bedrock you can find and then count 12 layers going back up. This might not take you precisely to layer 11, but it will be close.

The 2×1 Ladder Descent

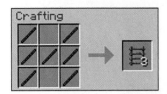

The fastest safe way to descend is in a 2×1 pattern placing ladders or vines as you go against one of the walls so you can climb your way out. Vines are plentiful in the jungle biome, but not elsewhere. You'll find a large jungle starting about halfway up the far eastern side of the Elysium world. You can use your map to navigate there sometime, but you'll need a couple of iron bars to make shears to snip the vines, so it's best to use ladders first. Ladders are made from sticks at the crafting table, with each set of seven making three ladder blocks. Vines and ladders have a significant advantage over jumping up and down stairs—besides being a fast method of vertical movement—because they don't use up any energy, so you won't see any drop in your hunger bar as you traverse them.

TIP

Use Sneak Mode to Pause

Enter Sneak mode ⊕ if you need to pause when climbing or descending a ladder or vine. While paused, you can place torches and do anything else required, including placing additional ladder or vine segments.

Dig out the block directly in front of you, as well as the one underneath. If all looks good, turn around and dig out the block you were standing on and the one underneath that, and you'll be down to a level pit. Place two ladder segments on the wall in front of you, and repeat. Attach torches to the other wall every 9 layers or so. You can also place blocks between the torches to break your fall. It shouldn't really be necessary because it's difficult to fall off a ladder—especially with Sneak mode activated—but staring down a 50-layer drop can induce feelings of virtual vertigo. You might be wondering why to not just dig a 1×1 descent. Making it 2×1 allows you to avoid the pitfall of digging the block out from underneath that drops you into a lava pit or cave. It's just a bit safer to dig 2×1 in Survival mode.

Figure 4.2 shows the view looking up to the sky from the bottom of a 53-layer pit.

FIGURE 4.2 Sunlight seems such a long way away when you're on layer 11, but ladders make for very fast ascents, and it takes only about 20 seconds to reach the Overworld.

TIP

Defying the Laws of Physics

Falling down the side of the shaft without the ladder is deadly, but like the acrobat at the circus diving off the high board into a pail of water, you can easily break your fall. Just dig out a block at the bottom of the non-ladder side of the shaft, pour a bucket of water into the hole, dig out a further two blocks under that so the water forms a pool three blocks deep (you'll need to jump into the pool to dig out the last block and then press ⊗ to swim to the surface). You'll survive extreme falls every time, as shown in Figure 4.3. You can also use this as the world's fastest one-way express elevator to get down in a hurry. If you do take fall damage, try increasing the water's depth, although a 250-layer fall can splash down with zero damage in water just three blocks deep.

FIGURE 4.3   Break an otherwise breakneck fall down a long vertical shaft with a few blocks of thud-absorbing water.

The Straight Staircase

The staircase is one of the most natural designs, and it's quick to move along it. You'll need to break three blocks for each one down, so it's not quite as efficient as the ladder descent, but it's the simplest option available if you are short on wood for ladders and are lacking in vines.

Start by digging down one block in front of you. Hop in the hole, and then follow this pattern:

1 Dig out the block at eye level in front of you and the two underneath that.

2 Move into the hole in front of you, and repeat.

As you go, don't forget to place torches every 9 steps or so, and if you hit any problems, either take a 90° turn to the left or right and continue or make a bit of space for a landing and do a 180° turn.

You can see a typical straight staircase in Figure 4.4.

FIGURE 4.4 The straight staircase descent is easy to go down and fast to move back up. You can improve it by crafting cobblestone stairs so that no jumping is required on the return journey, although you'll need to dig out an extra block for each step so you don't bash your head on the tunnel as you head up and down.

The Spiral Staircase

A spiral staircase takes a little more care to build, and you might get a bit dizzy going up and down with all the frequent turns, but it has a couple of advantages over the other methods:

■ The staircase descends vertically, which makes for more methodical exploration. It's also easy to build if you don't have the wood needed for a vertical access shaft.

■ This type of staircase winds down around itself or a central core, exposing more surface area and therefore providing greater opportunity to discover seams of ore on the way down.

Several versions of spiral staircases exist. The tightest staircase possible is the 2×2. You can build this following the same steps as for a straight staircase. However, each time you drop down one level, just turn to the right or left 90° and start again. Keep turning in the same direction to ensure that you drop down vertically.

A 3×3 version of the same staircase involves going down two steps straight, turning, going down another two steps straight, and so on. This leaves a single-column central core that you can remove to create an open light well, gaining more illumination from each torch you place. It's also a bit easier to keep your bearings if you remove the central core as you go, but there's always a risk you could fall into the core, so consider placing a 3-deep pool of water at the very bottom to cushion any inadvertent tumbles. There's a good chance you'll find some iron on the way down, so you can then build a bucket, fill it with water, smelt the iron in the furnace, fill it with water, and finish off the staircase. Figure 4.5 shows the end result.

FIGURE 4.5   A 3×3 spiral staircase provides a handy light well down the middle, single block core.

A 5×5 version is similar, but you go down four steps and then turn. This leaves a solid block of 3×3 in the middle. You can then dig out the central block in the pillar and place a ladder against the side when you're ready for faster ascents and descents. Open up blocks from the staircase into the core (except on the side reserved for a ladder) to allow in light from the torches. This style of staircase also exposes the maximum surface area, essentially mining out a block of 5×5 units all the way down. It is, however, a complicated method requiring that you keep careful count of the steps you dig on each side. I usually just go for a 3×3 if I need to descend vertically or a pit with ladders. If ladders are lacking, I'll use a straight staircase lined with cobblestone stairs so that heading up and down doesn't drain my hunger bar.

Layouts for Fast, Efficient Mining

There are numerous methods for mining, and some may lead to madness. You can wander around hacking at every rock in sight, but this can miss a lot of ore deposits, and it's pretty easy to get lost in a maze of your own making. You can also go for grandeur, hollowing out halls as you go, dwarfing the Mines of Moria. Fortunately, Minecraft doesn't yet have a Balrog, although the Enderdragon comes close.

A gigantic, modern, underground lair with powered rails allowing you to zip back and forth in minecarts also has its charm. (See Chapter 9, "Redstone, Rails, and More.") There's nothing wrong with that, and it does make for a fantastic creative challenge, but for your first serious dig, with what is probably still a quite limited set of tools, your aim should be to collect as much ore as possible with the least amount of effort and using the fewest number of pickaxes possible. That mine is called a *branch mine*.

Branch mines generally cover a rectangular surface area. You can choose any size you like, but you might find yourself limited by the terrain. Lava breakouts at Layer 11 are quite common, and if you end up at a firey pool such as the one shown in Figure 4.6, you have little option but to treat it as the end of the trunk—or that particular branch—unless it's easily worked around. The good part is that lava pools provide a lot of light, so mobs tend to spawn elsewhere.

FIGURE 4.6   Lava lakes usually act as a natural barrier to further mining, at least in the beginning. Pick up the lava in a bucket and use it to power your furnace. One bucket will smelt 100 blocks of ore! Later you can use buckets of water to turn the lava into an obsidian bridge and mine that for a Nether Portal. In the meanwhile, just work around them.

So what's the most efficient layout? The one I prefer is quite simple, easy to navigate, and effective. It relies on the fact that blocks of ore almost always appear in veins larger than a single block. Yes, even diamonds!

Branch mines use a horizontal central trunk, two blocks high by one block wide. Branches are then dug out perpendicular to the trunk, much like the branches of a tree, or at least a strangely geometrical one.

Because each block of ore can be identified from any of its six sides, a distance of two blocks per branch exposes at least one side of every block to the side and also above and below you. In other words, move one space along a branch, and you expose a total of six blocks: two on each side, one below, one above, and the two in front of you.

This is the most thorough mining method available because it exposes every single block within the area the mine covers. But it's not the most efficient because ore veins almost always take up more than 1 block, generally in clumps of 2–16 blocks. Think of the goal, therefore, as being to uncover veins of ore, not individual blocks. If you find 1 block in a vein, you'll mine it and therefore expose the next, and you can then follow the vein to its end.

Spacing each branch every fourth block, with three blocks in between, works best. Take a look at Figure 4.7 for a top-down view.

FIGURE 4.7 Space your branches every four steps (leaving three blocks between), off a primary central trunk, and place a base camp for convenient crafting and storage.

NOTE

Spacing Your Branches

If your mining targets are the more common ores such as the coal and iron that occur in larger veins, you could even space your branches with four or five blocks in between. You might miss some smaller deposits, but you will intersect all the larger ones. This is a fast, efficient technique you can use in the higher levels.

When you've completed mining layer 11, head back up using the same spacing principal vertically that you did horizontally, leaving a gap of three blocks, or layers, between the roof of your first trunk and the floor of the next. As you work higher, you lose most of the chances for redstone, but other ores are plentiful. And you can head down to bedrock the same way, taking extra care because there's a lot more lava about.

Staying Safe While You Mine

Your first mining expedition will undoubtedly turn up a lot of valuable ore. Don't risk losing it all by dying. Chances are you won't be able to make it back down from your last spawn point to pick up your valuables. Here are some tips that will help:

- Use Sneak mode so you can safely walk around the edges of lava lakes and other hazards without risk of falling in.

- Build a small base to act as a staging point. It's easy enough to create a new crafting table and furnace, but if you've also been able to construct a bed and don't have wool for another, consider bringing your bed down with you from your Overland dwelling. You can break it up with any tool and pick up the floating icon so that it slots into your inventory. Set up your base somewhere central to your mine, and sleep in the bed at least once to set a new spawn point. Figure 4.8 shows a minimal layout where everything fits into a cozy space. Spruce it up with a clock, so you know when it's daylight outside, and maybe a picture or two.

NOTE

The Mobs Might Not Let You Sleep

You might need to try several base locations before you can successfully sleep in a bed. Any mobs nearby, even if separated from you by a solid wall, will prevent you from catching a snooze and resetting your spawn point. Rather than searching for and clearing out caves, just pack up the camp and find a new site somewhere else in your mine.

- Place chests in your base or anywhere that's convenient in your tunnel system. Regularly return to the chests to drop off any valuable items you've found so that you can pick them up again if you respawn.

FIGURE 4.8   A mining base makes it easier to recover after a respawn, and it lets you improve tools, smelt ores, and store valuables and supplies for your adventures in the dark, dangerous depths of the Overworld.

The Bottom Line

Mining is the only way to gather many key resources, including the diamonds required to mine obsidian and get to The Nether region. Don't make the mistake of mining too high because you'll miss most of the good stuff. When you hit layer 11, you'll be amazed at just how quickly you amass a huge range of useful resources. Mine your way in layers back up, rather than starting at the top and working down, and you'll have a plentiful supply of iron for tools, coal for torches, and masses of cobblestone to expand your dwelling on the surface.

Minecraft places resources in 16×16 blocks that run all the way from bedrock to the sky. (These are known as *chunks*.) There are an average of just over 3 diamond blocks per chunk, and of course many times that of the more common ores. So if you don't find what you need, just dig across at least 16 blocks and try again. There's a wealth of material down there, and it won't be long before you have everything you need and will even be able to build an incredible powered rail system that can zoom you up and down from the surface as fast as a freight train, as well as carry resources for you.

Don't be discouraged if you don't find diamonds right away. It could take a couple of hours of real-time mining using the layout I described earlier. Sometimes, you'll get to layer 11 and the first block you break will uncover diamonds. Other times, it'll take a dedicated chipping away, using up as many as half a dozen iron pickaxes in the branch pattern before you've all but given up. Then, knocking away one more block among hundreds, there they are. It's always something of a thrill. Just keep at it, no matter what. They are definitely there, and it won't be too long before you see their glinting, delightlfully blue-hued surfaces (see Figure 4.9).

You might have noticed one thing, though, while you were toiling. Those caves you've no doubt uncovered look mighty tempting—all that exposed ore just waiting for you to collect. In the next chapter, you get battle-ready so you can head back down, take on the mobs, and take home the spoils.

FIGURE 4.9   A group of three diamond blocks—and there are three more underneath! If you're having incredible difficulty finding any, head to coordinates x:131, y:11, z:138 in Elysium.

Combat School

In This Chapter

- Mobs, meh! Learn their strange, wonderful ways and how to defeat 'em.
- Build snow and iron golems for additional defense.
- Wield a sword like a swashbuckler, dealing extra damage with critical hits.
- Don't bow down before them—use your bow instead for long-range attacks.
- Learn how to keep your quiver fully stocked. Arrows are everywhere, and they're easily crafted.
- Grow a thicker skin with all the information you need to craft the right armor.

It is perfectly possible to live a peaceful existence in Minecraft. Build a nice, safe mine; avoid cave exploring of any kind; create a self-sufficient farm that produces everything you need; protect your domain with mob-proof fences; keep it all well-lit to prevent spawning inside; and retire at the end of each uneventful day with slippers on your soft, uncalloused feet in front of a warm fire, sipping a bowl of mushroom stew.

Ah, the serenity...but there's only one problem with that: you'll miss out on most of the fun! Sooner or later combat becomes a necessity. It's not full-scale war, but having the right equipment, some key tactics, and a few fighting skills will let you progress much faster and further in the game than taking the purely passive path.

I've introduced a few of the hostile mobs previously, but now it's time to get into the specifics of tactics, weapons, armor, and defense.

Introducing the Menagerie

Minecraft mobs might be a pain in the derriere at times, but you'll never get to Valhalla without 'em. Let's take a closer look at each and the unique tactics you can use to defeat them.

Remember that, in most cases, hostile mobs switch to pursuit mode if they are within 16 blocks and have a line of sight to your location. As soon as they switch, they'll track you even if you move out of direct sight.

You can use this to your advantage, leading them to a location that's better suited for a counterattack or escape or even maneuver them into a position where they can be pushed off a cliff or into a lava pool, but do ensure you keep your own footing while doing so.

Each hostile has specific strengths and weaknesses. Although any tool can do damage, you'll do best sticking with a sword for short-range attacks and the bow for longer-range ones. Mobs are also vulnerable to fire, so lighting the ground with a flint and steel can weaken them enough that a final blow finishes them off or actually does them in altogether.

In this chapter, I run through the mobs you are most likely to encounter in The Overworld. See Chapter 12, "Playing Through: The Nether and The End," for complete details on those that inhabit The Nether and The End regions.

Zombies

The first mob you'll encounter in Minecraft will probably be the humble zombie (see Figure 5.1). The sound of one of them trying to beat down your door can set hairs on end, but their bark in single numbers is worse than their bite. Zombies are slow, and while a poorly handled encounter can definitely kill you, be the aggressor and you'll stay on top.

FIGURE 5.1 Zombies are slow but have a habit of spawning in large numbers.

There are a few different ways to deal with zombies. If you encounter them close to a cave entrance and it's sunny outside, just lead them out as soon as they enter pursuit mode, and they'll burn up in the light. Keep your distance, though, because they can still attack while they're burning and cause you fire damage. Zombies can happily exist in daylight when it's shaded, overcast, or raining or when wearing helmets on their heads—although they do look a little silly. (Then again, you can wear a pumpkin on your head to prevent Endermen from attacking, so let's not point fingers.)

For a more direct assault, keep your crosshairs on the zombies and hit first and hit often, pulling R2 continuously. They'll only sometimes land a hit in return, and probably just the one before they're overcome. You can also try to block their attack, and that of most other mobs, by holding L2 as they lurch toward you.

If you encounter more than one zombie along with other mobs sprinkled in for good measure, hack through the zombies first and spiders next, and then make your escape or retreat.

Zombies can also lay siege to villages at night and convert villagers into zombie villagers. You can generally survive if you can get inside a room, but zombies also can spawn inside during these *Walking Dead* moments, no matter the light level. And I have seen a villager open the door during a siege, only to let a zombie stagger inside. Villagers are not exactly the smartest things on a Minecraft block!

TIP

Watch Your Back

Consider placing a wooden door at the entrance to caves that connect back to your tunnel system. This will protect your base while you're exploring the cave. The door also protects your retreat route if you need to make a hasty exit, and you can always knock it down for retrieval and permanently block off the cave after the mobs have wandered off.

Zombies drop rotten meat when they're defeated. The meat is poisonous but can still build up your hunger bar. The best strategy here is to save up a few pieces and eat them all at once because you will still only get one hit of food poisoning. This is a great way to replenish your hunger bar from almost empty to full—your health will take a minimal hit from the poisoning and then start to replenish from the full hunger bar. Also, consider carrying a bucket of milk with you because this instantly cures all types of food poisoning. A quick swig and you'll be good as new. There's one other use for rotten meat: feed it to tamed wolves to keep up their health.

CAUTION

The Dead Stick Together

Zombies are the most "mobbish" of Minecraft's mobs. If you attack one, others nearby—even outside of the usual hostile range—might come swarming to help out their undead brethren.

Zombies can also, even if rarely, drop other items such as tools and armor.

Spiders

Minecraft will populate your world with two types of spiders and, for good measure, a skeleton/spider hybrid.

You'll encounter the large spiders shown in Figure 5.2 most often. (See the sections "Cave Spiders" and "Spider Jockeys," later in this chapter, for more information on the others.) The large spiders are jumpy, literally. They can leap two to three blocks in a single bound and can climb walls unless there is an overhang or a layer of a transparent block type they can't climb, such as iron bars or glass. They're fast, aggressive at night or in dark places, and a little bit tougher to defeat than your average zombie.

FIGURE 5.2   Spiders are fast and able to climb walls, but they're easy to defeat even with a wooden sword.

NOTE

Building Spider-Proof Walls

Spiders can crawl up almost any wall unless it contains transparent blocks. This isn't always practical. An overhang provides an alternative defense. Position a single block on the outside of the third level of any wall such that the block forms an upside-down ledge. Spiders can't get through single-block gaps, so these overhangs have to be positioned only every second space, somewhat like the battlements on a castle keep's walls. See Chapter 8, "Creative Construction," for examples of this and other defensive construction techniques.

Spiders are, however, very useful because they drop string, a vital ingredient for crafting bows and fishing rods. Every four pieces of string can also make one block (or bale) of wool. Gather three of those blocks and you'll have enough to craft a bed. Sleep in that to reset your spawn point and escape the night. Spiders can, therefore, be *very* handy if there are no sheep nearby!

They have one other drop: spider eyes. Treat these as a sort of extreme food if you can handle the concept. They're poisonous along the same lines as rotten meat but will give you a quick hunger boost, and those eyes make for a useful ingredient in some potions.

Spiders are just one block high and two blocks wide, so a 1×1 opening in a wall will keep you safe.

Their jumping ability gives them a slight edge in combat. The best strategy is similar to that of defeating zombies. Hit them as rapidly as possible, but also walk backward at the same time, preferably going uphill. This can help keep you out of range of their jump attacks.

CAUTION

I Always Feel Like Somebody's Watching Me

Ever had the feeling someone's watching you? In Minecraft, that someone is probably a spider with all eight eyes, bright points of red in the dark. Spiders don't require a line of sight to enter pursuit mode, so they'll be on your trail as soon as you get within 16 blocks, and they'll do almost anything to get closer. Lock yourself in your shelter for the night, but take care in the morning. If you hear the spider's hissing/slurping noise, it might be still waiting for you, hatred in every eye. Spiders won't attack you during the day unless you attack them first, but if one has been in pursuit of you at night, even if you hadn't noticed, it will carry a bit of a grudge and still attack you during the day. Spiders have a habit of lurking in ambush on your roof, waiting for you to "tra la la" out the door the next morning without a care in the world, until you feel their fangs sink into your back! Fortunately, the large spiders aren't poisonous, so just make sure you have your sword in hand, ready to fight back, and you'll be fine.

Skeletons

The sound of a skeleton's rattling bones usually gives this mob away a few moments before its arrow pierces your breastbone. Skeletons are sharpshooters, so the best approach is to stay out of the direct line of fire, ducking out to attack only when they're close enough. Do it commando-style, moving sideways to avoid the feathered missiles that will undoubtedly be coming your way. It's not an arrow-proof strategy, but it can help. (If you've been hit a few times, use ⬤ to switch to an external view and admire your porcupine-ness.) Figure 5.3 shows a skeleton with its ubiquitous bow.

FIGURE 5.3   Skeletons are sharpshooters, so keep your distance until you can strike, and don't let them sneak up behind you.

If you can get close enough, a sword will finish off skeletons quite quickly. For this reason, a good strategy is to try to wait somewhere protected, letting them get within striking reach, but behind any sort of barricade that will protect you from their arrows. Skeletons also burn up in direct sunlight, but not when it is overcast or raining.

Skeletons usually drop arrows when they die, making them an easy way to resupply your stock if you are also using a bow. You'll also often find arrows that have missed their mark sticking out of blocks. It's impossible to collect these, but do take care breaking any block that has gathered some arrows: the arrows will fall to the next block and can strike you on the way down.

Also, keep in mind that skeletons will try to circle around you, so they can sneak up on you from behind.

Cave Spiders

These invidious arachnids are found in abandoned mine shafts. They're fast, small, and poisonous, and they make large spiders look positively passive!

Cavers can slip through a gap one block wide and just half a block high, so a 1×1 block hole in the wall offers no protection at all. They're easily spotted by their blue coloring and smaller size (see Figure 5.4).

FIGURE 5.4   Inhabiting only abandoned mineshafts, cave spiders aren't common, but they are definitely among the top deadly mobs.

Cave spiders don't spawn naturally. They're spewed out of a spawning device, a small fiery cage that shows a miniature of themselves spinning around faster and faster until it seems they're flung out the side through centrifugal force. It's a bit like a washing machine's spin cycle gone mad.

If you are lucky enough to find an abandoned mineshaft, consider it a huge bonus. These massive structures can hold well over one dozen chests with all kinds of goodies inside. The cave spider and other mobs that may inhabit it can be a bit of a challenge, but go ahead and claim that mineshaft for your own. It's now *your* mineshaft. Just take care as you go, ensuring you are well prepared.

Here's what you need to know:

- A poisonous bite from a cave spider won't kill you. Like all poisonings, it can take you down to half a heart on Normal difficulty, but the damage from the bite itself, not the poison, can definitely do you in.

- Cavers are easy to kill but are smaller than other mobs, so you need to aim your cross-hairs with a bit more care and click frenetically.

- Fighting while walking backward works as well as with the large spiders, but cavers are faster so they will be able to launch more attacks.

- Cave spiders' habitat is filled with spider webs. These will slow you down, but cavers can slip through those webs at normal speed.

- Break the spawner. Kill the source, and you solve the supply. But keep your guard up because there is often more than one spawner in close proximity. Spawners exist in abandoned mineshafts, in the much smaller dungeons where the spawner may spit out other mob types and usually has a chest nearby, and also in Nether fortresses where they usually spit out blaze mobs. Disable a spawner by raising the level of light nearby with up to four torches.

- The good news: abandoned mineshafts are a treasure trove of resources waiting to be plundered. You'll find loads of chests, and the mine braces provide the only source of wood available underground.

Spider Jockeys

Sit a skeleton on top of a spider, and you get a spider jockey. Spider jockeys jump like a spider, shoot arrows like a skeleton, and are best given a wide berth. Fortunately, they're rare. If you see one, smash the skeleton if you can and deal with the spider next. You might not survive, but isn't that why you keep your valuables in a chest next to your spawn point? Rhetorical question: of course, you do that!

The skeleton will burn up as per usual in sunlight, leaving just an ordinary spider behind. See Figure 5.5 for an action shot!

FIGURE 5.5   A spider jockey burning up in the morning sun.

Creepers

If Minecraft has an anti-hero, it's the creeper (see Figure 5.6). Think of creepers as walking improvised explosive devices (IEDs). I talked a little about creepers in Chapter 2, "First-Night Survival." Rather than repeating that, let's get into some of the specifics.

FIGURE 5.6   Creepers appear to be fairly docile until they get close and provide a taste of their truly explosive personalities.

First, you can survive a creeper attack unless you are completely caught by surprise. If you turn a corner and there's one right in front of you, do your best to sprint away. Your attack on a creeper needs to be well timed, and you need space to sprint in, thwack it, and move back out again so that its fuse resets. The force of your blow should usually be enough to knock the creeper far enough that this happens with reasonable surety. A sword with a knockback enchantment (see "Sprucing Up Your Weapons" on page 196) also helps a lot against creepers but actually makes things worse when fighting skeletons.

Unfortunately, if you see a creeper swelling like a balloon (something it does just prior to exploding), it's probably already too late.

Try to ensure that you are not fighting the creeper near an important structure. Just about the worst situation occurs when stepping out the front door, straight into one. You'll end up with a crater where your door knocker used to hang. As one of the memes on the Web reads, "I just undid in 2 seconds what you spent 5 hours building." You are generally safe if you can keep a distance of at least two blocks, but they move quite fast.

Creepers do have an Achilles heel. If you find one swimming in water, you can easily deal with it by attacking from below, and not just by hitting their heel. Anywhere will do. Creepers are also scared of ocelots or their tamed version, the humble cat (see Chapter 7, "Farming and Taming Mobs").

As with most mobs in Minecraft, creepers can seem somewhat formidable at first, but with a little practice you'll find you can dispatch them fairly easily.

Creepers drop gunpowder, a key ingredient in crafting TNT blocks and making the throwable "splash" potions described in Chapter 10, "Enchanting, Anvils, and Brewing."

Slimes

Slimes are uncommon, which is unfortunate because they're also quite handy. They spawn only in underground areas between bedrock and layer 39, and even then only in about 10% of the actual chunks. You might recall that each chunk is a column of 16×16 blocks.

If any mob needs frenetic hitting, it's the slime. That's because each large one splits into up to 4 smaller ones and up to 16 tiny ones (see Figure 5.7). The tiny ones don't do damage but can be annoying as they swarm you. Just thwack them repeatedly until you've finished them all, and then switch to your fists to finish off the tiny ones so you don't needlessly wear out your weapons. All it takes is one blow to see them off.

FIGURE 5.7   Slimes split and split, seemingly ad infinitum.

Slimes drop slimeballs, a substance that makes ordinary pistons stickier than duct tape. Slimeballs are also useful in creating magma cream, which is useful in The Nether for protecting you if you need to swim across lava lakes.

Endermen

The Endermen are curious, otherworldy creatures surrounded by a purple haze (see Figure 5.8). The Endermen call The End region home, and you'll see them there in enormous numbers, but they also appear in The Overworld quite often, so I've also included them here.

FIGURE 5.8   Always look behind when the Enderman you're attacking teleports away.

Endermen keep busy zipping from place to place, lifting blocks and moving them. They may even steal part of your house!

They tend to teleport when attacked and have a habit of popping up behind you, which can make them tricky to defeat. Your best bet is actually to do your best to ignore them. They're not hostile unless you put your crosshairs on them, and as mentioned previously, popping a pumpkin on your head—while not offering any armor advantage, and definitely not winning you any beauty contests—essentially hides your eyes so that Endermen don't turn hostile.

Endermen drop ender pearls, an essential crafting component for Eyes of Ender. The latter is an unusual item that will help you find the stronghold that houses the End Portal needed to access The End region. Attack the Endermen's legs to prevent them from teleporting away.

Zombie Pigmen

Like Endermen, these inhabitants of The Nether region are neutral unless attacked. The main problem with doing that is that, just like wolves and zombies, attacking one causes them all to want to join the fray. If you do get zombie pigmen riled up, you might find it best to try to make your escape. They'll calm down eventually. Figure 5.9 shows their interesting visage—a mug shot if ever there was one.

FIGURE 5.9   With a pack mentality, zombie pigmen are best left to their own devices.

Defensive Mobs

Balancing out the host of hostile mobs are a couple of defensive ones that are unique because they are also the only player-created mobs. Neither of these mobs is created at a crafting table. Instead, you'll need to stack their blocks where you'd like them to spawn, always ensuring you leave the pumpkin block to last.

Snow Golems

Snow golems aren't the strongest line of defense because they don't cause damage to any of the Overworld mobs, but their furious rate of snowball throwing can be enough to keep zombies and other hostile mobs at a distance, making them useful around your home. Create your own snow golem with these simple steps:

1 Gather at least eight snowballs by collecting any snow lying on the ground with a shovel.

2 Craft two snow blocks using four snowballs for each.

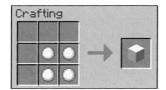

3 Create a stack of the snow blocks by placing one on top of the other.

4 Place a pumpkin on top of the stacked snow blocks to bring the snow golem to life, shown in Figure 5.10.

Unfortunately, snow golems have a tendency to wander, so place them behind a fence or walled area for best results, but ensure there's a roof over their heads because they don't survive rain.

FIGURE 5.10 Snow golems aren't particularly powerful, but who doesn't want a snowball-hurling automaton in their front yard all year round?

Iron Golems

Iron golems exist to protect villages and their inhabitants (see Figure 5.11). They're incredibly powerful, and you really shouldn't attack them or any villagers because they'll rush to the villagers' defense.

Iron golems spawn naturally in villages of sufficient size (approximately 21 houses), but you can also build one in a similar fashion to a snow golem:

1 Build up a collection of 36 iron ingots. (These golems are incredibly expensive!)

2 Create four blocks of iron using nine ingots each.

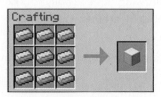

3 Place one block of iron on top of the other, and then attach two more blocks to opposite sides of the upper block in the stack. You are, effectively, creating a stack of iron blocks in the shape of a *T*.

4 Place a pumpkin on top of the middle upper block where the head would go.

Iron golems, besides smashing the heck out of spiders, zombies, and most other hostile mobs, have the endearing habit of giving red roses to village children. Unfortunately, they don't really care too much about your well-being, so unless your strategy is to help protect villages, iron golems are not really worth building due to the enormous amount of iron required.

FIGURE 5.11   Iron golems aren't directly on your side, but if you set up your house inside a village, you'll be within their circle of protection.

Weapons and Armor

Out in the wild? Getting stuck by skeletons? Zombies spawning everywhere? You can stand and fight, or you can decide to run. Either way, a decent set of weapons and a suit of armor will help you live by the sword, and survive.

Minecraft has two primary offensive weapons: the sword and the bow. In a pinch, other tools will also do. None of the tools are as powerful as the sword, but if you do run out of swords in combat, switch—in order of effectiveness—to the axe, then a pickaxe, and then if all else is lost remember that you can also beat something over the head with a shovel.

TIP

Delivering the Winning Blow

Deliver a *critical hit* to cause up to 50% more damage. This works for every weapon (and tool) except the hoe. The trick is to make the hit as you are falling, and the easiest way to do that is to jump first, timing it right so that you have passed the apex of your leap by the time you strike. I'm not sure if it helps to yell "Hiiiiyaaa!!!" as you do, but feel free to give it a try. You'll know you've succeeded when you see a little bloom of stars around the unfortunate recipient of your attack immediately after the hit.

Critical hits can be crucial for survival because they can kill some mobs in a single blow, saving your sword's durability. Put in a bit of practice when you can, and the timing of the hit (and the optional battle cry) will become second nature.

The same techniques that work in many other combat games also work in Minecraft. Keep on the move; don't just stand like a statue and flail. Float like a butterfly and sting like an infuriated wasp. Use ⬤ to circle around the enemy and dodge direct blows, ranged attacks such as from skeletons, and melee attacks (which essentially are full-body broadsides by slimes and the like). Always use height to your advantage when out in the open. It will help both with avoiding attacks and in delivering critical hits.

Swordcraft

The sword will no doubt become your go-to weapon. In a pinch, it's easy to quickly craft a sword from a few raw materials, and its damage and durability increase quickly as you upgrade from stone to iron to diamond. Table 5.1 lists the materials, the damage inflicted, and the durability of each material.

TABLE 5.1 Sword Materials

Material	Bare Fists	Wood	Gold	Stone	Iron	Diamond
Durability	Infinite	60	33	132	251	1562
Damage Points	1	4	4	5	6	7
Maximum Critical Hit Points	2	8	8	9	11	12

The damage points represent the minimum damage from a successful strike. Critical hits increase by a random amount up to the totals shown in Table 5.1. Iron and diamond swords are obviously the most powerful, especially if you keep in mind that attack is actually the best defense. The quicker you can kill a mob, the less time it has to deliver blows in return. Dispatch them fast, and move on with your health mostly intact.

Sprinting while hitting also knocks back the target, a vital move for attacking creepers, but not so good against skeletons because it gives them time to line up another shot.

The sword is unique among all weapons because it also provides a blocking move. Use L2 to block any attack, either direct or ranged, if you can spot that arrow or fireball from a Ghast in The Nether heading your way. This provides an up to 50% damage reduction at the expense of dropping your speed to a crawl, so block at the last possible moment or in tight corners where there isn't enough room for the usual evasive maneuvers.

Bows and Arrows

A fully charged bow deals more damage than an unenchanted diamond sword, making them very powerful weapons. Bows and arrows also enable you to attack from a distance, giving skeletons a dose of their own medicine and keeping you well clear of creeper detonation range. Figure 5.12 shows the bow in action.

FIGURE 5.12   Arrow in flight: Sorry, Porky.

Craft a bow from three sticks and three pieces of string (dropped by spiders) and equip it in any Hotbar slot. There is one other part to the equation: arrows.

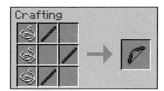

A piece of flint, a stick, and a feather will create a stack of four arrows.

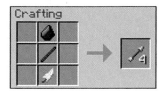

This isn't a lot, and you're going to need a lot of arrows to make a bow worthwhile—probably several dozen on any significant expedition.

A few techniques make this quite easy. The easiest is to go for a quick scout around in the morning when the sun comes up. Here's why:

- Skeletons often drop arrows when they burn up in the morning, so there's no crafting required.

- Zombies sometimes drop feathers.

- Chickens can die during the night, a victim of wolves or cacti. You can also kill any random chickens you find during your travels to get both meat and often 1–2 feathers per chicken, or you can build a chicken farm and start breeding them as described in Chapter 7.

Sticks are almost always readily available, but what about flint?

Every mined gravel block has a 1 in 10 chance of dropping a piece of flint instead of a block of gravel. It's completely random, meaning that every block of gravel, if mined, placed, and mined again, will eventually yield the flint. That changes everything!

Gravel usually seems to be a bit of an annoyance in mines because it's so common, keeps falling down, and for best results usually requires that you change from a pickaxe to a shovel. But from now on consider it a benefit. Gather all the gravel you can because each and every one contains flint, just requiring a bit of gentle encouragement to give up its precious yield.

Dig out a nice big room somewhere convenient underground, light it with torches, and fill in the middle with all the gravel blocks you've mined. Then have at 'em with a shovel. Mining gravel with an iron shovel is incredibly quick, so it won't take long. Placing just 10 blocks is likely to yield 1 flint (enough for 4 arrows!) and the same 9 gravel blocks ready for reuse. Add a new block to the mix and repeat.

TIP

Superfast Flint Mining

The quickest way I've found to recycle gravel for flint is to create a room with a set of four 8-block-long trenches that are 2 blocks deep with an additional step in the end so you can climb out. This creates a total of 64 gravel spaces—conveniently equal to a full stack of gravel in a Hotbar slot. Keep another full stack of gravel in a regular inventory slot. This is the replenishment stack. With the Hotbar gravel selected, jump into each trench, running backward while holding down **L2** to place the gravel in a continuous stream. Switch to the shovel and do the same forward while holding down **R2** to harvest the gravel and flint. Iron shovels provide the best combination of durability and speed if you don't want to needlessly craft a diamond shovel.

You'll get 6–7 pieces of flint each time you clear the room, which is sufficient to make between 24 and 28 arrows. Now replenish from the spare stack of gravel in the inventory, refilling the Hotbar stack, and repeat.

Ready for some archery practice? Follow these steps to fling arrows of misfortune:

1 Make the bow the active item in your Hotbar. Arrows can stay hidden in a regular inventory slot and are depleted automatically.

2 Use the crosshairs to aim at your target. You'll need to learn to account for the arrow's arc through the sky and to lead your target's movement. Aim directly at nearby targets and increasingly above their heads as they get farther away. If they are heading clearly in one direction across your line of sight, just target slightly ahead of that, leading the movement to make up for the time it takes the arrow to reach them. There's no hard-and-fast rule here: practice does make perfect.

3 Pull 【L2】 and hold to pull back on the bow. Hold longer for a stronger shot. When it's fully charged the bow will stop drawing back and shake slightly, showing that it's primed for a critical hit with a damage bonus.

4 Fire the arrow by releasing the trigger. Fully charged shots leave a trail of stars behind the arrow as it flies.

Arrows deliver substantial damage and are the safest way to deal with skeletons, creepers, and other mobs that also deliver ranged attacks or are just plan dangerous in close proximity.

Various enchantment effects can also greatly increase a bow's strength and versatility and also provide an unlimited supply of arrows.

Armor-All

Armor is crafted from leather, iron ingots, gold ingots, and diamond gems. Full armor suits require 24 units of source material, but each armor piece doesn't need to be made from the same material. It's best to think of armor not as a complete suit but as its individual parts: a helmet, a chest plate, leggings, and boots. Each can be made from a different material, depending on what you have on hand, and each adds to the damage protection value that protects your entire body, regardless of where you are hit. Your avatar is, to put it plainly, one giant hit box—like a punching bag that can also strike back.

I mentioned in Chapter 3, "Gathering Resources," that each armor icon represents an 8% reduction in the damage you'll take, so a 10/10 suit of armor will reduce the damage you take by 80%, whereas a 1/10 suit will absorb only 8%. Armor becomes less effective the more damage it absorbs, although the rate at which it deteriorates also depends on its material—leather being the weakest and diamond the strongest.

NOTE

Which Suit Suits You?

Finding 24 units of any of the materials that can be turned into a suit of armor isn't easy when you're starting out, but if you happen to have spawned near a few cattle, consider starting a farm as described in Chapter 7 and breeding the cattle rather than trying to constantly find more out in the wild. If you haven't found any willing bovines, mining for iron is the only reasonable option, but ensure you can build up enough of a stock of ingots for your tools before turning additional ones into armor.

Your heads-up display (HUD) shows the total defense points for your current armor. As with the other bars, each unit represents two points, decreasing by half an icon as each point depletes.

Table 5.2 lists the maximum damage absorption provided by each armor material. Various enchantments can also improve the damage absorption of each type, with gold fairing the best, followed by leather, diamond, and iron.

TABLE 5.2   Maximum Armor Protection Values

Type	Icons Displayed	Percent Protection
Leather	3.5	28%
Gold	5.5	44%
Chain	6	48%
Iron	7.5	60%
Diamond	10	80%

Having said that, not all the armor components made from one material provide the same damage protection. The chest plate always provides the highest protection, followed by leggings, the helmet, and lastly boots. The actual ratios differ somewhat between materials but, generally speaking, a chest plate is 3–3.5 times as effective as boots. This is also the recommended order for building armor.

I'll show you the recipes for iron armor, and you can just substitute whatever materials you have on hand. The same material must be used for each piece, but as mentioned earlier, you don't need to wear every material from the same type. For example, if you have been able to collect a lot of leather but only a handful of pieces of iron, consider using the leather for a chest plate and the iron for a helmet because this will give you the maximum damage protection from the available resources:

- **Chest plate**—8 units of material

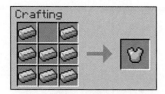

- **Leggings**—7 units of material

- **Helmet**—5 units of material

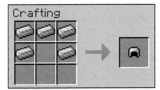

- **Boots**—4 units of material

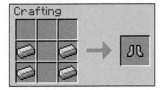

When you've crafted the armor, open your inventory window, select the piece, and press △ to automatically shift it to the correct armor inventory slot.

Press ⬅ to admire your new look (see Figure 5.13).

FIGURE 5.13   An almost complete set of iron armor, ready for battle, but we must still do something about those leather boots!

Color Coordinate Your Leather

Leather armor is the only armor that can be dyed. Although this won't help one iota with damage protection, it's possible to step out in style by crafting any of several hundred thousand different colors for the different armor pieces. Open your inventory window △, and ensure you are wearing the armor you want to color. Then pick up the dye and place it directly on the armor's icon in the upper-left section of the inventory window to apply that color. You can use any combination of dye to achieve the desired result. (See Table 7.2 in Chapter 7 for a full list of dyes and colors.) Repeating the same dye more than once tends to weight the final color toward that dye. Figure 5.14 shows the result.

You might be asking the question why bother? Well, that's true. It's fun to differentiate your character for multiplayer, but it makes no difference otherwise, and it's possible to change the entirety of your character's skin via the skinpacks that can be purchased on PSN.

FIGURE 5.14 Ready for a spot of village trading in colored leather chestplate and leggings and an iron helmet and boots.

The Bottom Line

Minecraft's hostile mobs are quite a piece of work. Literally. They're creatively constructed, have unique behaviors, drop vital ingredients that allow you to continue your journey, and present an interesting range of challenges. It can be tough to live with them, but you won't get through the entire game without 'em.

There comes a time, my friend, when loins must be girded, weapons honed, and armor polished to a mirrored gleam. Go forth and conquer!

Of course, don't do it blindly. Practice around your base first while sharpening your skills. Don't carry too much with you so you don't have to race back for it if you're killed in action. And keep the area around your base well lit to prevent too many hostiles from spawning nearby. This will give you a nice stream of stragglers wandering by at night, but in most cases not too many at once.

You can also use a flint and steel to set grass on fire near a hostile, and spilling a bucket of lava can provide a last-ditch option, as long as it doesn't also spill on you.

One final tip: until you have an excellent perimeter defense set up, lead any creepers away from your base and practice your attack runs there. If you die, so be it; death happens and might happen often. But you'll at least keep the side of your house from looking like it was hit by multiple RPGs.

In time, you will succeed, and picking off hostiles will seem like a walk in the park—maybe Central Park at 3 a.m., but a park nonetheless.

Crop Farming

In This Chapter

- Become self-sufficient with your first crops and optimize your farm.
- Learn the secrets of irrigation—it doesn't take much to do a lot.
- Harvest your farm with one click of a button.
- Build a fully automated water harvester.

Farming is fun. There, I said it. I don't mean turning your Minecraft character into Farmer Joe, chomping on a stalk of wheat while slopping out a pigsty. I mean farming the Minecraft way.

Farming in Minecraft refers to any system that creates renewable resources. This concept goes well beyond a simple wheat field. It includes growing a host of different crops that all have a specific purpose and creating automated, hands-off harvesting systems. In this chapter, I take you through the elements of a crop farm and how to transform harvesting from a painful chore to a single, simple action.

Choosing a Crop

Given you can farm just about anything, you might be wondering where to start. Let's go for the basics first because you can easily branch out from there.

Wheat is the most useful to farm initially because three wheat sheaves crafted into bread form a useful food staple, and wheat is also used for breeding cows, sheep, and mooshrooms. (Pigs are bred with carrots, while chickens prefer to be thrown a handful of seeds.) It's also easy to get started with wheat for two reasons:

- You can find the seeds just about anywhere by knocking down tall grass; you can then plant the seeds to grow wheat.
- Wheat will grow without water, but it does grow faster when well hydrated.

First, find your seeds. You don't need many. When harvested, they'll drop up to three times as many seeds as they take to plant. This means you can start with a small stock and quickly expand your plantation as the plants mature. Just harvest, replant, and repeat until the crop reaches your target size. Under optimal conditions, the crop will reach maturity in a few day/night cycles.

Before you get started, here are some tips to keep in mind:

- All crops except cocoa beans grow faster when planted near water.

- All crops except cocoa and sugarcane need their soil prepared with a hoe, converting dirt or grass blocks into *farmland* blocks. The soil can revert to ordinary soil after it is walked on, unless you sneak. Planting a raised bed makes harvesting easier because you don't need to worry about stepping on the soil and can therefore run down the aisle quickly, lopping off the produce.

- Use a perimeter fence at least one block high, or two of any other type of block to prevent mobs from overrunning your farm and trampling your carefully grown produce. This won't keep out spiders, but they don't trample crops.

- All crops grow better in light. Use torches at night to keep the area well lit to prevent mob spawning and to increase the speed at which your crop matures.

- Crops can also be grown underground using the same principles.

- You don't need an enormous farm to become completely self-sufficient. Figure 6.1 shows one example with every possible crop planted. Combine this with the next chapter's tutorial on animal farming, and you'll be about as close as you can get to having your own supermarket.

- After a farm is established, it doesn't require constant tending. Matured crops don't rot or decay and can be harvested any time you need to fill up your pantry.

FIGURE 6.1 The crop with the lot!

Each Minecraft crop has some unique characteristics. Table 6.1 provides a full rundown on each.

TABLE 6.1 Crop Types

Crop	Obtain Seeds by	Growth Conditions	Used in
Carrot	Look for the crop itself in village farms, and then directly replant.	Plant on a farmland block with hydration.	Consume as is to restore four hunger points, or use it to breed pigs.
Cocoa beans	Harvesting mature cocoa pods yields cocoa beans that are directly replanted.	Must be grown on jungle wood blocks. The blocks can be stacked with pods planted on each face.	Cookies, and for creating a brown dye.
Melon	Melons don't grow naturally, but seeds can be found in dungeon and stronghold chests. After you have a first harvest, place the melon slices on a crafting table to obtain additional seeds.	Same space requirement as pumpkin.	Melon slices (each block provides 3–7 slices, with each slice restoring 1 hunger point). Also used to create glistering melon, an ingredient for brewing potions. Nine melon slices can be reformed into a single melon block and used for construction.
Potato	Look for the crop itself in village farms, and then directly replant.	Plant on a farmland block with hydration.	Consume as a baked potato by cooking in a furnace (restores six hunger points).
Pumpkin	Placing a pumpkin block in a crafting slot.	Plant with clear space around each block to allow the pumpkin to grow.	Pumpkin pie (restores eight hunger points) and to create a jack-o'-lantern.

Crop	Obtain Seeds by	Growth Conditions	Used in
Sugar-cane	Breaking the top blocks of sugarcane when harvesting and replanting. Leave the lowest block for regrowth.	Must be planted on sand, grass, or dirt that is directly adjacent to water.	Used to craft sugar and paper. Sugar is used in cake, pumpkin pie, and some potions. Paper is used to make books, bookshelves, and enchantment tables.
Wheat	Knocking down tall grass. You can also obtain seeds by harvesting the wheat found in village farms.	Best with hydrated soil, but any farmland will do.	Bread, and with other ingredients also used in cakes and cookies. Wheat is also an important tool for farming animals.

Finding Seeds in Elysium

If you're playing the Elysium world started in Chapter 1, "Getting Started," here are a few tips for finding all the crop seeds. You can harvest all the seeds with any tool or just your bare hands, but you'll get the best results using an axe on the pumpkin:

- **Wheat, potatoes, carrots, and seeds**—The village has plenty of all three of these, ready for harvesting. There's also lots of grass nearby. Just knock down the grass to gather seeds. There's a small chance any particular clump will deliver up seeds, but keep at it and you'll soon have plenty. Harvesting the already-planted wheat will also provide you with seeds.

- **Pumpkins**—You'll find a good-sized pumpkin patch about 150 blocks east and slightly south of the village. It's so close that the village is visible from the patch. Just head east and look toward the right. You can see the patch in Figure 6.2. Harvest with an axe.

- **Sugarcane**—Head south from the village until you reach water; then look to the right and left. Two stands are visible in each direction. Follow the coast to either one. Harvest the cane by hitting the second block, not the base block. This will leave the root so the cane can keep growing but also give you what you need to take home.

FIGURE 6.2 Pumpkin patch to the east of the Elysium village.

- **Cocoa pods**—This is more of a journey. The nearest jungle is about halfway up the map on the eastern side. You can get there over land in a day, but the surest way to avoid monsters is to go via boat. Bring some food, about 12 wood blocks, a few torches, shears, a pickaxe, an axe, and an iron sword or two. Also craft a couple of boats.

  Pack them all up along with a spare crafting table, and head east of the village at day-break until you reach the coast. Place a torch as a marker; then put the boat in the water, hop in with a pull of the left trigger, and steer it north. Move ⓛ forward and back and left or right to steer. To speed up, press ⓧ. Stay within a few blocks of the coast because the edge of the map is very close, and rubbing your boat against it while zooming along will quickly break the boat, although so will crashing into the coast, so take it gently. You'll see the jungle in just a couple of minutes of careful travel. No need to go full throttle unless you need to zoom past some monsters. There's a good chance you'll spot cocoa pods from the boat quite close to the start of the jungle; otherwise, point your crosshairs at the boat and press **R2** to exit.

  Head into the jungle. When you find the pods (see Figure 6.3), hit them to gather the cocoa seeds. Chop into some trees to gather jungle wood so you can plant the pods back at your farm. While you're there, use your shears to gather as many vines as you think worthwhile. You can use these instead of ladders back home. When you're done, jump back in your boat and head home. If you get caught out at night, just dig a small shelter, light the inside, and wait out the night. If this all seems a little daunting, you could also consider saving your game and switching to Easy or even Peaceful difficulty, or just leave the cocoa pod gathering until later.

- **Melon seeds**—Melon seeds are found in dungeon chests and strongholds. See Chapter 11, "Villages and Other Structures," and Chapter 12, "Playing Through: The Nether and The End," for more information on these. It can be a tough job getting to and surviving either, so it's best to just focus on the other crops for now.

FIGURE 6.3 Cocoa pods attached to a jungle tree.

Establishing a Wheat Farm

The first step in establishing your farm is to choose a suitable location. You'll probably want something fairly close to your house and in a reasonably flat area, although you can also adjust the landscape as required by removing any stray blocks. You can even build out most of the farm on a single layer of dirt blocks that is suspended in air like a floating platform—perfect for that farm in the clouds!

CAUTION

Stay Close for Growth

As you've probably already noticed, Minecraft's world is quite large. If the game kept the entire lot in memory at once and kept all the different crops, mobs, and other blocks updating...well, let's just say you'd need something a lot more powerful than the latest consoles. Instead, Minecraft keeps just a small section of the world in memory at any one time—and that's the part that's around you to a distance of a few hundred blocks, and it keeps only that section up-to-date.

This becomes quite important for farms. You could build a gigantic, fantastic, grow-everything farm on a nicely irrigated, well-lit piece of land, but nothing will grow if you wander too far away. Keep your friends close and your farms closer.

To begin, mark out an area sufficient to fit your farm. A single block of water can hydrate a square of 9×9 farmland blocks, assuming it is positioned in the middle (see Figure 6.3). This is a space 4 blocks in each direction from the water block, providing a total of 80 farmable blocks after discounting the 1 in the center occupied by the water. Each block will provide 1 bushel, or a total across the plantation of 26 loaves of bread each harvest. That's a lot of produce—more than is needed—so instead consider starting with something a little smaller. A smaller area will also be easier to fence.

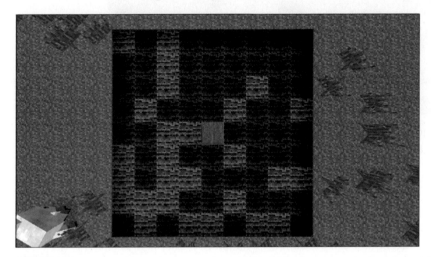

FIGURE 6.4 Hydration from a single water block extends out four blocks in each direction.

In Figure 6.5, I've laid out a smaller field of 36 farmland blocks. The central water block provides all the irrigation required. Placing paths isn't strictly necessary because there's no reason you can't trample up and down the field during the harvest, working your way in from the edges while using Sneak mode to ensure you don't trample the carefully tilled blocks back into ordinary dirt, but I prefer touches like that for aesthetic reasons. Also, particular blocks will mature earlier than others, so the path ensures faster access to matured blocks in the middle of the field that would otherwise require walking over planted ground to reach. There's no need to worry about this in early Survival mode. Just hoe some dirt blocks next to water and plant the seeds, then reap the harvest. You can make it more sophisticated later. Of course, if you're playing the Elysium world from Chapter 1, you can also harvest the village crops next to the spawn point to get started.

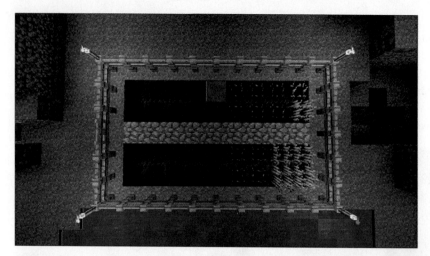

FIGURE 6.5 The seeds that come from harvesting crops allow almost any sized plantation to quickly multiply. There's no need to plant every block when you're starting your first field. These first six will, after just a few cycles of harvesting and replanting, become a full field of wheat.

The first harvest provided a total of 6 bushels of wheat and 9 seeds. The bushels produced 2 loaves of bread; the 9 seeds, after the next harvest, provided 9 bushels and 14 seeds. As you can see, it's a logarithmic progression: the next harvest resulted in 28 seeds and 14 bushels, and the one after that, 41 seeds and 28 bushels—more than enough to now plant the entire field with plenty left over.

Ready to create your own? Just follow these steps:

1 Find a suitable area, leveling the ground if necessary.

2 If the ground isn't bordering a water source, craft a bucket from three iron ingots, place it in your Hotbar, and fill it from any still water nearby. Just look for a nearby lake or use the sea off the coast. If the water is flowing, fill the source from the head of that flow.

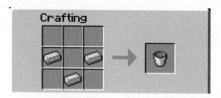

TIP

Creating a Permanent Watering Hole

Give yourself a constant source of water by digging out a 2×2 hole and filling the two diagonally opposite corners with water. The water source becomes self-sustaining, replenishing indefinitely no matter how many times you fill your bucket. This same trick does not work for lava.

3 Use a hoe to till any grass or dirt blocks into farmland.

4 Put up a fence or erect any other barrier two blocks high to keep out mobs. Fences are created from sticks, with each set of six making two fence panels.

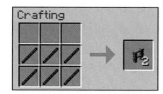

5 Fences are actually one and one-half blocks high so they can't be jumped. Add a gate for easy access.

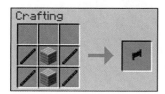

6 Add some torches to the perimeter to ensure mobs don't spawn inside the field and to keep your crops growing through the night.

7 Plant the seeds you previously collected by selecting them in the Hotbar and using L2 on the tilled blocks.

Give the crop a little time to grow. It can take a few day/night cycles. Wheat bushels are produced only from crops that have reached their final stage of growth. When the tops of the crop turn brown, they're ready.

TIP

Grind 'Dem Bones

Bone meal, crafted from regular old skeleton bones (assuming the aforementioned are not still actively using them to shoot arrows at you!), gives almost every crop a boost. The growth spurt won't take a crop instantly from seedling to mature plant, but it does push the crop forward one or more stages. Although bone meal can help melon and pumpkin plants grow to maturity, it won't speed up their crop formation. However, one dose of bone meal on a grass block will also encourage tall grass to grow in a 10×10 space. This is a great way to collect all the seeds you need to start a wheat field! A little bit of fertilizer can go a long way.

You can use any tool to harvest the wheat because harvesting does not impact durability. And your bare hands or anything else selected in the Hotbar will work just as well. Just L2 each crop block to pick up the results.

Figure 6.6 shows the final crop ready to harvest.

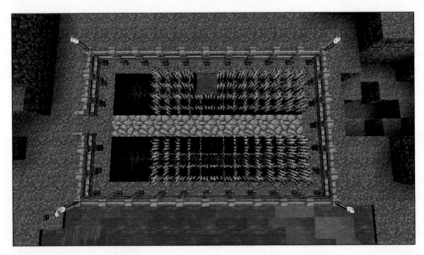

FIGURE 6.6   The wheat field is now fully planted, producing enough seeds to be self-sustaining and delivering 36 bushels every harvest. The wheat on the left is brown and ready for harvest. The wheat on the right is still green and so has a little further to go before it matures.

It won't take long before you are producing more than enough wheat and seeds. Keep them handy. You can use wheat to lure and breed the farm animals, and seeds do the same for chickens. See Chapter 7, "Farming and Taming Mobs," for more information.

Figure 6.7 shows an alternative farm layout with two raised beds to make harvesting easier. You can just run up and down the sides with the trigger pulled in, quickly collecting the wheat and seeds. When planting, do the same. The central water trough collects any harvested bushels and seeds that fall into it and sweeps them to the end of the rows, making for easier collection. However, you will need to run around to pick up any strays, such as those few shown in Figure 6.7, that didn't get knocked in. Arranging this system correctly is quite important. Follow these steps:

1   Make two raised beds nine dirt blocks long, leaving a single row in between. I generally make the beds two blocks wide.

2   Place a single block between the middle rows at one end of the middle row, and place a torch on top. You could also choose to place a jack-o'-lantern because they throw out a bit more light than torches, and if you squint hard, they look a tiny bit like a scarecrow's head. Throw some levers on each side to act as arms.

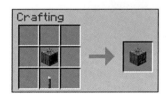

3   Pour a bucket of water against the end block so the water can create a stream that runs down the central channel ending after exactly eight blocks. It should be directly aligned with the ends of the two raised blocks.

4   It isn't absolutely necessary to build a nice cobblestone path all the way around, as is shown in Figure 6.7, but it's nicer that way.

5 Fence off the area any way you think will work best, and then hoe and plant the blocks. You'll find it easiest to work on the inner section of each bed, first running along the edge holding down **L2** with a hoe selected to till the blocks, and then with seeds selected using **L2** again to quickly plant them.

6 When harvest time comes, just use any tool to knock out the wheat and seeds. Most that are flung away from you will wind up in the water and wash down toward each end of the beds. Because the beds are hydrated, you can also run up and down them to pick up any seeds or wheat left behind without too much worry about reverting the beds to dirt blocks. Dry beds revert much faster!

7 Knock the mud out of your shoes (just kidding), and go bake some bread!

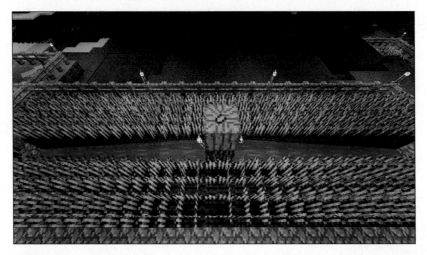

FIGURE 6.7 Raised beds make it easier to plant and harvest, and the central water conveniently washes harvested crops that aren't picked up down to a single collection point at the end.

Automated Farms

Automated farms can save a lot of the tedium involved in harvesting crops, even if they don't help with the planting. There are, essentially, an endless number of ways to build these, with some variations according to the crop, but each relies on one of three methods:

- Pistons cut across the top of the crop, sweeping the harvest into a channel of water that carries it to a convenient central location for pick-up.

- Pistons move the block on which the crop stands, shaking the harvest loose.

- A torrent of water floods the entire crop, carrying the harvest down to a single location. The water can be controlled using sticky pistons or a water dispenser.

NOTE

Want to Be Moved? Use a Piston

Pistons are one of the most useful features of Minecraft's redstone system. I'll show you how to use them here for farming, but you'll also find a lot more detail on these and all the other juicy redstone equipment in Chapter 9, "Redstone, Rails, and More".

Figure 6.8 shows a piston farm that uses the first two methods mentioned earlier: using a piston to cut the top of the crop and shaking the farmland itself to break loose the harvest.

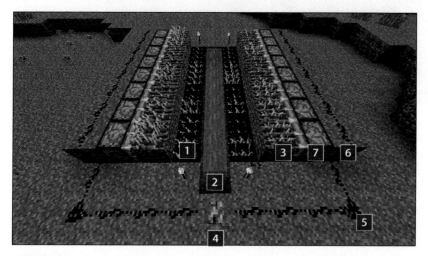

FIGURE 6.8 This wheat farm uses two types of piston farming to automate the harvest.

1. A row of standard farmland block, hydrated by the water flowing from a water source block positioned up the far end of the central channel.
2. Collection point for the harvest.
3. The raised row of farmland blocks.
4. The lever provides an on/off switch and power to the pistons.
5. Redstone dust placed on the ground to deliver power to the pistons.
6. Pistons placed on their sides must be powered by a raised block behind them that carries the redstone current the rest of the way.
7. A row of sticky pistons.

The principles used in Figure 6.8 are fairly simple. Pulling the lever causes the sticky pistons to extend (see Figure 6.9). This pushes the raised farmland across the top of the lower rows, harvesting those crops by scraping them into the central water channel. At the same time, the movement of the raised farmland causes its crops to shake loose. Return the lever to its off position, and the pistons retreat. Because they are *sticky*, they also pull the attached farmland block back into its original position.

FIGURE 6.9 The happy harvest. It's still a bit messy, but it completes the harvest more or less instantly.

The only problem with this method is that a lot of the harvest falls outside the collection channel. Also, as you can see from Figure 6.10, when the pistons return to their original positions, the entire lower section has to be hoed once more and the upper farmland blocks revert quite quickly because they're not hydrated. That's a fairly easy fix, though, with some strategically positioned water blocks at each end of the upper rows, shown in Figure 6.11.

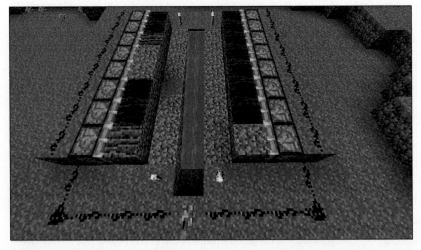

FIGURE 6.10 After harvesting, a lot of the farmland reverts to dirt or grass blocks. The water harvesting method described later solves this issue.

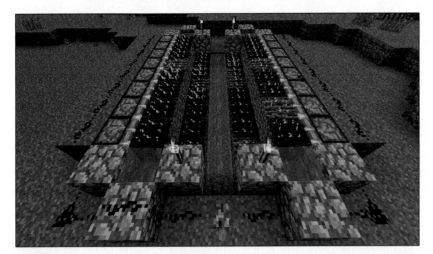

FIGURE 6.11 The corner water blocks help hydrate the upper farmland rows. Actually, in this layout, water in one corner is able to hydrate the nearest raised blocks on the other side because they are still just four blocks away. The gap in the middle is ignored. This can help greatly with creative and efficient farm designs.

NOTE

Semi- and Fully Automated Farms

Automated farming doesn't mean quite the same thing for every crop. Melons, pumpkins, and sugarcane can be farmed in a fully automated manner because the stem of the plant stays behind when harvesting. With a timer-delayed circuit, you can just set it all up and walk away. It will operate indefinitely. The other automated farms for wheat, carrots, potatoes, and cocoa pods really only handle the harvesting for you. You'll still need to replant seeds for the next crop and break out the hoe to repair any farmland that has reverted to a standard grass or dirt block after harvesting.

Setting up an automated farm can be quite resource intensive. The basic piston used for cutting a crop requires three wood plank blocks, four pieces of cobblestone, an iron ingot, and one redstone. If you've mined extensively and knocked out enough wood, you'll probably already have plenty of these, but it can get trickier when building the sticky piston used for pushing farmland and controlling the flow of water. These are built from a standard piston and a block of slime, and these spawn extremely rarely, as described in Chapter 5, "Combat School." However, you could also, when you're ready, start to explore some of the deeper cave structures where you might be lucky enough (if fighting a giant blob of slime can be considered such) to find a few oozing their way across the floor.

An automated farm can also be a great way to learn about some of Minecraft's more advanced features. It might all seem a bit confusing at first, but once you have down the basic moves, the rest are really just repetitions of those building blocks. It won't take you long to start developing some quite amazing layouts. Let's take a look at the various methods step by step.

TIP

Getting Creative with Farming

Practice makes perfect, right? Automated constructions can definitely take some time to build and understand. If you're low on resources but really want to try building some of the examples shown in this chapter, consider starting a new world in creative mode and run riot with the unlimited resources. You can then switch back to your current world and continue in "Survivor or Bust!"

Creating a Piston Harvester

The simplest piston harvester is easy to build. Figure 6.12 shows a push-button–operated harvesting piston. Levers and redstone provide a way to connect multiple systems so they all operate together, but let's take a look at this first design.

FIGURE 6.12 Automated farming isn't so alarming. It's quite simple, schematically speaking. No need to get up to your ears in a redstone engineering degree.

1. Water hydration and collector

2. Farmland with crop

3. Piston facing the crop

4. Cobblestone block, although almost any block will work

5. A wooden push-button crafted from a wood plank block

Building this is easy and is a great way to get a basic understanding of how all this automated stuff works. Just follow these steps:

1 Dig a hole for your water supply, and fill it from a water bucket.

2 Hoe the grass or dirt block to turn it into farmland, and plant some seeds.

3 Create a standard piston. Minecraft always places pistons so that the face of the piston points toward you, snapping toward the closest of the six possible degrees of orientation, so place this one by standing on the block next to the water supply facing the farmland block. Place the piston on the far side of that block.

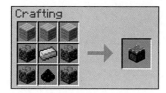

4 Place a dirt, wood, cobblestone, or other kind of solid block behind the piston.

5 Craft a wooden button from wood planks, and place it on the side of the block behind the piston.

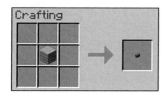

Position yourself close to the button, point your crosshairs at it, and use **L2** to press it. The piston swiftly powers up, sweeping the crop off its farmland block. The results might spring directly into your inventory, depending on how close you are standing, or they might float around waiting for you to collect them. Buttons send a brief pulse of power, so the piston will retract after a short delay.

Well done! That's all there is to creating a simple piston harvester.

One piston an automated farm does not make, but it's remarkably easy to extend this design into one that is much more effective. Follow these steps:

1 Replicate the same pattern side by side, but still leave just the one button on the side of the first block.

2 Then run a little trail of redstone dust (use **L2** on the top of each block with redstone selected in your Hotbar), and you'll create a circuit that links each block from the first to the last. Figure 6.13 shows the final picture.

3 Click the button again to push each piston out in unison. Lovely, isn't it?

FIGURE 6.13 Set up a row of pistons with a line of redstone dust to create a synchronized one-click harvesting row.

Sticky Piston Harvesting

Sticky piston harvesters work on the same principle as the simple piston harvester with one key advantage: the harvesting power of the piston is doubled because it can also push and pull back a farmland block, shaking its harvest loose (see Figure 6.14).

Start by crafting a sticky piston using a standard piston and a slimeball (the sticky part). Then follow the same routine as for a simple piston harvester, but place an additional dirt block directly in front of the piston, hoe it to turn it into farmland, and plant seeds on it and the farmland block in front.

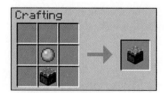

There's just one problem with using the button system. It's fine for a single row of crops, but what if you wanted to create a system where the entire farm's harvesting is automated with a single click?

Running redstone along the ground provides a central control panel and a coordinated system across multiple crop rows. It has many benefits and takes only a few more steps.

Just decide on a central point, put the button on a block, and run a redstone trail back to the pistons from either side of that block. A redstone current runs for only 15 blocks, so if your trail is longer than that, insert a redstone repeater to boost the current.

FIGURE 6.14 Sticky pistons stick like glue to the block in front, keeping it attached as the piston moves back and forth. This handy property also makes them an easy way to construct sliding doors and windows and all kinds of other fascinating machines. More on that in Chapter 9.

Creating a Water Harvester

Using water to harvest wheat has a major advantage over the regular piston harvester: the water washes away the crops but doesn't revert the farmland to a regular dirt block.

There are two basic methods:

- Use a piston to drop water from a raised water source so that it flows out over the farmland.
- Use a dispenser containing a filled water bucket to send out a stream of water.

Figure 6.15 shows a farm built using the first method.

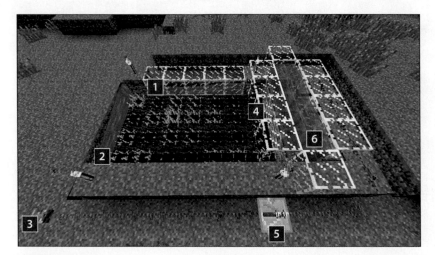

FIGURE 6.15 A water-harvested wheat farm: the glass blocks are just for illustrative purposes and can be replaced with dirt, cobblestone, or any other type of block.

1. Hydration source
2. Collection stream
3. Lever set to "On" because this type of harvesting drops water only when the power goes off
4. Row of pistons in their extended positions holding back the water
5. Redstone repeater required to amplify the power due to the length of the circuit
6. Water source used for harvesting, suspended by the extended pistons

The layout of the piston system is a little difficult to detect in a completed working farm, so Figure 6.16 shows a simplified view. The water source is held in place by the surrounding blocks. In Minecraft's geometry, the extended piston beneath also prevents it from flowing down. However, as soon as that piston is retracted, the pathway through the block under the water opens, allowing the water to flow out over the crops.

Levers work better than buttons on this type of layout because you want the water to keep flowing until the crop has been washed away, and the pistons, anyway, need to stay powered with the lever in the "on" position when the water shouldn't be flowing. It's almost like a negative circuit. Levers are easy to make: you'll just need a block of cobblestone and a stick.

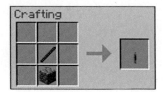

FIGURE 6.16 Close-up of the piston and water source block.

When creating this type of farm, make sure you build up all the surrounding components, including the pistons—powered and therefore extended—before you place the water sources in the upper reservoir. Otherwise, you'll end up wading through a constant flow of water, fighting the current, as you build the rest of the farm. You also can't place redstone dust in water, and flowing water will wash away any you *have* placed, which can make the wiring something of a challenge.

The other method described relies on a dispenser block. Again, Figure 6.17 shows a simplified view that you can easily extrapolate into a complete farm.

The dispenser layout is easier to build than the water-drop used previously but also more resource-intensive because dispensers require redstone, an undamaged bow, cobblestone, and (in this case) a bucket filled with water.

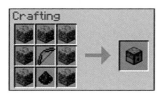

Place the dispenser with its outlet facing the crops. Then use L2 to open the dispenser's own inventory window. Place a full water bucket in one of the slots. Your dispenser is locked and loaded! By the way, dispensers are a lot of fun. You can load them with all kinds of items, shooting out arrows at mobs, pumping out lava, and even getting them to shoot fireballs. They're great for traps because they can operate with trip wires and pressure plates. If your multiplayer games are player versus player (PvP), you could turn one of your intrepidly exploring friends into something more akin to a skewered kebab! All in good fun, of course.

Finally, rather than using a lever, I've used a wooden button attached to the side. Just click the button to start the flow of water, and click again to stop it. Connect a number of dispensers in sequence by running redstone dust along the top of each block. That single button still controls them all and will let you smoothly harvest any number of crop rows. One final note: water flows eight blocks from its source, but if there's a single downward step, it will flow another eight blocks, and so on. Use this to your advantage by arranging a regular terrace in your farms, and you can run the crops to a length limited only by the edges of your world.

FIGURE 6.17 Simplified layout for a water-dispenser harvester.

Harvesting Other Crops

Sugarcane, pumpkin, melons, and cocoa pods each work best using a slightly different and nondestructive method of farming.

Sugarcane can be harvested using a standard piston raised above ground level (see Figure 6.18). This piston is operated from a lever made from cobblestone and a stick.

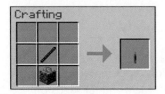

The piston shears off the sugarcane, leaving the original stalk still implanted so that it can grow again.

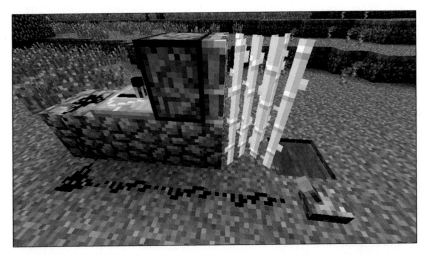

FIGURE 6.18 This cane-shearing piston is operated by a lever.

You can harvest all the other crops by placing pistons beside the main stem's growth blocks. As with sugarcane, the piston shears off the crop, leaving the original plant untouched.

UNDERGROUND FARMING

If you've found that you prefer to spend most of your time building a mine, you also might like to farm full time with an underground estate. The principles are the same as for any farm. Just hollow out a large enough space and place plenty of torches to keep things well lit to assist with crop growth and prevent mobs from spawning. Underground farms have the advantage that they can be properly secured from hostile mobs so that you can tend the crops any time of the day or night without fear of being sniped by a skeleton over the fence or straying too close to a lurking creeper.

The Bottom Line

Crop farming is an important part of Minecraft because the results play a huge role in crafting, brewing potions, and satisfying hunger. And, as you know, a full hunger bar restores health, so you absolutely shouldn't contemplate venturing out for extended periods without also carrying a good supply of food. Without potions, it's the only way you can quickly restore health.

You can start with very simple layouts, choosing the crops according to whatever you can gather from nearby biomes. If there's no tall grass for wheat seeds, look for a nearby village and become a one-person raiding party. You can probably pinch some potatoes and carrots while you're there. Avoid food poisoning by baking your potatoes in a furnace before consuming—unless you are in desperate straits.

Besides wheat, cocoa pods can become cookies—very useful when you need a quick bite. And pumpkin can be baked into a nutritious pie, although both do require the addition of wheat to complete. Melons also provide a steady source of nutrition, although only satisfying 1.2 hunger points per slice—and finding their seeds is an adventure all in itself. Cocoa beans, pumpkins, and sugarcane all require at least wheat to become food grade.

Of course, cows, pigs, and chickens are all good sources of food.

There is one other natural harvest worth mentioning: the fungi. Find some red and brown mushrooms, and you can make a hearty mushroom stew that also provides a huge 7.2 points of saturation. First, create a wooden bowl from three wood plank blocks (bonus: you'll get four bowls from this!), and then use the mushrooms and bowl at the crafting table under the Food tab. Yum! And if soup really is your thing, a mooshroom trimmed with shears, or milked with a wooden bowl, will help ensure a supply that will have you producing the hearty stuff faster than a Campbell's factory. Turn to Chapter 7 to learn more.

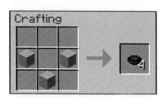

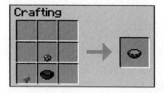

Farming and Taming Mobs

In This Chapter

- Create a passive mob farm for a constant supply of eggs, meat, and more.
- Tame ocelots to scare off creepers, and use wolves for self-defense.
- Fancy a spot of fishing? Hop on a boat and tap one of Minecraft's unlimited food resources.

Crops are nice and easy to grow, and there is very little hassle involved. If you wanted to live a vegan life, crops could provide everything you need, but you'd also miss out on some key resources that will help get you to the end game.

Minecraft's passive mobs (those that don't actively seek to kill you) can provide food, ingredients for crafting, decorative items, and—very handily—defense and attack assists.

In this chapter I show you how to make the most of Minecraft's animal kingdom.

Farming and Working with Friendly Mobs

Mob farms create replaceable resources through breeding. Each animal is a little different, so I've compiled the list of characteristics in Table 7.1.

The most useful are all shown in Figure 7.1, a working farm with sheep, chickens, cows, and pigs. Fortunately, all the animals are self-sufficient and never starve to death, so all you need to do to keep the numbers up is breed one pair for every other one that goes to the friendly mob farm in the sky when you need some of their rather handy resources.

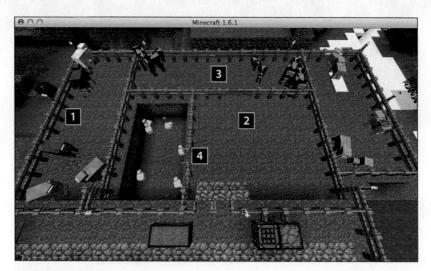

FIGURE 7.1 A passive mob farm.

1. Sheep and pig pen, with one sheep dyed blue.
2. Corralling yard provides an additional lock to prevent the mobs from escaping as you enter their individual yards.
3. Cattle pen.
4. Gate to chicken yard—access gained from a ladder against the wall just below the gate (chickens haven't yet learned to climb ladders).

Farming involves a few basic steps that I'll take you through in more detail as this chapter progresses:

1 Do like Noah, and collect at least two of each creature.

2 Lure them back to your farm using the appropriate food.

3 Ensure their enclosure is secure with a one-block-high fence or a two-block-high dirt or other type of wall. (Chickens need a two-block-high fence or a three-block-high wall.)

4 Get the animals in the mood for breeding using the specific food for that species (no need for candlelit dinners for two).

5 Wait 5 minutes and they'll be ready to breed again, so repeat step 4.

6 Wait 20 minutes (one Minecraft day/night cycle), and the newborn will have matured and can also start breeding.

In just a few day/night cycles, you'll have the farm fully established.

By the way, there's no need to go all Texan and build a giant cattle-yard. If this is just for your needs and not a cooperative game, two breeding pairs of each type will provide plenty of resources.

TABLE 7.1 Passive Mob Leading and Breeding Guide

Animal	Lead or Tame with	Breed Using	Provides
Cows	Wheat.	Wheat	Leather, raw beef when killed, and milk.
Sheep	Wheat.	Wheat	Wool; can be dyed to create different colors of sheep.
Mooshrooms	Wheat.	Wheat	Mooshroom stew (by milking) and red mushrooms from shearing.
Pigs	Carrots.	Carrots	Pork chops; pigs can also be ridden with the help of a saddle and a carrot on a stick.
Chickens	Seeds.	Seeds	Chicken, feathers, and eggs.
Wolves	Tame by feeding them bones.	Pork chops, raw beef, steak, chicken, and rotten flesh	Tamed wolves will follow you (unless told to sit) and attack any mob that attacks you or any that you attack.
Cats (Ocelots)	Approach carefully with a raw fish in hand without sudden movements of the crosshairs; when the ocelot approaches you, give it the fish.	Raw fish	Both ocelots and cats scare the creeps out of creepers, but cats will stay nearby whereas the wild ocelots wander about as they choose.

Farms take a little bit of planning; otherwise, they turn into an exercise in herding cats. Ensure that all animals have to go through a corralling yard to help prevent escape. This is a double-gate system, with the same purpose as an air lock, and it can be shared by all pens. It can be quite tricky to get out and close a fence gate with the herd wandering around at random. Herds have a habit (or perhaps a secret strategy) of preventing you from closing the gate before one or two have slipped through. The second yard will stop those that do make a run for it from escaping the entire farm. You can try to lead them back by enticing them with food, but that just attracts the rest of the group, making for double-trouble. In the worst case, you might consider treating escapees as volunteers for the chopping block.

Farm animals don't need to be fed, but wolves do. Their tails act as a health indicator. If a tamed wolf's tail sticks straight out, it's in full health; it gradually drops down as its health decreases. Bring it back to the straight and level using any sort of meat, cooked or not. You can even feed tamed wolves the rotten flesh that zombies drop. By the way, never attack an untamed wolf, especially with other wolves nearby. Before you know it, you could well be beset by the entire pack.

Finally, don't let any ocelots into the chicken coop: feathers will fly as they slowly consume your avian friends. Ocelots are a lot better behaved once tamed.

NOTE

Your Farm Is (Mostly) Safe from Hostiles

None of the hostile mobs intentionally attack farm animals, although collateral damage from creepers exploding near you is a possibility, and if you are caught off guard by a skeleton firing arrows over the fence, you could—but I'm not saying you should—use a cow for cover.

Breeding Animals

Breed animals by taking their favorite snack in hand and pulling L2. You'll know you're on the right track when you see the floating love hearts appear above them (see Figure 7.2). To create offspring, feed two of the same species that are standing close together. Minecraft doesn't have any sex determination, so any two will do. They'll quickly find each other and, well, I'm not sure how to describe it, but it looks like kissing. A short while later, an infant will appear, taking 20 minutes of real time to reach maturity.

FIGURE 7.2 Love is in the air.

Breeding two sheep whose wool is dyed results in an offspring of the same color. (If the parents are different colors, the offspring's color is randomly chosen as one of the parent's coloring, although some combinations produce a new color.) Dyed wool is used to make colored wool blocks, a useful decorative item, so use sheep breeding to generate as much as you need without having to source more, and shear the sheep to obtain the wool without killing them. It's also possible to dye leather armor (see Chapter 5, "Combat School") and the collars of tamed wolves.

NOTE

Dying for Dye?

Minecraft has 16 dye colors made from a combination of original materials and crafting. For example, if you've plucked a rose on your travels, go to the Decorations tab of a crafting table and you'll find you can produce rose red dye. A dandelion produces yellow dye. The Lapis Lazuli ore produces a deep blue dye, and cocoa beans produce brown dye. Combine Lapis Lazuli dye with bone meal (crafted from the bones dropped by skeletons) to create a light blue dye. Table 7.2 lists them all, and you'll find all the craftable ones under the decorations tab of the crafting interface. Although wool and wolves colors are limited to just the 16 colors of the available dyes, leather armor uses a mixing system that provides thousands of possible colors.

TABLE 7.2 Dye Guide

Name	Ingredients	Recipe	Description
Black	Ink sac	Kill a squid to obtain up to 3 ink sacs.	Colors the applicable items black.
Brown	Cocoa beans	Harvest the beans from jungle trees and apply directly.	Colors the applicable items brown.
Green	Cactus	Cook the cactus in a furnace to obtain the dye.	Colors the applicable items green.
Blue	Lapis Lazuli	Mine Lapis Lazuli ore to obtain the dye.	Colors the applicable items blue.
White	Bone meal	Place bone on the crafting grid to obtain bone meal.	Colors the applicable items white.
Cyan dye	Lapis Lazuli and cactus green		Colors the applicable items cyan.
Dandelion yellow	Collect a dandelion		Colors the applicable items yellow.

Name	Ingredients	Recipe	Description
Gray	Ink sac and bone meal		Colors the applicable items a light gray and can be used to create light gray dye.
Light blue	Lapis Lazuli and bone meal		Colors the applicable items light blue.
Light gray	Gray dye and bone meal		Colors the applicable items a light gray.
Lime	Cactus green and bone meal		Colors the applicable items lime. Obtain cactus green by smelting a cactus block in the furnace.
Magenta	Purple and pink dyes		Colors the applicable items magenta.
Orange	Rose red and dandelion yellow		Colors the applicable items orange.
Pink	Rose red and bone meal		Colors the applicable items pink.
Purple	Lapis Lazuli and rose red		Colors the applicable items purple.
Rose red	Collect a rose		Colors the applicable items red.

Riding Pigs

Pigs can't fly in Survival mode, but they can be ridden, and they don't need taming first. Just place a saddle on a pig's back (you'll have to look for saddles in the chests in dungeons because they're not a craftable item) and hop aboard. The pig will move randomly, which isn't a lot of use, but if you craft and hold a carrot on a stick, you can steer the pig normally.

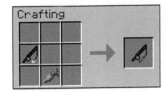

Pigs have another neat trick. Push a saddled one into a minecart, jump on its back, and the pig will power the cart, actually moving faster than powered rails. It's another fast way to get around, especially if you don't have the gold available for those rails. (See Chapter 9, "Redstone, Rails, and More," for more on railed transport.)

Fishing

Fishing is a great way to ensure a steady supply of food, and it gives you the raw fish required to tame ocelots, turning them into rather cute house cats.

First, build a fishing rod from three sticks and two pieces of string.

Any body of water will do, but casting in a way that hits a solid block doubles the decrease in your rod's durability, so always try to cast into deep water. You can do this standing on land, in water, or even sitting in a boat (see Figure 7.3).

Cast with **L2** and watch the bobber carefully. As soon as it dips below the surface, use **L2** again to reel in the line. With a little luck and good timing, you'll need to duck as the fish comes flying toward you.

It's generally better to fish in the rain. You'll catch an average of 4 fish per minute. Otherwise, expect to catch around 2 per minute with each rod catching 65 fish before it breaks.

Fishing rods can also catch and pull in other entities, at least to a limited extent. They're probably most useful in this regard for reeling in the dreaded Ghast in The Nether region.

FIGURE 7.3 After a hard day's mining, why not relax in a boat doing a spot of fishing? Boats are also a very fast method of transport—great if you're near an ocean biome.

The Bottom Line

Passive or—as I prefer to think of them—*friendly* mobs are more than just field-dressing. They're an important part of Minecraft's gameplay.

They can, however, be a little tricky to find. If you're lucky enough to spawn in a place with more than a few, go out, hack and slash for some fast food, and then work on luring in the rest to set up a farm. Try to resist giving the sword-arm too much of a workout because they won't respawn, and you could end up left with just a single example and no way to move on to a breeding pair. Actually, more likely is that you could clear out all examples in the immediate area and find it just surprisingly arduous to lure any others back from further afield.

You'll find sheep and cows heading toward well-lit, grassy areas—pigs as well, although they also seem to appear quite a lot in hilly areas. Ocelots and chickens seem to prefer jungle biomes. Oh, and perhaps the oddest friendly mob in Minecraft, the mooshroom, can be found hanging around their namesake: the relatively rare mushroom biome (see Figure 7.4). You'll find the same in Elysium at coordinates x:-224 y:-40.

There is one other friendly mob out there: the squid. It can't be bred, so farming is out of the question, but if you kill one you'll find its ink sacs do make for a mean black dye.

FIGURE 7.4 Shear mooshrooms to gather red mushrooms.

Creative Construction

In This Chapter

- Time for a block party! Build your first aboveground base.
- Decorate your pad with chairs, tables, and paintings.
- Chill out Zen-style with flowing water, pools, and fountains.
- Warm things up with a fireplace or two, not forgetting the BBQ.
- Follow step-by-step while building an underwater abode.
- Protect your perimeter and take pot-shots at mobs with a water trap.

This chapter is packed chock-a-block with construction ideas, from a few starting tips on finding sources of inspiration to a detailed list of all the things you can add that go beyond the basic functional elements.

Construction is easy—put one block on top of another. But take heed: once you start, it's hard to stop. Every step is like opening another door, and you'll soon find your imagination running riot.

Even if you have no particular architectural talent (and I must confess that I am absolutely astonished by the incredible feats some have achieved with soaring gothic cathedrals and entire cities that are nothing short of a wonderland), all construction starts with a single block.

Leaving the Cave

If you've been busy mining, farming, and doing all the other Minecraft-y things that get you established, you probably haven't had the time to build a glorious aboveground structure or decorate your home with a few nonfunctional items. Well, now's as good a time as any to take a bit of a break. Unleash Minecraft's bevy of building blocks and unlock your creative potential.

Some of the incredible creations players have already made include

- Highly accurate models of famous real-world locations and buildings including cathedrals, towers, castles, palaces, and cultural landmarks. Think the Reichstag, Taj Mahal, Louvre, Westminster Abbey, Sydney Opera House, Empire State Building, and so much more.

■ Fictional locations either as faithful replicas or as near as can be achieved, including Tolkien's Middle Earth; Caribbean pirate towns; and, in the ultimate homage, levels and locations from other video games, movies, and TV series (see Figure 8.1), and, of course, the U.S.S. Enterprise from *Star Trek*. Trekkies are everywhere!

FIGURE 8.1   King's Landing from *Game of Thrones* built in Minecraft with incredible attention to detail. (Image courtesy of WesterosCraft)

■ Giant pixel art depicting almost anything at all: statues and sculpted creations that are nothing but a glorious exploration of the maker's creative capabilities.

The list can go on and on, but I'll curtail it here. Suffice to say that anything is possible.

NOTE

Get a Whole New Look with Texture Packs

In a standard installation, Minecraft has an organic, pixelated appearance, but it's possible to completely change the look of every block. Texture makes this easy and can change the way your creation looks from the default to rustic, realistic, modern, hi-tech, or even cartoon-like. You'll see the ones available for purchase on the PlayStation when you start a new world, with free trial versions also available, although you won't be able to save a world with a trial texture applied.

Each Minecraft block is one cubic meter, so many replicas are built to a 1:1 scale—even the entire center of historic Beijing from the ancient city walls torn down by Mao all the way back toward the Forbidden City, with—it seems—almost every *hutong* in place.

Many of these creations are too much for one person, so they have sprung up on multi-player servers where players using the PC edition of Minecraft all pitch in.

So, having set the scene, what's the easiest way for you to get started without necessarily budgeting the next six months to a building project?

You can take several approaches:

- **Extend your current shelter**—Keep all the basics in place while building out and up a little at a time.

- **Start from scratch aboveground**—Pick a location close to your current spawn point, or strike out to a better location with your bed in hand to reset your spawn. Figure 8.2 shows an example.

FIGURE 8.2 Home sweet home perched far above the madding crowd.

- **Head to the nearest village**—A village is a handy location to set up home if you don't mind the villagers' constant creaky grumbling that makes them sound like they need a quick squirt of WD-40. Once established, you can harvest their farms without them getting upset. Just don't forget to replant their fields for the next time because the villagers, a lazy bunch, don't do that themselves.

- **Dive**—Not all shelters need to be aboveground or deep in a cave. I've included a tutorial on building underwater later in this chapter.

TIP

Floating Blocks

Minecraft ignores basic physics on almost all the standard blocks except for sand and gravel. This enables the creation of gravity-defying structures. Stack them as high as you like, build out to a platform, and then remove their lowest layer to create a floating structure in the sky. Imagine a fortress connected to the ground with just a single block. It's perfectly possible.

There are as many approaches to building aboveground as there are different worlds in Minecraft. The easy way is to use a box design. It doesn't take much effort and is something of a natural starting point. But you could also go for a walk around your actual neighborhood grabbing photos with your phone or camera. If you'd prefer not to have a run-in with Neighborhood Watch, check out some online real estate sites. They often have multiple photos and architectural plans. YouTube also hosts numerous videos. Visit www.youtube.com and search for "Minecraft creations" to see some truly amazing builds.

Unleashing Your Interior Decorator

Not everything in Minecraft has to be functional. Figure 8.3 shows that all kinds of components can be put together in different ways to create a homey ambience, both indoors and out.

FIGURE 8.3 The living room with wide-screen TV, modular lounge with coffee table, tanning bed, dining table, and fireplace. There's also a kitchen tucked in the back-right corner.

I've put together a collection of ideas for you, but this is also one of those things where your own creativity and experimentation come into play. Try some of these in a world set to Creative, and let the juices flow:

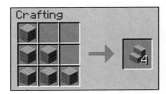 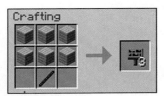

- **Chairs**—Chairs are made from staircase blocks. Craft a staircase from six wood blank blocks. The chairs can be as long or as short as you want, from single seats to a modular lounge. Placing signs or trapdoors (in their open position—use **R2** to toggle them) on the sides creates armrests. Extending the base of the chair with a slab creates a deck-chair effect that's perfect around a pool or on a sun deck. Figure 8.4 shows a view of chairs around a dining table (see the next bullet).

NOTE

Placing Signs

Signs placed against a block attach to the side of that block. Signs placed on top of a block become freestanding with their orientation fixed so that they face you at the time they're placed.

- **Dining table**—Create a table by placing a single fence block, which becomes the stand. Then place a pressure plate on top of the post to form the table's surface. Pressure plates don't create a seamless surface, so for larger tables consider using squares of carpet instead. Surround the table with a few chairs to complete the picture. Remove some squares of the table's surface, and pop some cake down in their place to finish the picture, as shown in Figure 8.4. If you want to make a giant dining table, use regular blocks and then place pressure plates or carpet in front of each seat to act as placemats.

FIGURE 8.4 A dining table with Antoinette-approved centerpiece. Let them eat cake.

- **Floors**—Inset colored wool or use different types of blocks to create tiled flooring.

- **Beds**—Think of the standard Minecraft bed as just the starting point. Put two side-by-side for a double, or make a king-size bed out of three and some blocks behind for a headboard. Then place some slabs at the foot to get the proportions right.

- **Bedside table**—Use a standard construction or wood block or a bookcase—anything that matches your color scheme. Then put a torch on top in the middle of the block. The torch will burn permanently, but if you put a redstone torch in the middle and then a lever on the side of the block, you'll have a light you can switch on and off. Replace the redstone torch with a redstone lamp for much brighter lighting.

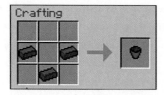

- **Indoor plants**—Choose a plant such as a flower, sapling, cacti, or leaf block cut from a regular tree with shears or a tool enchanted with silk touch. Pick a base block such as grass, dirt, or sand; plant it; and attach signs or trapdoors to its sides to give it a nice boxed look, as shown in Figure 8.5, or create a flower pot from three bricks. Smelt clay to make the bricks, then craft the pots and plant them with flowers, saplings, ferns, and mushrooms. You can place them on almost any surface, and they make for some rather nice window ledge decorations.

- **Hedges**—Leaf blocks also work well in decorative construction. Use them to build hedges lining a path or parkway. You can even use them for the walls of a tree house. The blocks won't decay, unlike regular leaf blocks that are no longer attached to their trunks. Gather leaf blocks in Survival mode by cutting them from a tree with shears.

FIGURE 8.5 Planter boxes and hedges add a leafy touch to rooms and balconies. Saplings are also safe to plant indoors because they won't grow without empty blocks above.

- **Fantasy trees**—Use wood and leaf blocks to create unique trees dotted around your estate. You can even place them inside a giant atrium, creating your own Crystal Palace.

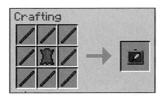

- **Item frames**—Crafted from eight sticks and one piece of leather, item frames serve a decorative and practical purpose as single-item storage. Place the frame on any wall and then take the object you'd like to store in hand and place it in the frame. Store that enchanted diamond sword you plan to save for later combat, or maybe a diamond pick for when you need to retrieve more obsidian. Use **R2** to retrieve both the frame and the object at a later date. Use an item frame and a clock to create a wall clock, or place a map in the frame for permanent reference.

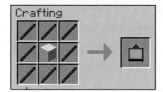

- **Paintings**—These are purely decorative. They have the same recipe as an item frame, but with the leather swapped for any piece of wool. Placing paintings is a little bit random because Minecraft tries to scale the painting up to suit the flat space available, with some limits. There's a built-in inventory of 26 pieces of art in various shapes and sizes. One way to try to force a correctly sized painting is to first surround the target area with other blocks and then use **L2** to place the painting in the lower-left corner of the target space. You can keep removing and then replacing the painting until you have the correct size, and then remove the additional blocks.

- **Fountains**—Build fountains as simple or complex as you like. Place a water source on top of any other structure. Glass blocks work quite well for this, but almost any block will do. Create a hollow fountain by removing the blocks after you've placed the water. Also, don't forget to put a surround around the base so the cascade doesn't turn into a flood. Figure 8.6 shows one example.

- **Ponds and pools**—As long as water drops one level every eight blocks, it can flow on forever from a single source. Use this to create water features that flow down and through your house into a pond. Add a few floating lily pads in the still water to complete the effect. Pools are a nice touch that can look good surrounded by almost any smooth blocks, especially with the addition of the deck chairs mentioned previously.

FIGURE 8.6   This small indoor fountain feeds the swimming pool located on the recreation level of the house.

- **Netting and wisps**—Cobwebs gathered with shears or silk touch can stand in as netting between two posts. Tennis, anyone? Use redstone to draw lines on the court. Cobwebs can also suggest smoke billowing from a chimney or for the lashings and cargo nets on ships.

- **Bookshelves**—Although bookshelves have an official use for enhancing enchantments (see Chapter 10, "Enchanting, Anvils, and Brewing," for the full details and crafting recipes), they're also an excellent decorative item. Stack them up where needed to build a library or add some interesting ambience to any living room. Slabs also work well and are easier to make than the bookshelf item. Stack them up to create multiple shelves and dress the sides with regular blocks, or just run them straight to the wall to make them appear as built-in shelves.

- **Raised and lowered floors**—Slabs are half a block high, making them ideal for creative flooring and embedded fixtures. Although items placed on a slab seem to float, two sets of slabs can lead down to a sunken lounge or indoor pool. And if your design extends to the bathroom, create a slab floor leaving a one-piece hole against the wall. Place a cauldron in it and fill it with water to make a recessed sink. Slabs are also a useful way to hide redstone wiring. They'll float one block up with the redstone running underneath out of sight, saving an additional layer of trench digging. More on this in Chapter 9, "Redstone, Rails, and More."

- **Fireplaces**—You need to know just two things about fireplaces. Netherrack (a block from The Nether) burns forever. Set it on fire with a flint and steel, and bask in the glow. The other thing, perhaps slightly more important, is that fire is catching. Don't surround your fireplace with wood blocks. As a matter of fact, don't have anything flammable within at least two blocks of it—or more, just to be sure. Use nonflammable materials such as cobblestone and bricks. Fireplaces look great with a glass pane in front of them (see Figure 8.7). They also make a pretty decent BBQ (see Figure 8.8) or fire pit outdoors. S'mores, anyone?

FIGURE 8.7   A modern fireplace set inside a wall with a pane in front. The fire provides a dynamic animation, making a room feel warm and alive.

FIGURE 8.8   This BBQ is made from a mix of brick blocks and staircases. Note that the trapdoor, like a normal door, doesn't burn, so it is safe to position above the fire.

Construction is one of the indulgent pleasures in Minecraft. In Creative mode, you'll have access to the full range of available materials, but there is also something to be said for building an amazing structure in Survival mode. Having to find the materials first really adds to the experience.

Building Underwater

There's not a lot of justification for undertaking the effort to build an underwater house—except that you can! It's a fun challenge. An underwater house provides great visibility, is immune to hostile mobs including the creeper, and, well, it's just pretty darn cool. This type of house can take a little bit of extra work, but it's fairly easy, and you can let your imagination take you anywhere you want to go—from the equivalent of a reversed aquarium, with you as the sole internee, to a full remake of Bioshock's Rapture. Figure 8.9 shows a small underwater base.

FIGURE 8.9   Make like a dolphin and head underwater to build your aquatic base.

Building underwater is a methodical process. The trick is to consider it the inverse of mining. Instead of removing material, you actually want to fill in the entire shape of your structure to displace the water, place the final shell of the building around that (for example, glass blocks), and then remove the internal material to create the living area. There's no method of pumps or pipes to suck water out or pump air in, so this displacement system is the only viable method.

There are a few ways to go about it.

In Creative mode, it's just a matter of taking the time and a bit of care. You can stay underwater as long as you need.

Survival mode adds a twist because running out of air is a constant risk. It becomes vitally important to keep a close eye on the oxygen bar and your health bar. Swimming up from the bottom of a lake always takes longer than expected, causing hits on your health, so the real trick is to find a way to create an air supply down below.

At a minimum, ensure your kit includes these items:

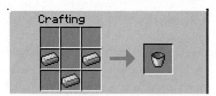

- **One bucket**—Crafting a bucket takes just three iron ingots and can give you a quick gulp of air in an emergency.

- **Doors, ladders, and signs**—These blocks displace water but leave space for you to stand and grab a breather. You can make do with just one of these, but it's best to pack a few. As you'll see later, ladders or signs will really help give you some breathing space as you drain the water from the initial perimeter tunnel.

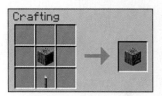

- **Light sources**—Torches go out in a soggy fizz as soon as they hit water. Jack-o'-lanterns work best and can be smashed up and repositioned as required. Glowstone from The Nether also works well. See the sidebar "Light Up Your (Underwater) Life" for another option.

- **Construction equipment**—Bring the usual suspects: a couple of shovels for digging sand, dirt, and gravel and some pickaxes for the harder stuff. An axe also makes it easier to reposition other equipment such as doors.

- **Soft blocks**—You need several full stacks of dirt, wood, sand, or gravel as temporary filler material to remove the water from your construction. By the way, I use the term *soft blocks* to refer to the temporary blocks you'll use during construction—those you can remove quickly with a shovel while underwater.

- **Construction materials**—You need lots of glass blocks for the outer shell, as well as any other material you want to use.

- **Food**—It's important to keep a full hunger bar underwater so that your health recovers quickly if you run out of air.

Survive with an Island Spawn Point

Underwater construction can be a hazardous business, so place a bed nearby and take a nap before you begin. If your spawn point is nearby, you can get back down quickly enough to pick up any dropped items should you suffer a watery demise. If you are building too far offshore, use a boat to return quickly or build an island platform on the surface, perched on top of a single block tower. It just needs to be big enough for a bed and a torch to prevent mob spawns at night.

There are plenty of methods for getting started, including tunneling in from the side of a lake, but these aren't always practical. The most comfortable I've found is to just jump right in. Here's how:

1 First find a location. At a minimum, the water should be four blocks deep. This gives you two blocks of standing room, a glass roof (because it looks awesome!), and one block of water over the top, but you also might want to go deeper. There are no practical limits; the only concerns are having sufficient air and light, but keep the structure on the conservative side initially. Figure 8.10 shows the exterior view of the structure shown in Figure 8.9.

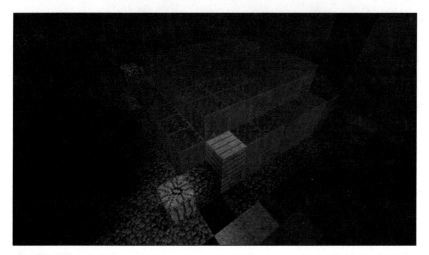

FIGURE 8.10   Keeping your initial structure to a conservative size helps you get used to building underwater while providing plenty of room to breathe. This one, when the shell is in place, will be 9×9 and 3 blocks high.

2 Keep the bucket in your Hotbar, along with a door or, if you are using ladders or signs, have some soft blocks and one of those at the ready.

3 Head to the bottom, and keep a close eye on the oxygen bar. It depletes in 16 seconds.

4 Place the door as soon as you reach the seabed (see Figure 8.11). If you are using ladders or signs, create a stack of two blocks and then put the ladder or sign on the top block. Any of these actions creates a permanent air pocket you can step into and breathe. Incidentally, jumping into a lake with any of these items at the ready is also a good way to escape hostile mobs at night, and you can poke at the bottom-side of any curious creepers swimming by. What's not to like?

FIGURE 8.11 Doors create a two-block-high breathing space. The jack-o'-lantern provides a waterproof source of light.

TIP

Light Up Your (Underwater) Life

Things get gloomy in the deep. Anything more than seven blocks down comes close to pitch black, even during the day, and torches need a full block of clear air to stay lit. How can you light up the murky mire? Jack-o'-lanterns and glowstone are good solutions. Light tunnels also work well. Place blocks and ladders above your first air-pocket block until you reach the surface. The light flows down the tunnel brightening up the sea floor and provides a convenient access shaft for your submerged traversals (see Figure 8.13). Potions of Night Vision also clear up the murk, allowing you to see much farther underwater.

Now that you have a survivable location on the seabed, it's time to get started on the structure.

Building underwater takes a few steps and a lot of care:

1 Plan out the perimeter. I find it easiest to create an air tunnel around the perimeter using dirt blocks and ladders at eye height, filling in the interior as I go. Figure 8.12 shows an example. All the ladders are recoverable later, and I generally put them on the interior wall so that I can work on the exterior without worrying about removing a ladder and getting swamped by an inrush of water.

FIGURE 8.12 A one-block-wide tunnel and ladders keep the water at bay. I've removed all the stray water sources in the lower half of the tunnel by swamping them with sand blocks dug out earlier.

2 As you fill in the interior, also start building up the external shell on the outer side of the tunnel. Use your final construction materials such as glass blocks because this will form the permanent structure. Keep some soft blocks at the ready to plug up any water breakthroughs. The wall needs to be only two blocks high. Given that you're on the bottom of the sea, you can always dig down later to create more height. Place some torches as you go to create additional light, although they won't attach to glass.

NOTE

Flooded In? Head to the Source

It's quite typical to find your tunnels still half flooded even after all the walls are done and every ladder is in place. The damp ankles are caused by water source blocks that still exist on the floor of your perimeter tunnel. To remove them, place any kind of soft block wherever you can see anything that looks like the head of the water spring. This kills the water source, and you can then quickly shovel out the soft block. Rinse and repeat until all the source blocks have been extinguished and your tunnel has dried.

3 With the interior full and the external wall done, it's time to attach the ceiling. This is easy. All you need to do is jump out of the tunnel into the water and run backward across the interior fill, placing glass blocks—or your material of choice—as you go. Unless you've planned an enormous structure, it's easy to do a row or two without having to stop for air, but be ready to dash to an air pocket, just in case. Fill in any gaps you spot in the interior as you go.

4 You're almost there! Just dig out the internal material to fully open the space. Breaking up the soft blocks dislodges the ladders so they can be scooped up into your inventory and perhaps used to create a laddered pillar all the way to the surface.

5 Finally, make an access point. You can place a door or just use a pillar and a ladder outside the wall (see Figure 8.13). Add any finishing touches to the interior, and you're done!

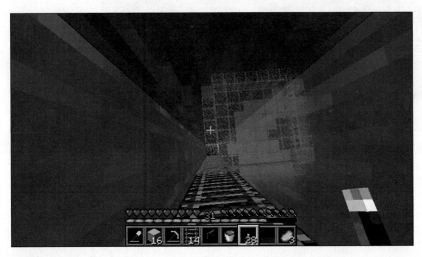

FIGURE 8.13 Looking down a long access ladder from the sea's surface to the undersea dwelling.

After you've built one room, the rest is even easier. Place a bed down in the first and sleep in it to reset your spawn to the ocean floor; then take it bit by bit. You should have just about all the materials you need, except maybe wood. And you are on the ocean floor, so there's plenty of sand for glass, and there's nothing stopping you digging straight down and mining up other materials as required.

NOTE

Underwater Enchantments

Two enchantments help underwater work. The first is *respiration*, which applies to helmets and increases the length of time you can breathe underwater while also reducing suffocation damage; in addition, it improves your underwater vision. The second is *aqua affinity*, a speed boost for tools when you're mining underwater.

One of the key advantages of underwater dwellings is that they don't require protection, at least not until the squids launch their revolution. But those houses on land do. In the final part of this chapter, I take you through some key strategies for protecting your other perimeters.

Protecting Your Perimeter

There's nothing worse than stepping outside your front door only to hear the quick hiss of a creeper's fuse running down and to find two seconds later a massive crater that has taken out half your house. (Creepers can take out a block of dirt that measures 5×5×5.) If the explosion doesn't kill you, the next influx of hostile mobs probably will. In any case, rebuilding will be a painful experience, especially if you've gone all out with a delicately aesthetic blend of textures and materials. (A cobblestone wall—okay, that's not so bad, but that's the Building 101 course.)

There is an easy way to step out in the morning and enjoy a breath of fresh air without a pang of fear interrupting the ritual. It's the perimeter—your stake in the world. Varmints be gone! The simplest is just a wooden fence, not forgetting the gate so you can actually get in and out, but I've also included some other ideas below.

Becoming a Ditch Witch

Ditches provide protection without interrupting the view. They were even a feature of English country gardens, known as the *invisible fence*, designed to keep the sheep from trampling the peonies without the fence line blotting the landscape.

In Minecraft, no mobs except spiders can cross a ditch that is two blocks deep and just one block wide, but creepers can still detonate if you're nearby. Build three blocks deep, and they won't trouble you unless you fall in. Or dig two blocks deep and put a fence around the inside edge of the ditch. You won't need to worry about an inadvertent stumble, and creepers will stay nicely defused.

So what about spiders? I don't worry about them too much. They're easy to kill and provide string for bows; fishing rods; and, with sufficient numbers, enough string to make the wool for a bed—handy if sheep aren't around.

TIP

Mobs Go with the Flow

Place water sources in strategic locations in the ditch to wash the mobs downstream away from critical areas. This can help you build a smaller perimeter because you can force them to bunch at the far end of your property (see Figure 8.14).

If spiders still give you the shivers and you want to keep your AAA insurance rating, build a ditch for all other mobs and then a wall behind it with an overhang. Or if you want to get a little fancier, make the third layer of the wall iron bars or a glass pane and put a final layer on top. Spiders can't get a grip on bars or glass, so you'll still be able to look out on the marauding hordes.

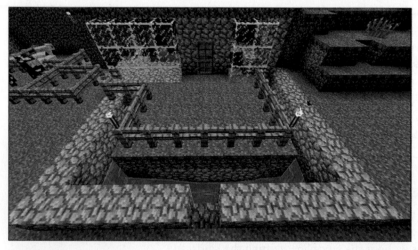

FIGURE 8.14 A ditch with water flowing to a central point (the middle-front here) sweeps any mobs away from the entrance so they can exit through the gap in the front.

CAUTION

Knobble Their Knees

The ditch gathers all kinds of mobs. Some such as zombies and skeletons burn up during the day, but others such as creepers stay. Leave an easy egress of steps out of the ditch to the exterior if you want your ditch to self-clear and aren't using a mob pit and water-clearing method described later in the "Mob Pitfalls" section. Or cut in a tunnel under the wall at eye level for you and knee level for the mobs so that you can hack at their feet to collect their drops while being safe from attack. This works best if the tunnel ends two steps back from the edge of the ditch so that creepers don't detonate, with a smaller one block continuation to the ditch. Your sword can still reach them just fine.

Alternatively, put your house in an unassailable position atop a small stone tower. Enter through a door in the base, build a stairway or ladder going up at least three blocks (or many more if there's a good view!), and create as large a platform as you like. The overhang from the platform keeps spiders at bay. Use other perimeter fences to provide protection for farmland if you don't want to build them all in the air.

CAUTION

Don't Forget the Torches

It's easy to forget while focusing on the defensive perimeter around the house that an unlit roof also provides a mob-spawning platform at night. If you're wondering how that spider surprised you in the bedroom, it could be because it simply dropped from the sky and climbed in through that opening you left leading out onto a sunny morning verandah. (Been there, done that!) Always place a few torches on your roof to keep things clear. Torches can also help you spot home when you're out and about exploring the Overworld.

Mob Pitfalls

Mobs may be a nuisance, but they're also a boon because they carry all sorts of useful items from enchanted weapons to food. Why not reap the benefits of their fall?

Here's how to do it:

1 Dig a ditch two blocks deep and nine blocks long around your perimeter.

2 Create a vertical pit in the ninth block. The most effective height is a drop of 22 blocks because this leaves spiders, skeletons, and creepers with just 1 point of health—enough to dispatch them with a single punch and gather the resultant experience points that

help with enchanting. However, if you don't mind using weapons instead, the pit can even be just 2 blocks lower than the water flow.

3 Place a water source at the other end. It flows for 8 blocks, pushing mobs toward the pit. You can also place a second water source coming in from the other direction, providing a total of 19 blocks of coverage around your perimeter, and the water can flow around corners if required.

4 Choose a safe location inside your perimeter or even inside your house, and tunnel down and toward the bottom of the pit so that your eye height ends up at the same level as the lowest part of the pit. Any mobs that stray into the ditch gradually wash down toward the pit, fall in, and gather at the bottom. Head down the access tunnel to safely finish them off and collect the spoils. Figure 8.15 shows a trapped creeper.

FIGURE 8.15 Creeper knobbled: the water keeps it in place while you attack its knees with impunity. The sign prevents the water from flowing down your own tunnel.

TIP

Ding! Your Zombies Are Ready

For extra points and convenience, add a wooden pressure plate to the bottom of your pit, connected to a redstone lamp sitting somewhere in normal sight. When a mob hits the bottom of the pit, the pressure plate sends a signal to the lamp, lighting it up.

If you have no particular interest in collecting mob drops, fill the pit with lava. Keeping a mob's feet to the flame will see the mob off quite quickly, but it also burns up any items. You can use cacti in the ninth hole of the ditch for the same purpose, serving up death by a thousand cuts. Just place a cacti block instead of digging the pit, but keep in mind that the cacti can also destroy any dropped items.

Thick as a Brick

The defenses previously mentioned are designed to keep mobs at a distance, but the final line in the sand, or cobblestone, will be your own building's walls. This is also an aesthetic choice. Design your castle's keep, so to speak, more than one block thick. A direct creeper hit can take out a couple of layers of cobblestone and up to five layers of other materials. If you really do want that log cabin look, consider creating a sandwich of wood outside, an internal cobblestone section, and then a wood interior. Switch these around to suit your own needs. A couple of layers of external cobblestone with a wood interior is much safer than a single layer of wood. Sandstone has little blast resistance, so definitely create a 3-ply if you like the sandstone look.

Keeping with the concept of a castle's keep, attack is also part of any defensive strategy. Knock out a 1×1 block in a wall and then fill it with a slab, leaving just a half-block gap. Fire arrows at targets through the slit. You'll have an excellent field of fire, and skeletons will have a much more difficult time getting a clear shot at you.

Finally, obsidian is the toughest minable in Minecraft. It's a little difficult to collect, but in Chapter 10 you'll find a guide that makes it easy.

The Bottom Line

It takes a little bit of time to build a beautiful home, but it does provide a pleasant interlude between mining, farming, and fighting mobs. Enjoy the time. As you master the various techniques, you'll no doubt develop your own and create soaring, graceful masterpieces in the sky.

This chapter has been about letting your imagination take flight. In the next, you explore a completely different side to Minecraft: redstone and rails. It might be enough to make you think about construction from a completely different perspective.

Redstone, Rails, and More

In This Chapter

- Create automated contraptions with redstone power sources and components.
- Build cool circuits with redstone wiring.
- Understand different types of power to avoid wiring problems.
- Create a perimeter warning system, piston-powered doors, repeater loops, and more.
- Learn to use AND, OR, and NOT gates.
- Use redstone to build powered rails for a minecart transport system.

Redstone and rails create an entirely new Minecraft experience:

- **Redstone**—This is one of the ores you probably have seen in mines. When dug out and placed on the ground, it provides a way to transmit power between different devices, like a strand of electrical wire does, and is used for operating pistons, controlling doors, and doing all sorts of other neat tricks.
- **Rails**—These are tracks on which minecarts run, and when those rails are powered by redstone, they provide a system like an electric train track that can transport goods between different areas. They also give you, when sitting in a minecart, quite a thrill ride.

Redstone is a brilliant, almost magical system that draws on some real-life parallels with electrical circuits but is different enough to be absolutely confusing—even baffling—at the same time. It will challenge you to rethink everything you may already know. Is it worth it? Absolutely.

The trick to understanding redstone is to try your very best not to bring any real-world assumptions with you. It's a different type of energy from electricity. For example, it runs on a single strand so it doesn't have positive and negative wires, and it can be created by many types of devices, even a lever stuck in the ground or a wooden button attached to the wall. Redstone has its own rules, its own behavior, and its own results. Some of those are almost beyond imagination. I'm betting when

Mojang started thinking about adding a few logic circuits to redstone, they didn't think someone would spend possibly months of his life building a simulacrum of a computer complete with a 1,000-pixel graphical display, the entire system filling hundreds of acres and using tens of thousands of components.

In the same way that the building blocks of Minecraft deliver an architecturally infinite construction playground, redstone adds a whole new dimension. In some ways, it harks back to the genesis of the electronics industry, simulating the breadboarding of electronics with wires and vacuum tubes. Very retro.

This chapter is an introduction to redstone and transport. It teaches you the essentials, and you won't need an engineering degree to succeed. Even if you're not switched on by some of the more complex aspects of this extraordinary system, it is definitely worth coming to grips with a few core techniques. They go well beyond the water harvester from Chapter 6, "Crop Farming," and you'll have fun exploring this creative new world.

Seeing Red: A Beginner's Guide

Certain aspects of Minecraft are completely intuitive and can be understood in the usual process of discovery. Redstone is different, but it's not so hard. The complete redstone system is made up of just a few core concepts: power sources, wire, modifiers, and output devices.

TIP

Use Creative Mode

I recommend that you test and explore this chapter in a world set to Creative mode. It's just so much easier as a learning exercise to place and wire up components this way, especially the more exotic ones.

After you get a grip on redstone essentials and start to figure out how to put these building blocks together into more interesting systems, you will never think of Minecraft the same way again.

Power Sources

The power sources provide the energy to power devices or to signal that an event has occurred, such as a mob (or someone in multiplayer) walking across a pressure plate, or stumbling across a tripwire. Figure 9.1 shows the complete set.

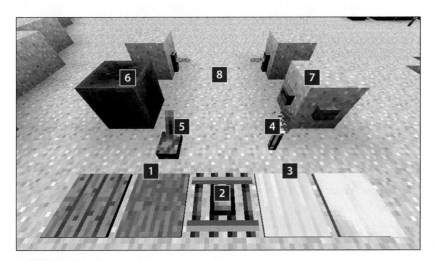

FIGURE 9.1 Redstone power and signal sources.

1. Wooden pressure plate
2. Detector rail
3. Stone pressure plate
4. Redstone torch
5. Lever
6. Wooden button
7. Stone button
8. Tripwire hooks connected with string

Signals and power sources provide the same redstone energy and are somewhat inter-changeable as terms, but consider signals to be intermittent providing that energy when an event occurs, such as someone or something stepping on a pressure plate. Power sources provide a continuous flow of power like a signal switched on permanently. Here's the most essential information on each type of signal or power source.

 Redstone torch—The torch is Minecraft's electric utility—clean, green energy, even if it's red. It provides a continuous source of power but also has a few handy tricks up its sleeve. Feed a power source into a torch and it will turn off, making it a useful switching mechanism for almost every circuit. You'll see many examples of this later. Craft a torch from a stick and a chunk of redstone.

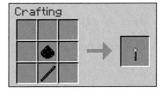

Lever —Minecraft levers act like on/off switches, but spruced up with their own built-in power generation. Like buttons, they're also safe from being flipped by any of the nonplayer mobs. Levers can be placed on any side of a block, including the underside.

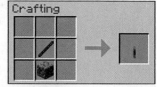

Button—There are two types of buttons. The stone button provides a 1-second pulse of power, whereas the wooden button delivers a pulse for 1.5 seconds. Craft a button from one wood plank block or a block of stone obtained by mining stone with a pickaxe charmed with silk touch or by smelting cobblestone back into a stone block. Buttons can be placed on the sides and top of blocks.

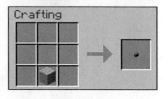

Pressure plate—Similar to buttons, pressure plates come in wood or stone variants, both delivering continuous power while activated. Stone plates react to mobs, a low-level fly-by in Creative, and a minecart containing a mob. Dropped items, all minecarts regardless of contents, the lure on the end of a fishing rod, and arrows also trigger wooden plates.

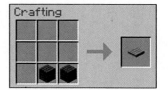

 Tripwire hook—Use string and two tripwire hooks to create a devious detection system with two tripwire hooks placed up to 40 blocks apart in a straight line. Join them by placing string between. The string creates a tiny, difficult-to-see texture between both hooks, making it a favorite trap creator. It's also an efficient way to "string up" a perimeter alarm. The hooks generate power while any mob is standing on or in the same block occupied by the string.

CAUTION

Don't Run Off the Rails

Pressure plates disrupt a contiguous minecart rail, so they are most reliably used at the end of the line. Detector rails provide a better alternative.

 Detector rail—Detector rails send off a signal as a minecart rolls over the top. This can be used to turn off other powered rails to prevent collisions, open doors, fire a dispenser, and so on.

Redstone Wiring

 Redstone is harvested from redstone ore with an iron, gold, or diamond pickaxe. When placed on the ground, the redstone transforms into a trail, also called *redstone wire*, that carries power or signals between other components.

Redstone wire has some interesting properties (see Figure 9.2):

■ Laying a trail is quite easy because the wire automatically connects adjacent nodes. Just click on blocks using the 🔲 where you'd like to place the wire, and it bends around corners, goes up and down solid block ramps, and creates three- and four-way junction points as required. It's sticky stuff, so prevent separate circuits from connecting by keeping them separated by at least one block; otherwise, they'll join together to form a lattice. If space is tight and you must run two separate strands side-by-side, use a parallel run of repeaters instead.

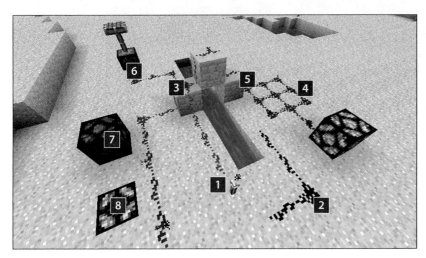

FIGURE 9.2 Redstone properties.

1. Powered wire emits a glow and sparkles.

2. Unpowered wire has a dull red color.

3. Wire transforms automatically into junctions as you place nearby nodes.

4. Connecting nearby blocks creates a lattice but continues to transmit power without short circuits.

5. Wire can also climb up and down blocks arranged in a stair-step pattern.

6. Devices can activate at the end of a wire at the same level...

7. ...but don't activate when when they run alongside.

8. Wire does power the block below, lighting up this adjacent glowstone lamp that is sunk into the ground one block.

- Water and electricity don't mix. The water just washes away the redstone wire turning it back into collectable redstone. Be prepared to climb over or tunnel under any water blocks.

- Powered wire sparkles with a red glow that gradually diminishes until the current runs out in 15 blocks. You'll need repeaters or torches to boost the power for longer circuits as described next.

- The current runs in the space above the block on which the trail appears but provides power (see the following) to the block underneath and the block directly in front of the end of the wire. Think of the wire as actually occupying the space above its depicted location. That space must be contiguous with the exception of slabs or transparent blocks such as glass, ice, leaves, and glowstone. Figure 9.3 shows a blocked current.

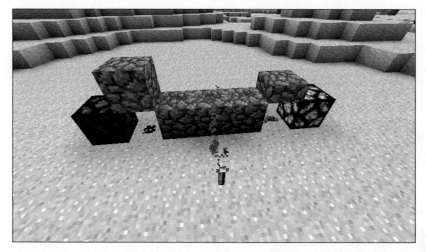

FIGURE 9.3   Blocks can break a wire's current: the block on the left prevents the current from flowing down and to the glowstone lamp, while the slab on the right (taking up just half an actual block space) allows the power to flow through it and down to the ground, lighting up the lamp. Replace the interfering block with a slab as shown on the right, if keeping a similar texture is important, or replace it with a transparent block such as glass, as shown leading out the back of the junction.

Powered Blocks

Redstone power propagates from the source as *strong* power. Strong power can light up redstone wire and activate devices. Feed strong power into a normal opaque block such as dirt, cobblestone, or wood, and that block will propagate *weak* power, which can only activate devices. Basically, it's not strong enough to reconnect with a redstone wire and continue acting like a partial insulator. Figure 9.4 illustrates this concept.

FIGURE 9.4 Strong and weak power.

1. The cobblestone emits weak power, sufficient to activate the lamp and other devices, but not enough to power the wire leading to the second lamp.

2. Running wire over a block continues the current through the space above the block.

3. The lever provides strong power to the block, firing up the wire.

It's also worthwhile mentioning that a wired connection between a power source and a device isn't always necessary. Most of Minecraft's blocks—the opaque ones—can be powered directly by a source. This enables the creation of very small circuits. I included one example of this in Chapter 6, where the piston was powered by a button placed on a block directly behind it. I'll show you some other examples later in this chapter.

Most redstone sources are attached to a block of some kind. For example, buttons are placed on the vertical surface of a block such as a wall, a lever to any surface, or even the ceiling. Generally speaking, the source powers the block to which it is attached (the *anchor* block), and this can then activate any devices adjacent to it. This is why a button placed on a block beside a door opens that door. It's not the button acting directly on the door through some hidden link. Rather, pushing the button powers the block to which it is attached, and that block being adjacent to the door triggers it to open.

NOTE

Torches Power the Block Above

Of course, there is an exception to this rule. The redstone torch powers the block above it rather than the block to which it is attached.

Now, here's the important part. All sources except the redstone block also strongly power the space they occupy, not just the anchor. This provides a choice of two blocks to which you can attach components: do so either at the anchor block or at the block occupied by the power source item. Figure 9.5 shows how this works.

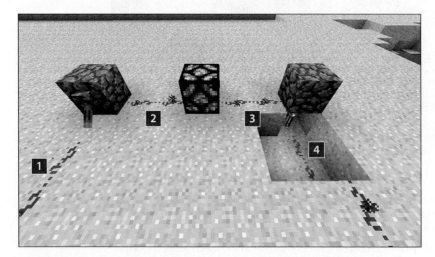

FIGURE 9.5   Sources provide strong power to two blocks each.

1. This wire is powered by the space occupied by the lever.

2. This wire gets its power from the block to which the lever is anchored.

3. Redstone torches power the block above, so this wire gets its power from the cobblestone block above the torch.

4. The torch also powers the space it occupies, firing up this redstone wire.

Keeping the two-block rule in mind gives you many more options for linking components and running circuits. In other words, more power to you!

Repeaters

 Redstone repeaters can amplify a strong or weak current and add a 1- to 4-tick delay that is useful for adding timing to circuits. (A "tick" is equivalent to 0.1 of a second.) The repeater also acts like a diode, ensuring current flows in only one direction.

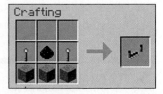

The power-boosting function allows current to flow through solid blocks such as walls without finding a way to go over or under them. This in itself can solve some otherwise difficult design problems. Figure 9.6 shows two examples.

A repeater's current always flows in the direction of the single fixed light on the repeater. You might be able to make out a faint triangular texture on top of the repeater that shows this direction. Place the repeater by facing in the direction you want the current to flow, and it will align correctly.

FIGURE 9.6 The repeater on the left picks up the weak current reaching the block and amplifies it back to strong. Without this, the block just emits a weak current insufficient to light the wire on the far left. The repeater on the right turns the block into a strong emitter, lighting up both redstone trails.

Click the repeater to add a delay to the circuit. The default is 0.1 seconds, increasing to 0.4 seconds with each click until the light has slid fully back to the base of its channel.

Repeaters are also useful for running current in tight spaces because they can be placed next to each other without forming the lattice effect that placed wire develops. Place them in parallel series, as shown in Figure 9.7.

FIGURE 9.7 Two sets of repeaters keep current separate. Terminate the sets with blocks, and use the sides of the blocks to run the separate strands to their destination.

Output Devices

All those power sources, wiring, and modifiers are a bit useless without the circuit actually doing something. Minecraft provides a large number of devices, activators, gadgets, and more. Figure 9.8 shows the full set, described in the following list.

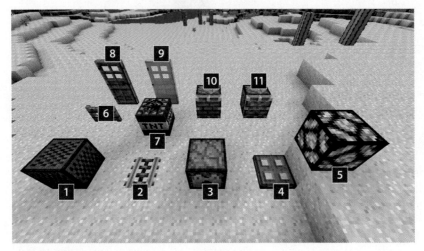

FIGURE 9.8 All of Minecraft's output devices.

1. Note block
2. Powered rail
3. Dispenser
4. Trapdoor
5. Redstone lamp
6. Fence gate
7. TNT
8. Wooden door
9. Iron door
10. Piston
11. Sticky piston

- **Redstone lamp**—The lamp, as you've seen from many of the figures in this chapter, is a handy way to check the output of circuits. It also happens to make a pretty good light source, although crafting one requires glowstone from The Nether. Glowstone is plentiful, but obviously you'll have to venture into The Nether first.

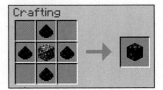

■ **Doors**—The *de rigeur* entryway. Doors come in iron and wood variants and switch between a fully open or closed state instantaneously, meaning one can't hit you in the rear on the way out. Iron doors can only be opened with some sort of power input. They also keep zombies out when playing on Hard difficulty.

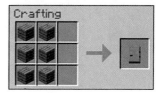

■ **Trapdoors**—Although a little obvious for use in a trap, a pressure plate in front of a trapdoor will save you from fumbling for the trigger as you approach.

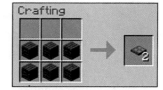

■ **Pistons**—Both the regular and sticky variants are incredibly useful. You'll see some examples soon.

■ **Powered rails**—Sure, you can power a minecart by jumping on board while riding a saddled pig, but is that any way to get around? You'll be the laughing stock. Powered rails provide a more stylish way to move you and your minecarts from A to B.

■ **Fence gates**—They open, they shut, and they're good for keeping the livestock in place.

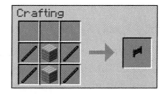

■ **Dispensers**—The dispenser pumps out almost anything that has been put inside it. Typically used for firing arrows, supplying a flood of water, and, well, an enormous range of things, they're an indispensable (sorry) part of any automated system.

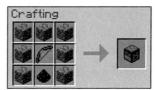

- **TNT**—TNT is the most destructive force in Minecraft, except for a creeper that has been hit by lightning, and that's incredibly rare. Set it off manually with a flint and steel or automatically with a pulse of redstone power. Craft TNT with gunpowder collected from slain creepers (that's easier to say than to do) and regular sand.

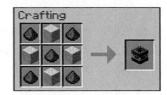

- **Note blocks**—Note blocks add a nice aesthetic to the game and are an easy way to create audible notifications or warnings of certain events. Once placed, use **L2** to change a block's pitch. You can even create your own doorbell with a string of blocks hooked up using repeaters to create delays. Try placing them on different types of blocks to also adjust the instrument used. Bring out your inner composer.

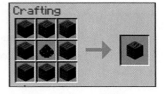

The output devices make quite a collection. You'll use them in various ways later.

You can make advanced circuits and mechanisms by combining all the components in different ways. The redstone system can do a lot more than connect a button to a light or a lever to a water dispenser.

Automatic Doors

Let's start with something simple and useful. You've probably already experimented with powered doors. Place a wooden or stone button on the wall next to any single door, and it will spring open. You can do the same with two doors placed side-by-side, but a single button placed on one side won't open them both. Wouldn't it be nice if you could link that button to both doors so they both swing open the way you'd expect?

All you need is a little redstone dust. Follow these steps and refer to Figure 9.9:

1 Position the doors. The order you place them is important. Place the left door first, and then the right. This causes the right-hand door to flip around, becoming a mirror image of the left.

2 Place blocks to surround the doors as shown, a stack of two on each side.

3 Position the button on the upper-left block. Wooden buttons provide a 1.5-second pulse of power, whereas stone buttons provide a 1-second pulse.

4 Run a trail of redstone dust from the base of one door pillar to the other in a U-shaped bend until it drives directly into the base of the other. The redstone receives its current from the space the button block occupies, transmitting the current to the opposite base block and powering that and triggering the opposite door to open.

The only obvious problem with this? It isn't attractive. You can't throw a welcome mat over it to hide the wire, but there are other ways to improve that.

FIGURE 9.9 A simple circuit to link two doors.

Let's remove the wiring and start again. Take a look at Figure 9.10. It's still the same concept, but the wiring now runs from the side of the button's anchor block, down a few blocks to where it can be hidden by ground cover, and back up the other side in a mirror image. Follow these steps:

1 Dig out the blocks shown to re-create, although you can leave the forwardmost row in place—I just removed those to better show the circuit.

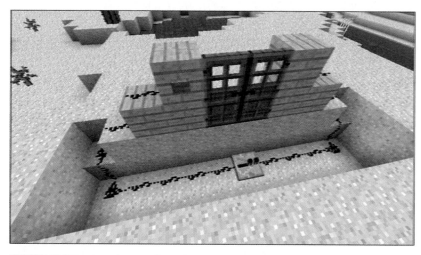

FIGURE 9.10 It takes only a few minutes to rerun the wiring so that it can be hidden from sight. Going two blocks deep leaves room for a layer of flooring above flush with the ground.

2 Add the two single side blocks on either side of the door jambs, and run redstone along the top of the blocks and down into the trench.

3 When you reach the middle, stop and place a redstone repeater to amplify the current because it needs to run a touch longer than 15 steps. Place it facing in the direction the current should run (in this example facing toward the right), and then continue the redstone wiring out and up the steps on the other side.

4 Time to test! Click the button, and both doors should spring open. The left one first, followed by the right after a tiny tenth of a second delay caused by the current as it runs through the repeater.

5 Now let's cover this back up. Start by filling in the main trench using any material you prefer, even glass blocks if you want to see the current fire up each time you enter, but leave the two blocks at the far end empty for now.

6 Figure 9.11 shows the blocks at the end of the trench. One is one block deep, and the other is two blocks deep. Place a slab instead of a full block over the space that is two blocks deep. This allows a surface flush with the ground while also letting the current run underneath.

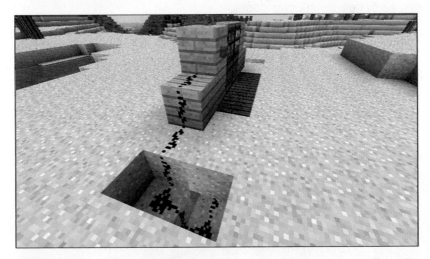

FIGURE 9.11 Cover the space on the right with a slab to allow the current to run down and into the trench.

7 Build up other blocks around and on top of the wiring until you've achieved the desired result. Figure 9.12 shows an example that turns the entry into something a little grander while also hiding all the wiring.

FIGURE 9.12 A completed portico. I've used fence posts and wooden slabs to create the roof.

8 Position a couple of pressure plates behind the door for an easy exit. The plates aren't quite perfect. Each one opens just the door in front of it. For extra props, dig a trench two blocks deep under the plates and lay some redstone under both plates that connects somewhere with the other wire originating from the button. This ensures that no matter which plate is jumped on, the original double-opening circuit will receive the hit and swing both doors open.

TIP

Forgot to Shut the Door on Your Way Out?

Place a wooden pressure plate inside every door leading outside even if you don't do any other wiring. You won't need to click the door to get out, and the door will automatically close behind you every time.

This is just one example for connecting doors and running wiring; there are many ways to slice this. The wiring could run over the top of the door. It could also be made shorter on the delivery side by placing a redstone torch two blocks under the door and powering it through an inverter, but the repeater significantly simplifies the design. And, of course, the entire thing could be flipped so that the wiring runs behind the doors.

Let's get a touch more sophisticated. Swinging doors are great, but if you have in mind something more high tech, perhaps a modern fortress decked out with everything that opens and shuts (literally), you might consider leveling up to doors that glide open before you. They're not whisper quiet, and they don't even give that swoosh sound of the doors in every sci-fi show. However, they do look great, and you can make them from any material, including glass blocks, so they'll add a certain something to any construction.

Sliding doors add an extra circuit to the loop. The pistons have to stay powered and therefore extended for the door to stay closed. But pressing the button delivers power rather than cutting it off, and flipping a lever will just keep the doors in one state or the other. What this circuit needs is a method of keeping the pistons powered constantly—but a way of interrupting that only when the button supplies its own current. This setup is known as an *inverter*, or a *NOT* gate, and is provided by a redstone torch attached to the button block.

Figure 9.13 shows the basic layout, with all components identified. The image shows the pistons powered. They'll be retracted at first, but you can place the actual door blocks either in the middle or up against the pistons, and they'll work just fine as soon as the pistons are extended for the first time.

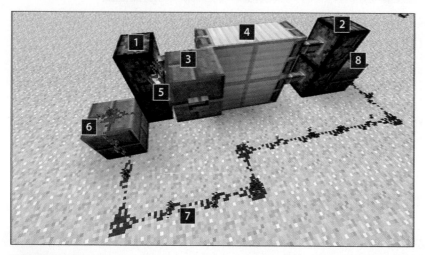

FIGURE 9.13 Place these components to create the mechanics of a sliding door.

1. A double-stack of sticky pistons.

2. The second stack of sticky pistons required for the opposite slider.

3. Block with button attached.

4. Blocks for the door—I've used iron for that fortress look.

5. Redstone torch attached to button block forming an inverter.

6. Start of redstone wiring.

7. The wiring must step around the block beneath the button's own space so it isn't fired when the button is pressed.

8. Place the trail up and onto the block behind the second piston stack.

I've shown the wiring at ground level for simplicity, but bury it the same way as for the wooden doors example and then build up the rest of the entryway to hide everything. Figure 9.14 shows one example, but feel free to achieve any look you like. Piston doors provide quite an entrance into a fortress buried into the side of a hill, where you can place natural terrain to hide the inner workings. You can also flip the workings 90° and make doors open vertically or add some vertical doors and pistons on top of the horizontal ones to create a three-way iris.

FIGURE 9.14   One approach to hiding piston door wiring.

Try the same design with an added latch circuit: run wire from pressure plates through the latch, feeding the power into the side repeater from a lever inside. Use the pressure plates to get in and out quickly, and then use the lever to lock the doors closed at night.

One final example of piston-controlled devices: Figure 9.15 shows a set of three automatic iron block storm shutters hidden within a wall cavity. (I've opened up the inner wooden wall and floor so you can see the workings.) A system like this controlled by a lever provides more blast resistance than glass, and you can open it to take pot shots at mobs. Wire this to a lever and bury the wiring under your floor.

FIGURE 9.15 Sliding windows created with sticky pistons. The repeaters keep the current feeding directly into the base block under the pistons. Without them, the wiring would revert to a lattice and stop working.

Vertical Currents

Although redstone wiring can easily climb and descend steps, there are times you'll want to send it vertically instead. The easiest way to do this is to use an alternating series of redstone torches, ensuring the final one is in sync (not inverting) with the current at the base of the tower. See Figure 9.16 for an example.

FIGURE 9.16 Redstone torches power the block above, so they are an easy way to create a vertically ascending current.

TIP

1×1 Vertical Ascending Alternative

Current (or really the current's signal) will ascend in a 1×1 pattern by placing redstone torches on top rather than on the side of each block. This requires a temporary tower behind the planned ascent that you can remove when you're done, but it's also ideal if you can just place the ascent against a wall. Attach blocks to the tower or wall every second space. Fix redstone torches to the top of each block, and they'll pass their signals to the block above until you can draw power from a final torch placed into the side of the uppermost block.

The only way to descend a current is through a 2×2 staircase (see "The Spiral Staircase" on page 74). You might want to use this in Survival mode as well as for ascending currents because it provides an easy way to get up and down the circuit.

Advanced Circuits

The creators of Minecraft did something interesting when they designed the redstone system: they made it possible to mimic the binary logic system that is at the heart of every integrated circuit that runs your electronics. Minecraft's system is nowhere near as crazily complicated as today's CPUs, and it's more like a breadboard of wires studded with vacuum tubes, but the basics are there. Let's take a look at some prototypical logic gates and how they're used to do useful things.

NOT Gates, aka Inverters

NOT gates take an input value and flip the output value. For example, if the incoming current is on, the output of the NOT gate is off. If the current is off, the output is on. Redstone torches act like this. By default, they supply a current, but if the block they are attached to is powered by another source, the torch flips off. NOT gates are also known as *inverters* because they invert the current.

We've already used an inverter to flip the current from the torch with a button in the sliding doors example. They have many other uses, though. For example, two inverters in a row act as an amplifier, just like a repeater (see Figure 9.17).

FIGURE 9.17 Inverters as amplifiers: the foremost inverter pair is a more compressed version of the furthest set (two inverters in sequence).

OR Gates, or Any Input Will Do

OR gates provide a positive output if any of the inputs is also true. This is a natural function of redstone wiring. Just connect two or more wires to a T-junction, and the single output will always be on if any input is on—or off if all inputs are off. Figure 9.18 shows an OR gate with three types of input, any of which can light the lamp.

FIGURE 9.18 The OR gate is represented by the junction point of the wiring. In this case, the lever is providing the power that lights up all the wires, but any of the three inputs will achieve the same result. Use repeaters or inverters on each strand if it's important that the current flows in just one direction always.

OR gates have many uses primarily because they allow multiple inputs to feed into the one circuit. For example, a row of pressure plates or strands of tripwire around the perimeter can hook up to a single wire that runs into your house, creating a perimeter alarm system. You can also add a timed circuit to a note block to create an audible beeping alarm.

I'm sure you'll find many other uses.

> ## NOTE
>
> ### If It's Not OR, It's NOR
>
> NOR gates operate as OR gates but with the output signal inverted. Think of it as NOT+OR. In these gates, the output signal is TRUE only if both inputs are FALSE. Just place an inverter on the single-wire output from the OR gate to create a NOR.

AND Gates, Two True

AND gates output current (or a value of TRUE) only if both inputs are also TRUE. In real life, this is often used in security systems where two keys must be inserted to open a vault. You can do something similar to create a secure room, and this can be especially useful in Multiplayer mode. Place a lever close to the door (although not so close it can directly activate it), and hide a lever in another part of the structure. String them together and feed the output to the door. Now the obviously placed lever by the door won't work unless the hidden lever is also flipped on.

The AND gate is a more complex construction using three inverters for two inputs and one output. Figure 9.19 shows the gate with both inputs on, and Figure 9.20 shows the same with one input off.

FIGURE 9.19 AND gate with both levers switched on. This cuts both torches above the levers, ensuring no current flows to the inverter on the side of the block. That inverter therefore sends power to the output wire lighting the lamp.

FIGURE 9.20 With one lever turned off, current flows from its torch to the output inverter, cutting its own current.

Repeater Loops

Loops set up a pulsing circuit. They're possible with just some redstone torches, but redstone repeaters make them more compact with adjustable timing by changing the repeater delay.

Figure 9.21 shows a prototypical design with a single repeater adjusted back to provide a 0.4-second delay. The torch adds one more tick to that, making this a 0.5-second loop. This causes the lamp to cycle through an on and off state every second. You can extend the circuit, adding more repeaters, to increase the delay. Replace the lever with wire connected to any other power source or signal to hook the repeater up to other circuits.

FIGURE 9.21 The repeater loop works off any type of input.

Rail Transport

Minecraft's rail transport system, as with much else therein, can be as simple or complex as you like. It is definitely part of the charm and the challenge. It can operate in a simplistic way, but the tendrils of redstone work their way deep into the rail system. Powered and detector rails provide key hooks that integrate rail and redstone into a homogenous whole.

Rail travel is the fastest way to get from A to Z, via B to Y if you prefer the scenic route. The carts travel at an average speed of 8 meters (or blocks) per second and can climb hills, traverse valleys, and—depending on how you design the track—offer something of a rollercoaster thrill ride in between. You won't break any land-speed records, but it's definitely faster than walking, and the rail system is a great way for moving items, resources, and yourself.

The system is limited by your imagination. In this section, I introduce you to the basic components, track-laying strategies, and some more advanced hints and tricks—enough to get you more than chugging along.

Have Minecart, Will Travel

A rail without rolling stock is about as useful as a car jacked on bricks.

Several versions of the standard carriage are shown in Figure 9.22. It would be wonderful if these were glorious celebrations of the gilded age of the iron horse. They aren't—not even steam-punk—but they do the job. Let's take a look in the stable:

- **Minecart**—This is the bare-bones version of the rolling chariot. Hop aboard by pointing at the minecart and pulling L2. Do the same again to exit. An occupied minecart rolls much farther than an unoccupied one. However, unless you are just going to roll downhill, you'll need some power and a launch system to get underway. More on that in a moment.

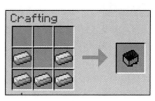

- **Minecart with furnace**—This is also known as a *powered* minecart. Burn, baby, burn! The furnace cart is powered by coal or charcoal and can push other carts in front. It's bidirectional: just click L2 on one with the fuel in hand facing in the direction you want it to go. You can also change its direction at any time using R to turn the view to your desired direction and then L to move there. The engine runs for 3 minutes on each piece of fuel (enough to travel about 600 blocks), and you can fuel it for a long haul by pressing L2 with fuel multiple times, building up a stack. A single powered cart can push numerous others, although some glitches can occur, leaving carts jammed or stranded.

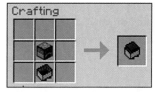

FIGURE 9.22 Minecarts.

1 Standard minecart

2 Minecart with furnace

3 Minecart with chest

 ■ **Minecart with chest (storage minecart)**—Add a chest to a standard minecart to gain 15 fully stackable slots. This minecart rolls with the same momentum as an occupied minecart, regardless of the contents of the chest.

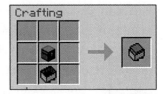

If you plan to build a bunch of minecarts and treat them like a train, keep in mind that they don't latch together, but instead can be used to push each other along. This works best with a powered cart doing the pushing. But even if you're just propelling yourself in a standard minecart, you'll find that you can push a practically unlimited string of storage carts ahead of you simply by bumping into them—shunting them along, as it were—as long as you stay on the flat. A powered minecart can push about four carts up a hill, but this doesn't always work out well in practice because the minecarts sometimes get stuck as the chain works its way around corners and over slope transitions.

NOTE

Destroying and Reusing Minecarts

By the way, you can destroy minecarts with a few hits from any tool and place them back in your inventory for reuse. You can also load them into a dispenser placed at the start of your track for easy one-click deployment.

TIP

Build Now, Rail Later

Real-life cities tend to be a mess of transportation compromises. Roads and rail fight for space with buildings, sidewalks, parks, and utilities, not to mention utility infrastructure. Take a page from their book: tunnel. Put your rails underground rather than demolishing your hard-built structures, and pop aboveground with access points when you can. The ability to run rails on a 45° slope makes your life much easier than that of a town planner, and subways with underground concourses add their own ambience to a vibrant landscape.

Rolling on Rails

Minecraft has three types of rail. Some are more resource expensive than others, but fortunately they don't need to be used all the time. Here's a quick guide:

- **Normal rail**—Six iron ingots and a stick of wood will create 16 rail track segments. Place them, and the system will take care of bending them around corners or up and down terrain. Only normal rails can bend into curves.

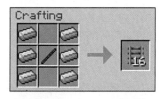

- **Powered rail**—The powered rail is expensive: for 6 gold ingots, a stick, and a lump of redstone, you'll get just 6 segments. Use wisely! Fortunately, you don't need a lot because a single rail can boost an occupied minecart or storage minecart for 80 blocks on level ground.

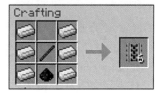

(Unoccupied minecarts lose steam after just 8 blocks.) The rail is itself powered by any redstone source, but some work better than others, and I'll use them in the examples that follow. These rails light up when powered and so are easy to recognize. When this type of rail is unpowered, it will slow you down, making it a good option for placing at the start and end of a track for a soft landing. Just 1 block can stop a minecart, even trundling down a slope. Powered rails provide a boost in the direction the minecart is moving. If stopped on a slope, the minecart will always head down the slope when the rail becomes powered. If the minecart is stationary and at the end of a track with a block in front, the rail will instead give the minecart a kick in the direction it can travel. This is really the key to making a station where you can board a cart without trying to jump on one trundling past. Powered rail segments chain together up to 8 segments from any powered source. Generally speaking, 1 powered rail is needed for every 4 steps up a slope, although you can work this as 2 rails in every 8 to make it a bit easier to manage the power supply. On the flat, you should place 1 powered rail every 37 blocks to keep an occupied minecart zipping along at a moderate pace, or use 2 powered rails to stay at high speed.

■ **Detector rail**—These rails are like a standard rail combined with a pressure plate, emitting a redstone current when a minecart rolls over the top. You can use this current or signal for any-thing really, including controlling hoppers, open-ing doors to a tunnel, setting off a note block, switching tracks at a T-junction, and so on.

Making Tracks and Stations

It's easy to lay tracks: just place them where you need them on contiguous blocks. If you make a mistake, you can easily dig up the tracks and reuse them. This allows for some trial and error, especially when working out the minimum placements required for the expensive powered rails.

TIP

Zig-Zag to Speed Up

Whereas a cart travels on level ground at a maximum of 8 blocks per second, a slight sideways dodge boosts this to 11 blocks. Lay diagonal tracks in a continuous zig-zag pattern to get this free speed boost. They'll look a little off on the ground, but the minecart will travel over them smoothly. Lay the tracks on diagonally adjoining blocks, and they'll connect with a series of corner tracks, creating the zig-zag pattern for you.

TIP

Efficient Powered Rails

The cheapest way to permanently power a rail is with a lever rather than a redstone torch. You just need a piece of cobblestone and a stick to craft the lever. Then place it by the track and flick it on. If you prefer to leave your power sources hidden, place a redstone torch under one of the blocks holding a powered rail, and the rail will transmit the power to any adjoining powered rails.

As you lay tracks, you need to consider inserting powered rails. The first place to start is really at the beginning of the track. Create a small launch station using Figure 9.23 as a guide. The station works like this:

1 The single powered track at the end acts as the launcher, gaining its power from the button attached to the wood block.

2 Place a cart at the end, hop aboard, and push the button.

3 You'll accelerate out of the dip and then get a speed boost from the track powered by the lever.

4 When returning, that same powered track gives your cart a speed boost sufficient to nestle it back against the block at the end of the line, ready for the next launch.

FIGURE 9.23   A simple minecart station that returns carts to their ideal starting positions.

Halfway Stations

One final note before I leave you to your own track-laying devices. So far, you've seen stations at the end of a track, but what about those along the way? Creating a midpoint station provides a convenient stop 'n' go system. They use the same principle as the end stations, with powered rails in an unpowered state to slow you down. Create them by digging a trench 1 block deep and 2 blocks long, and place the track in it so it forms a V-shape, as shown in Figure 9.24. The minecart will stop on a downward-facing track in the direction of travel, and a quick click of the button on the side will get you moving again. The lever provides an override that permanently powers the tracks in case you decide you don't always need to stop here. If you do have to bail out as you go flying by, you can be thankful that empty minecarts stop after 8 blocks or so, rather than 80! It's easy to collect again and be on your way.

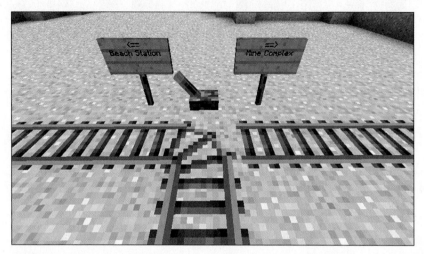

FIGURE 9.24   Switch the lever to turn the halfway station on and off.

CAUTION

Protecting Tracks from Mobs

In Survival mode, you are as vulnerable riding in a minecart as you are at any other time. Carts don't, unfortunately, run over hostile mobs, turning them into mincemeat. They just stop or bounce off them. Either way, it's a problem. If you are serious about using minecarts to get around, consider building them underground in well-lit, protected corridors, or put up fences when your minecarts have to run aboveground.

The Bottom Line

As you've seen, redstone offers many interesting possibilities. Like so much in Minecraft, redstone is limited only by your imagination. Although redstone differs enough from electricity to give an engineer conniptions, it's a lot easier to work with and you're not going to die from an electric shock if you cross wires. You'll just get a nice little wire lattice forming instead.

Redstone also plays nicely with the rail transport system, providing fast transport and an easy way to move items and other resources around. Rails are quite resource intensive, so in most survival worlds you'll probably start with something simple and efficient. In pure Creative mode, however, there really are no limits at all.

Enchanting, Anvils, and Brewing

In This Chapter

- ■ Learn Minecraft's enchanting ways.
- ■ Safely store your hard-earned experience levels.
- ■ Spruce up your weapons, enhance your armor, and improve your tools.
- ■ Hammer something out on the anvil for better repairs.
- ■ Mix up some magic in the brewing stand.

By now you may well have made it all the way to a diamond sword, your base might be nothing short of a warlord's fortress, and you're probably so armored up you can take on a corps of creepers without breaking a sweat on your squared-off brow.

All's good in the Overworld...but it could always be better.

This chapter walks you through a few extra skills involving a special crafting table, obsidian generation, and a few wee drams of potion.

Enchanting Wiles

Experience points (XPs) accrue through the normal course of the game, providing small green nudges to the experience bar shown in your heads-up display (HUD). (Those colored orbs flying toward you after you bravely slay a mob or patiently smelt a batch of iron all devolve into experience points.) When the bar fills, it delivers an XP level, a type of currency, and promptly resets. Spend that XP wisely through enchantments, and you can power up your weapons, armor, and tools.

Enchantments improve an object's core abilities. Among other things, they can help a pickaxe mine with more efficiency, make a sword cause more damage and become unbreakable, make your armor practically (although not completely) impregnable, and build up a lot of other vital improvements that will help you in The Nether and End regions.

Enchantments also add capabilities that are a little more mystical: the respiration enchantment can dramatically increase your underwater survivability, a bow with infinity enchantment will never run out of arrows (at least not until the bow breaks), and your enchanted boots will let you leap off tall cliffs with nary a thought for a distinct lack of feathers. Enchantments also have a practical use: they can help your tools gather more resources from every mined block, or even pull out whole blocks in their original form instead of just digging out dropped components.

So how do you start enchanting? There are several ways to go about it:

- Use an enchantment table to apply a random enchantment to an item, at the cost of XP.

- Combine an enchanted book with an item at an anvil. This will cost some XP but at a discounted rate to creating the original enchanted book. This is a bargain if you've been fortunate to find an enchanted book in some of the chests scattered around the world in villages and dungeons and so on.

- Combine an item with an enchanted item of the same type at an anvil. If you combine two items with different but compatible enchantments, the final item gains both enchantments. You can also use anvils to repair and rename items in a process not dissimilar to using them to enchant items.

Let's start with the enchantment table first, as shown in Figure 10.1. We'll get to the bookshelves surrounding it shortly.

FIGURE 10.1 An enchantment table surrounded by 15 power-boosting bookshelves.

Enchantment tables take up one block, just like a crafting table, but creating them is a little more difficult because they require two diamond gems, a book, and four obsidian blocks.

NOTE

Think This Is Hard?

If making an enchantment table seems challenging, I must forewarn you that it's got nothing on creating the brewing stand later in this chapter! Consider this a warm-up with lava.

Of all the ingredients, you might find obsidian the most difficult to obtain. It lurks in some village chests, but otherwise you need to discover it in a natural setting or create it yourself with a steamy combination of water and lava.

Creating and Mining Obsidian

Obsidian is naturally formed when *flowing* water meets *still* (not flowing) lava or, more specifically, a lava source block. Fortunately, these are used to form still lava lakes and so are quite plentiful. This is a key condition because any other variation of water and lava flowing or not, in either order, just results in cobblestone or stone—and that's not going to put a spell on anything.

Obsidian is practically indestructible, making it a great construction material, but it's a little risky to mine given its close proximity to lava and the latter's proclivity for turning your character into an instant Korean BBQ.

But enchantment tables don't require very much obsidian, and I'll show you a sure-fire technique for getting there. Just follow these steps:

1 Fill some buckets with water. You might need only one, but take some backups just in case.

2 Now find a lava pool. If you're lucky, you've spotted these on the surface, but your surest bet is to head down to the lowest levels of your mine where you've probably already stumbled on several. Lava is most common below layer 11, counting up from the unbroken bedrock that exists at layer 0. If you're still looking, head back down your mine and dig some additional branch lines until you do. It shouldn't take long.

3 If you find a lava pool with water that has already flowed over some part of it (Figure 10.2 shows an example on the surface), you can try to block the water source, fencing it off with cobblestone or any other handy blocks to dry up the flow and then mine the obsidian exposed underneath. Figure 10.3 shows the result. A further border of cobblestone dropped into the lava lake along the obsidian border allows you to mine the obsidian without fear of getting swamped by the molten magma. Don't forget to use sneak mode when near lava so you don't fall in. (If you do fall and catch on fire, jump into the nearest water as quickly as possible. You might just save your skin.)

FIGURE 10.2 A natural lava pool into which water is flowing. Obsidian has already formed where the water meets the lava, as shown by the thin black line under the front edge of the water flow.

FIGURE 10.3 Fencing or blocking off the water flow with a cobblestone barrier exposes the obsidian.

4 If there's no water nearby, stand back a little and pour water from one of your buckets so that it spills down onto a bordering block and then flows over the lava. This won't work if you pour the water directly on the lava. The best way to do it is to stand at least one block up. Place a block and jump on it if a block isn't there already, or there's no nearby ledge. This ensures you don't get washed toward the lava or backward into another danger zone.

TIP

Is the Lava the Only Source of Light?

Place some torches around before you extinguish the lava so you're not left standing in the dark when the lava is converted to obsidian.

5 Let the water flow as far as it can, converting the lava lake to an expanse of obsidian, and then fill your bucket from the water source block to remove the water and expose the obsidian, as shown in Figure 10.4. Repeat until the entire pool is converted. If you can't pick up the water source block, place other blocks around and you'll eventually dry it up.

FIGURE 10.4   Water poured from a bucket has converted the entire lava pool to obsidian.

6 Take your diamond pickaxe in hand and start mining obsidian! Obsidian takes a while to break, so be patient. There's also a good chance you'll expose more lava under the obsidian as you go. Pour some more water on top of that lava to convert any surrounding blocks to obsidian, and then scoop the water back up into your bucket to use again. Mine more obsidian than just the 4 blocks you need for the enchantment table. Try to gather at least 14 blocks in all because you'll use the remaining 10 to create a Nether portal in Chapter 12, "Playing Through: The Nether and The End," and you'll need to visit that before creating a brewing stand later in this chapter.

Crafting Books

Books are used to carry enchantments created at the enchantment table, and also, through bookshelves, for boosting the powers of that table. (They can also help you play Minecraft!)

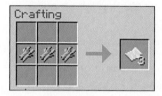

Books are made from three pieces of paper and a piece of leather. Start by crafting the paper from sugarcane, and then convert the paper into a book.

Go ahead and make as many as possible because you'll need up to 45 books to create a full set of bookshelves to surround the enchanting table. (Don't drop everything to do this, though: you can build up to it, starting with just a few.)

Casting Enchantments

Now that you have the raw ingredients, it becomes much easier. Follow these steps:

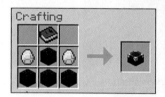

1 Create and place an enchantment table. Leave a perimeter of two clear spaces between the table and any walls for future bookshelves, as shown previously in Figure 10.1. As you approach the table, the book flips through a few pages in a rather nice animation.

2 Press **L2** to view the enchantment interface.

3 Place the item you want to enchant (a weapon, a tool, or armor) in the empty slot beneath the book. A list of three possible enchantments will appear to the right, as shown in Figure 10.5.

4 The actual enchantments listed are unreadable and randomly generated. The only information provided is the bright green numbering that shows the number of enchantment levels that will be expended for each enchantment. The enchantment you get is, essentially, up to a roll of the dice. An enchantment can run up 30 XP in cost, but the higher the level, the better the chance you have for gaining a more powerful enchantment. Any enchantments for which you don't have sufficient XP are grayed out, and an enchant table without nearby bookshelves can offer enchantments up to only level 8.

FIGURE 10.5   Enchanting a diamond sword. If you don't see an enchantment at the desired level, just move the object you are enchanting out and back again to generate a new set of three possibilities.

5 Select an enchantment from the list. Stay at the lower levels for now, saving your experience for additional enchantments.

6 Drag the enchanted item back to your inventory. Move the pointer over the item to see the actual enchantments applied.

TIP

Chancy Enchantment Tables

The formulas used by Minecraft for generating the list of enchantments aren't exactly obvious. Too many random factors are involved to provide a generic table of probabilities. A few sites online use the actual program code to generate a guide. To gain some more insight, visit www.minecraftenchantmentcalculator.com/. When you select the material, tool, and enchantment level, this neat utility will roll the die 10,000 times, collate the results, and give you a list of possible enchantments along with their likelihoods.

Improving Enchantment Chances with Bookshelves

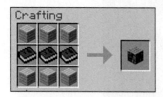

Bookshelves open up higher levels of enchantment, although you still need to have the same or a higher actual experience level. Craft them from three books and six wood plank blocks—any wood will do. You can also find large libraries packed with bookshelves in strongholds, as well as in the home of a village librarian. Break them up with an axe to gather the books, and then recraft them into new bookshelves.

The level up from bookshelves works the following way:

- Each bookshelf unit boosts the level by 1–2 points, with 15 bookshelves delivering the highest enchantment level possible.

- The shelves must be placed two spaces from the table with nothing in the intervening space. Torches, snow cover, and anything else will block the boost from the shelf.

- Even with a full set of bookshelves, you'll continue to see enchantments at the lower power. There's a random distribution of levels from the lowest to the highest possible between the three enchantment slots.

- The bookshelves must be on the same level as the table or 1 block higher. A single layer of 15 shelves looks like Figure 10.1, but you can also stack the shelves 2 blocks high against the walls (see Figure 10.6) to achieve the same power boost and leave the other 2 sides clear.

- Stacking objects such as chests and torches directly on top of the bookshelves won't block their usefulness. You can also place another bookshelf on the two-wall layout to make the shelves symmetrical, even though it won't improve the actual enchanting. Any objects placed between the shelf and the enchantment table will, however, block the shelf's boost to the available enchantments.

TIP

Choosing and Storing Enchantments with Books

Books provide an opportunity to be more selective with the enchantments that are applied to an item. Enchant the book at the table in the usual way. The result is still random until it's complete, but it carries an identifiable enchantment as soon as you drag it back into your inventory. Combine the one you want with an item at the anvil for a small additional cost in XP. Store any others in a chest so they stay safe.

FIGURE 10.6   A slightly different bookshelf layout that still provides the maximum power boost to the table.

Earning and Managing Experience

Experience points are earned through different actions and then "spent" through enchanting. What's the quickest way to gain XPs fast, and how can you maximize your return on XPs? Read on:

■ Killing mobs, mining, smelting, cooking, fishing, and breeding friendly mobs will gain you XPs. And if you cook the food, it becomes more nutritional. A quick way to gain lots of XPs is therefore to breed animals—increasing the population as quickly as possible—and then kill any extras, picking up their dropped meat and cooking that in your furnace. Breeding chickens is easy because the seed is available anywhere there is tall grass. Creating a mob trap as described in Chapter 8, "Creative Construction," and then killing the mobs at the knees is also a good way to quickly gain XPs, but cows may prove more useful as you can also use their leather to create enchantable books. However, you'll gain more XP killing hostile mobs than friendly ones.

■ Try to stay long enough to collect the colored experience orbs that gradually float your way after an XP-earning event.

■ Enchant gold weapons and armor. Gold benefits the most from enchanting and has a better chance of getting a higher-level enchantment than iron or diamonds.

■ Start with low-level enchantments first, in the 1–10 range on the enchantment table. There's little difference in the enchantments that can be had at the cost of 1 XP or 10 XP, so stay low and grow.

- The first 16 XP levels are the easiest. At 17 and above, it becomes gradually more difficult to climb each level, so if you want to enchant a lot of items quickly, keep your XP below 17, spend it, and then build it up again.

- All XP levels disappear on death, and while some experience orbs may drop for collection after your respawn, at best they'll be sufficient to build you back up to only level 5.

Sprucing Up Your Weapons

Show your foes the thin edge of the wedge with a range of powerful weapon enhancements. You'll be amazed at how quickly you can dispatch a zombie with a sharper blade or how far you can fling a creeper with the knockback enchantment. Table 10.1 shows the full list.

TABLE 10.1 Combat Enchantments

Enchantment	Maximum Level Attainable	Table Items	Anvil Items	Description
Sharpness, Smite, and Bane of Arthropods	V	Sword	Axe	Increases inflicted damage. Sharpness works on all mobs; smite on the undead; and bane of arthropods on spiders, cave spiders, and silverfish. An anvil is required to gain Level V on diamond weapons. Note that you can apply only one of these enchantments at a time.
Knockback	II	Sword	None	Knocks back an entity farther than a sprinting attack. Combine with sprinting for even greater efficacy.
Fire Aspect	II	Sword	None	Sets the target of your attack on fire for 3–7 ticks according to the level, but it has no effect on mobs from The Nether.
Looting	III	Sword	None	Improves the number of items killed and the number of mobs dropped and improves the chance of zombies and zombie pigmen dropping additional items such as iron or gold ingots.
Power	V	Bow	None	Increases arrow damage from 50% to 150% according to the level. Level V is available only through using an anvil.
Punch	II	Bow	None	Increases the knockback that a mob experiences from a hit with an arrow.
Flame	I	Bow	None	Sets the arrow on fire, causing fire damage to any mob hit except for those from The Nether.
Infinity	I	Bow	None	Provides an infinite supply of arrows until the bow breaks, but those arrows can't be collected in Survival mode for reuse.

Enhancing Your Armor

Iron Man is a trademark, so I won't run that gauntlet, but armor enchantments do give you the Armor-All of defense, allowing blows to slide off your polished pauldrons like so much Teflon.

All of the "protection" enchantments combine to an upper limit set by the item's material. Table 10.2 shows the full list, keeping in mind that the upper limit for enchantments runs from lowest to highest as follows: iron, diamond, chain, leather, and gold.

TABLE 10.2 Defensive Enchantments

Enchantment	Maximum Level Attainable	Table Items	Anvil Items	Description
Protection, Fire Protection, Blast Protection, and Projectile Protection	IV	Helmet, chest plate, leggings, and boots	None	"Protection" reduces the damage passed on for that piece up to a total for all pieces, varying according to the material. The other enchantments help more specifically against fire, explosions, and ranged weapons. These enchantments are mutually exclusive.
Feather Falling	IV	Boots	None	Reduces damage experienced from falling farther than three blocks.
Respiration	III	Helmet	None	Increases the time you can breathe underwater by 15 seconds per level while also delaying suffocation damage by 1 second per level. Also improves underwater vision by reducing the opaque blue haze.
Aqua Affinity	I	Helmet	None	Removes the speed penalty associated with underwater mining.
Thorns	III	Chest plate	Helmet, legging, and boots	Provides the chance of the armor causing damage to an attacker, at the cost of the armor's durability. The effect is noncumulative, so the highest-scoring armor piece wins.

Improving Your Tools

Of all your activities in Minecraft, resource collection is one of the most important. The enchantments in Table 10.3 imbue your tools with the ability to gather new types of resources, improve their speed and efficiency, and help them last longer.

TABLE 10.3 Tool Enchantments

Enchantment	Maximum Level Attainable	Table Items	Anvil Items	Description
Efficiency	V	Pickaxe, shovel, and axe	Shears	Increases mining speed from 0.3 times faster to almost 4 times according to the level.
Silk Touch	I	Pickaxe, shovel, and axe	Shears	Allows certain blocks to drop as themselves instead of their usual derivatives. Applies to grass blocks, coal ore, diamond ore, cobwebs, ice, and nether quartz ore, among others. Cannot be used at the same time as Fortune.
Fortune	III	Pickaxe, shovel, and axe	None	Provides a better chance that a breakable block will drop more items and increases the rate of flint production from gravel.
Unbreaking	III	Pickaxe, shovel, and axe	All weapons, other tools, fishing rods, flint, and steel	Improves the tool's durability by reducing the chance of wear from normal use.

Enchantments can be amazingly powerful, but they last only for the durability of the enchanted item, so use those items only when you really must.

Hammer It Out with the Anvil

The anvil has many talents. It can repair and rename items, apply enchantments from books, combine two enchanted similar items, and combine the enchantments in two enchanted books, as long as the enchantments are compatible.

Anvils do, however, require a lot of iron: 31 ingots in all.

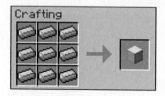 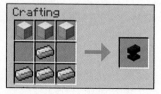

Start by crafting 3 blocks from 27 ingots. Then combine the blocks with another 4 ingots to create the anvil.

Place the anvil somewhere handy (see Figure 10.7), and nowhere it's likely to drop on your head. Falling anvils do cause damage and, for reasons Wile E. Coyote could well attest, prove quite popular in multiplayer traps.

FIGURE 10.7 The anvil is the largest chunk of iron in the game. Fortunately, there's no damage from stubbing one's toe.

The anvil provides a single interface for all its different actions. Press **L2** to open the Repair & Name window shown in Figure 10.8.

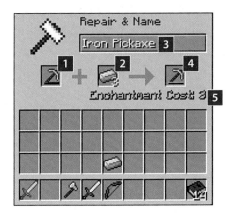

FIGURE 10.8 Repair, combine, or enchant items at the anvil, at a cost.

1. First item slot
2. Second item slot
3. Renaming box
4. Output slot
5. XP level cost to complete

Here's how you use the anvil:

- **Repairing an item**—Place the item to be repaired in the first item slot and the raw material in the second item slot. The item can be any item with a durability value. Figure 10.8 shows an iron pickaxe being repaired courtesy of three iron blocks at a cost of three XP levels. (You may need to place more than one of the raw materials in the slot to bring the item back to full or close to full durability.) In the example, the pick was so worn out it required three iron ingots to bring back to almost full durability.

- **Combining two**—Place the items to be combined in the first and second item slots. The items must be compatible and the total XP cost less than 40 to be successful. This applies to weapons, tools, and armor as well as enchanted books.

- **Enchanting items**—Place the item to be enchanted in the first slot and the enchanted book in the second slot. The enchantment from the book transfers to the item.

- **Combining enchantments**—Place the enchanted weapons, tool, armor, or books in each slot and pick up the item with the combined enchantments from the output slot.

- **Renaming items**—Use the renaming box to name an item while carrying out any of the other anvil operations, or as a singular operation on its own. There are two reasons to rename an item. First, each repair on an item accumulates a 2 XP level penalty, and this eats into the total 40 XP that can be expended during any anvil operation. However, renamed items remain at a maximum 2 level penalty no matter how often they are repaired, so a renamed item gets an XP price-freeze. Second, a renamed sword with particular enchantments is easier to find while rummaging in a chest among a collection of enchanted swords whose icons are otherwise identical.

Brewing Potions

Let's brew up some trouble. Potions give you an offensive and defensive advantage that will keep limb attached to limb in the Overworld, but more importantly help you complete the other regions. They can give you a useful speed boost, rebuild your health, give you the strength of Popeye, and—through splash potions—give you something like a hand grenade you can toss at hostile mobs to cause additional damage. (The following tables list them all.)

Although potions don't require an eye of newt or toe of frog, they do, like a hell-broth, require a trip to The Nether for some core ingredients.

The first essential ingredient is *nether wart*, the starting point for almost all the potions. It grows in pits dug around the bases of staircases in Nether fortresses (see Figure 10.9) and also in random locations outside of fortresses. Those planting grounds and the Nether itself also contain the *soul sand* you'll need to start a Nether wart farm back home. Fortunately, soul sand is quite plentiful, growing in dull gray tracts around many of the lava lakes you'll find.

FIGURE 10.9   Nether wart growing in soul sand at the foot of a staircase in a Nether fortress.

The other elusive component is the blaze rod, required for creating the brewing apparatus. Obtain this by defeating a blaze, one of the hostiles that inhabit Nether fortresses. This, admittedly, is something of a challenge. You won't do it in five minutes. I've written Chapter 12 to help you prepare for that journey, handle the hostiles, and get you home in at least one piece. Treat this first venture into The Nether as a quick snatch-and-grab. You don't want to spend too much time down there until you're truly prepared. You might want to get a range of protection enchantments such as fire protection and feather falling on your boots. It really just depends on how far you appear from a fortress and the terrain you'll therefore need to cross. An unbreaking enchantment on tools can also save you some trips back to the Overworld until you've had time to create a well-stocked Nether-base.

Head over to Chapter 12 now, and come back when you have a blaze rod, Nether wart, and soul sand. You'll also need some glass blocks (smelted from sand) and a supply of water, although even a single block of water will fill an endless number of bottles. Figure 10.10 shows my own brewing chamber.

NOTE

Nether Not Yet?

Try some of the potion recipes that follow in a different world set to Creative to learn how they work and test the results. Sprint around with a 40% speed boost (it's quite an exhilaration after the normal plod/sprint).

FIGURE 10.10 The "Home Brew Club" with brewing stand, crafting table, water supply, Nether wart farm, furnace for creating glass bottles, and a chest for storing the results.

TIP

Plant Those Nether Warts First

Nether wart grows only in soul sand, but it doesn't have irrigation or light requirements. Given the challenge in collecting Nether wart, use any Nether wart and soul sand you collected from your trip to build a Nether wart farm. Do this *before* you start using the Nether wart for brewing. The simplicity of growing it means you can put the farm just about anywhere, including inside a small chamber reserved for your potable magic.

Brewing Up a Storm

Brewing up a batch of potions is actually quite easy and will continuously deliver rewarding results. You've already done the hard part: getting the initial ingredients together. The rest is easy, making the creation of potions a useful, easily replicated exercise.

Follow these steps to get started:

1 Craft a brewing stand from three cobblestone blocks and a blaze rod. Place it somewhere convenient.

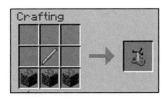

2 Create at least a few glass bottles from three glass blocks. Fill the bottles from your water supply.

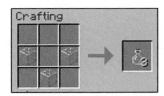

3 Use on the base of the brewing stand to open the brewing window, and then place the glass bottles in the output slots shown in Figure 10.11. (You can place from one to three bottles, depending on how much of any potion you'd like to create. In this first instance, we're creating the base *awkward potion*. Because this potion is required for most others, it's efficient to create three of these at a time.)

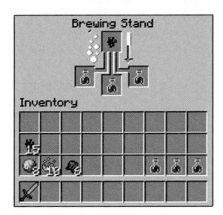

FIGURE 10.11 Drag the brewing ingredient to the top slot and the bottles (water or another potion) to the three output slots.

4 Place one Nether wart in the top of the stand. After a short while and a brief brewing animation, the three water bottles are converted into three bottles of awkward potion. There's no visual change to the bottles, but hovering your cursor over them shows their new name in the tooltip.

NOTE

That Was Awkward...

Awkward potion is inert. It's the wallflower of potions. Turn it into something more out-going by adding one of the secondary ingredients to create the potions in Table 10.4. These potions are usually referred to as *positive potions* because they have a benefi-cial effect on the player's character. There are also negative variants of most of these that you can throw at mobs to cause damaging effects, with some caveats discussed in the Note "When Positive Becomes Negative."

TABLE 10.4 Positive Effect Potions

Potion	Effect	Secondary Ingredient	Obtained from
Swiftness	+20% speed for 3 minutes.	Sugar	Sugar cane
Strength	+130% damage for 3 minutes.	Blaze powder	Blaze rods—each will make two blaze powders
Healing	Instantly restore two hearts.	Glistering melon	Melon + eight gold nuggets (one gold ingot produces nine gold nuggets)
Regeneration	Restores 9 hearts over 45 seconds.	Ghast tear	Ghast drops
Fire Resistance	Complete protection from fire and lava for 3 minutes. You can even swim across a lake of lava as long as you get to the other side in time! Also provides protection from ranged blaze attacks.	Magma cream	Magma cube drops or by combining blaze powder with a slime ball
Night Vision	See perfectly at night and underwater for 3 minutes.	Golden carrot	Carrot and eight gold nuggets
Invisibility	Become invisible to all mobs for 3 minutes.	Potion of Night Vision	

Use the potions the same way you eat food: select the potion and hold down **L2** to drink it. The potion of healing takes immediate effect, while others last for the specified duration. Open your inventory screen to see all the active potions and their remaining durations, as shown in Figure 10.12. You'll also see a bubble effect come up in the view through the main gameplay window while any potions are in effect.

FIGURE 10.12 Active potions show their remaining durations in a box to the left of the inventory window.

Enhancing Potions

Potions provide a particular boost over a specified duration. Add a third brewing cycle to a potion to modify its boost *or* its duration, and convert it into a throwable *splash potion* or a negative potion:

- **Glowstone dust**—Doubles the effectiveness of the potion where possible, typically at the expense of duration. Applies to Swiftness, Healing, Regeneration, and Strength. Replaces the use of redstone dust, as discussed next.

- **Redstone dust**—Doubles the duration of the potion but replaces the use of glowstone dust.

- **Gunpowder**—Converts the potion into a splash potion at the cost of a 25% weaker effect. You'll see the shape of the bottle change, looking a little like it has grown a small hand-grenade pin on the side. Throw splash potions at mobs or down at your feet if you want to get an immediate effect from the potion without taking the time to drink it.

- **Fermented spider eye**—Add this curious crafting to transform the potion into a negative potion. Table 10.5 lists all those available along with other negative-effect potions that can be brewed without using a positive-effect potion as the base. Craft this ingredient from a spider eye (dropped by spiders), a brown mushroom, and sugar.

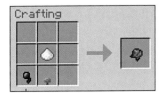

Glowstone and redstone cannot be combined through additional brewing cycles; only the last one used takes effect. However, gunpowder and fermented spider eye are often used together to create a throwable version of a potion that will have negative effects when it hits the enemy. You can add them after glowstone or redstone dust to enhance the effects of any throwable positive or negative potion.

TABLE 10.5 Negative Effect Potions

Potion	Initial Potion	Effect
Slowness	Swiftness	–15% speed for 1.5 minutes
Weakness	Strength (or brew a base potion using a water bottle and add a fermented spider eye)	Reduces melee damage by half a heart for 1.5 minutes
Harming	Healing	Causes 3 hearts immediate damage
Poison	Awkward potion (add a normal spider eye through brewing)	Causes up to 18 points damage over 45 seconds but does not cause death

NOTE

When Positive Becomes Negative

Not all negative potions have deleterious effects on mobs. Throwing a potion of harming at the undead (zombies and skeletons) helps them heal. Whoops! Throw potions of healing instead to cause them harm. This is particularly useful when you're in a tight battle with these particular mobs because you can just toss a potion of healing at your feet and improve your health while causing harm to any of those currently in close combat.

The Bottom Line

Minecraft's magical effects are potent and powerful.

Start with enchantments because their toughest barrier to entry is a natural by-product of cooking, smelting, and taking care of mobs. You'll gain XPs step-by-step.

Use the anvil to manage your enchantment inventory by storing them in books, repair items when needed, and combine enchantments for even more powerful results.

Potions provide your final boost, and they are the most powerful enhancements in Minecraft.

The next chapter is a small step back from combat preparedness but is important nonetheless. Your world contains villages and a host of hidden structures with items and resources that will help you push into the game's other dimensions.

Villages and Other Structures

In This Chapter

- Meet the village people, and trade your way up in the game.
- Discover dungeons, strongholds, temples, and more.
- Craft a map.
- Clock on and off. It's easy!

Minecraft is far more than static terrain and a few hordes of wandering mobs. You'll also find villages teeming with people and, dig deep enough, mysterious underground structures containing hidden treasures and loads of useful resources including chests packed with items that can't be found anywhere else. This chapter takes you on an exploration of the structures above and below the pixelated earth.

Village Life

Villages are a haven for useful resources. Finding a good-sized one early on can provide a useful leg-up with chests containing handy items and rows of harvestable wheat, carrots, and potatoes and the opportunity to trade emeralds for other items courtesy of the proboscisally endowed villagers. (Okay, that's not a real word, but you'll understand when you see the villagers.)

The only problem with villages is that they are not too common. They appear only in the desert and plains biomes—and not too often at that. It is, however, rather neat that the villages in the two biomes use construction materials native to those biomes, so you'll see a lot of wood and cobblestone in a village located in the plains (see Figure 11.1) and a lot more sandstone in one situated in a desert.

FIGURE 11.1 Villages spawn with a varying number of buildings and farms. This one is located in a plains biome near the Elysium spawn point.

Villages add a useful dynamic to the game. They're not essential, and you can get by just fine without them, but knowing how to make use of them will help.

Here are the essentials:

- Villages can appear in almost any form from a single dwelling (or even just a sad lonely well) to a dozen buildings or more. The buildings are any of 10 different designs from small huts to large taverns and churches.

- Your interaction with a village's inhabitants affects your popularity within that village, and attacking a few or—even worse—killing them can result in your being attacked by an iron golem, although golems appear only in larger villages. Villagers won't attack you back, no matter how mean you are to them.

- Villagers increase their population by producing children. As long as two adult villagers are present, you can increase the population and therefore the trading opportunities by adding doors to any structure, where one side of the door is in a clear space able to receive sunlight. The most efficient method is to add numerous doors side-by-side to a simple box structure. (The formula built in to the software results in approximately one villager per 3.5 doors.)

- Villages are a lodestone for zombies, resulting in a possible zombie siege where hordes of zombies swarm the village at night. The zombies spawn anywhere in the village itself, including inside rooms, and attack any villagers present. Dead villagers can then turn into zombie villagers, increasing the havoc (see Figure 11.2). Cure a zombie villager by throwing a weakness potion at him, followed by a golden apple, and try to keep him segregated because the cure takes a few minutes to complete. Fortunately, as night falls you'll see most villagers scurry for cover to their favored village building. They'll also do this if it starts to rain. Iron golems fight the good fight by attacking zombies, and they get rid of them very quickly, but iron golems spawn only in villages with populations of at least 10 villagers and at least 21 houses (although really you just need doors, not complete houses, as described earlier). Creating the conditions to spawn an iron golem is therefore a good reason to increase a village's population, especially if you decide to take up residence!

TIP

Sleep Through the Siege

Beds don't occur naturally in villages, but if you place one in a village and sleep through the night, you'll spare your villagers from a zombie siege because time doesn't tick over when you're sleeping. It's a neat way to keep zombie infections to a minimum.

FIGURE 11.2 Zombies can spawn in and around a village at night in large numbers, resulting in scenes like that shown here—a zombie siege in full swing!

- Villagers trade goods, and this is the real reason for a village's usefulness. Look for a trade where you can obtain emeralds by harvesting wheat or performing some other simple task, and then use the emeralds to pay for other types of items. Talk to as many villagers as you can to find the best trade. Some offer rare Minecraft items, while others might have something more mundane. You can also deconstruct bookshelves in a library to obtain books, and you can happily loot any chests you find without dinging your popularity with the villagers.

Emerald City: Your Ticket to Trade

Villages contain up to five types of villagers (see Figure 11.3). You'll see farmers, librarians, priests, blacksmiths, and butchers. However, this is just visual dressing: the villagers themselves don't offer trades according to their professions.

FIGURE 11.3   The Village People: from left to right: blacksmith, priest, librarian (this one's a little shy), butcher, and farmer.

You also might spot some village children running around, but they don't participate in trading.

Place your crosshairs on a villager and pull **L2** to open the trading window shown in Figure 11.4. Each villager starts with a single trade, either offering to sell you something for emeralds or offering to buy something from you in return for a payment of emeralds. You can't change the trade; villagers stick with their offer until you've performed the trade once and then open additional offers.

Villagers are rock-hard hagglers, so their offers won't budge. However, every unique villager represents another possible trading opportunity, so increasing the overall population can lead to a much more useful set of offers and a better price.

Trades are made by ensuring you have the required items and then pressing ⊗; your inventory updates automatically. If you lack the required items, you'll instead see a red background behind the trade and the relevant items. Upon a successful trade, the villager lights up with an animation similar to that when a potion is taking effect, along with some green sparkly flashes.

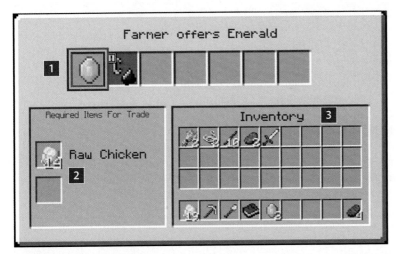

FIGURE 11.4 The goods you'll receive are shown in the top bar, with the goods or payment required on the left.

1. Various trades on offer
2. Items required to make the trade
3. Items in your inventory

TIP

Emerald Farming

You can find emeralds in the ground in the extreme hills biome, but the easiest way to get a decent quantity is through trading. But take care: not all trades are reasonable, and some are downright ridiculous. Look for trades where the required items are readily replicable. For instance, if you've built a chicken farm, it makes sense to look for trades that require raw chicken. The same goes for other types of items. You can also move into a village, but take extra care at night so you don't get caught on the wrong side of the door if a zombie siege begins, and light up any rooms that are dark so zombies don't spawn inside; then build up the village fortifications. The villagers also don't mind if you move into one of their houses to stay safe or build your own nearby, and you could do them a favor by fortifying their village to help alleviate the effects of a zombie siege and keep other mobs away.

CAUTION

Not All's Well with the Well

Village wells are deep, with lips too high for a standard jump. If you plan to spend a lot of time in a village, consider placing some blocks below the first layer of water in the well. Also, knock out one block from the wall so you can climb out if you happen to fall in. Alternatively, leave the block in place and use the well as a zombie trap. Plenty can fall in during a siege, and the shade from the roof prevents them from burning up during the day, so you can then attack them at your leisure. By the way, you also might find a different type of well standing on its own in the desert. It's a useful source of water if you spawn in that biome and plan to call it home.

Other Structures

Villages usually have a chest or two tucked away, but your Minecraft world also contains other structures that provide a more valuable treasure trove.

NOTE

Structures Within

Minecraft has many types of structures that are the result of specific programming code that is separate from the general terrain generation. Some of these (caverns, ravines, and basins, I'm looking at you!) are negative structures, adding space to the terrain in ways that expose various types of ore and often provide a geological gasp of wonder. Others, such as the rivers that flow between biomes, are a clever combination of several techniques that both add and remove particular blocks, blurring what would otherwise look like jarring edges between the biomes. This Note serves no other purpose except to say that this is rather clever coding, particularly the rivers. Cajoling software to create apparently natural geology is tremendously difficult. So, here's to you, Mojang, for your natural beaches, soaring overhangs, and delightful waterways!

Most of these structures contain chests with all sorts of juicy loot, but they also often contain hostile mob spawners of various types. Disable the spawner by placing a few torches nearby to raise the light level above that required for mob spawning. You can also attack the spawner with a pickaxe to break it apart. With the spawner disabled, you're now free to loot in peace!

Before we dive into dungeons, let's take a look at two other types of aboveground structure, as they are also well worth a look.

Desert Temples

Desert temples appear in the desert biome. A temple looks like a stone pyramid with two turrets out front (see Figure 11.5), although it is often partially buried under sand dunes. Although architecturally interesting, it's their four chests hidden beneath the floor of the main chamber that make them useful.

Head toward the central chamber. In the middle, you'll see a block of blue wool. The chamber with the chests sits directly beneath this, but so does this structure's biggest danger: a pressure plate connected to nine TNT blocks. Go back a few blocks and dig out a block to see the chamber. Then dig down one of the walls to get to the base shown in Figure 11.6, break the pressure plate to make the chamber safe, and raid the chests. While you're there, you might also want to dig up the floor and retrieve the TNT blocks.

FIGURE 11.5 A desert temple in its full glory. You're as likely to find them partially or even almost completely buried, so keep an eye out for any orange-colored blocks while traipsing through the deserts.

TIP

Can't Find a Temple? Try a New Seed

Not every type of structure appears in every world. For example, desert and jungle temples don't appear in Elysium, the seed we created in Chapter 1, "Getting Started." Search online for "Minecraft PlayStation Seed", and you'll find many suggested seeds you can use to view and explore these structures. The various videos, blog posts, and so on that turn up with this search also typically include the coordinates of all the main structures.

FIGURE 11.6   The treasure room of a desert temple. Be careful of that pressure plate! You might find some such rooms already blown up, typically caused by a mob spawning inside and trampling on the plate.

Jungle Temples

Indiana Jones faced a trap-laden jungle temple in *Raiders of the Lost Ark*, and you can, too! The jungle temple is a mossy, vine-laden structure that, for obvious reasons, occurs in jungle biomes (see Figure 11.7). Each temple contains two chests—one hidden behind a set of levers and, on the lower level, another protected by two sets of tripwire connected to a couple of arrow-shooting, face-piercing dispensers. Use shears to cut the tripwire and access the first chest. Then head back to the levers. These form part of a puzzle that opens a sliding block beside the stairs in the entry level. Jump down to get to the next chest. Alternatively, just smash through the wall behind the levers to get to the chest.

Even if the chests don't contain anything particularly valuable, the jungle temple's construction provides many useful blocks and items, including three sticky pistons, two dispensers, arrows, tripwire hooks, redstone, string, and more. Unlike Indy, you won't need to deal with any giant rolling boulders as you plunder the temple. Bring in the wrecking crew and have a ball!

FIGURE 11.7   Jungle temples can take some spotting, hidden as they are by the tall trees and foliage, but they're well worth finding. Just be careful of the traps.

Dungeons

Dungeons are smaller rooms buried underground that house a mob spawner and usually one or two chests. Although they can appear anywhere, a dungeon is most easily spotted when its wall intersects with the side of a large cavern or abandoned mineshaft. Look out for the greenish moss stone shown in Figure 11.8.

The chests can hold a lot of useful loot, so disable the spawner and enjoy.

FIGURE 11.8   A dungeon connected to a cave system. Some are more useful than others. This one's chests contained enchanted books, a saddle, lots of gunpowder, and more.

Abandoned Mineshafts

I first mentioned abandoned mineshafts (see Figure 11.9) in Chapter 5, "Combat School" (see "Cave Spiders" on page 86). They are quite liberally scattered underground and often intersect caves, making them easy to find. Each is different, often sprawling across huge multilayered levels. Explore them for their chests, rails, and timber, but look out for cave spiders while you do so. One small bonus: you'll find lots of cobwebs near cave spider spawners. Try to disable the spawner as soon as possible.

Harvest the webs with a sword or shears to obtain string, or use shears enchanted with silk touch to pull in the actual cobweb. Cobwebs slow down all mobs except cave spiders, so they are useful in traps. However, they won't slow you down if you're riding a minecart, so you can use them to defend tunnels by slowing down mobs while you speed ahead.

FIGURE 11.9 Abandoned mineshafts are renowned for their cave spiders but can contain all the other Overworld's hostile mobs, along with water and lava hazards. They're a great source of rails and wood, as well as other finds from chests.

Strongholds

Strongholds are large underground structures. They come in a variety of sizes, often with numerous rooms and chests. More importantly, they also contain the End portal needed to reach The End region. The portal is protected by a silverfish spawner. Disable that, activate the portal, and you'll be on your way to a fight with a very large dragon.

Finding strongholds takes a specific technique. I cover this and the portal in Chapter 12, "Playing Through: The Nether and The End."

Nether Fortresses

These huge constructions feature exclusively in The Nether region and contain unique ingredients for brewing potions and finding strongholds. Getting to The Nether and surviving long enough to find a fortress is a journey in itself. As with strongholds, I show you how to conquer Nether fortresses in Chapter 12.

Mapping, or There and Back Again

You'll likely make some significant tracks as you journey across the Overworld. One handy tool can help you. Maps, in a word. You'll have a map in your inventory when you start a new world, and that one map can display the entire extent of the world in the PS3 edition, although more are required on the PS4. But if you lose it, you'll need another. Plus, maps placed in an item frame also provide a piece of handy wall art, so it's good to have more than one. Follow these steps to start making more maps:

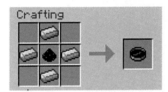

1 Create a compass. The compass on its own isn't too useful—it *always* points to your world's original spawn point. This never changes, even after you change your own spawn point by sleeping in a bed, but if you've built your base quite close to that original spawn, it could be useful. Just keep it in a quick access slot and follow the red needle. But let's continue on our current path and use the compass instead to make a map.

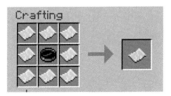

2 Combine the compass with eight pieces of paper at a crafting table to make a new map. (Remember: Paper is obtained from sugar cane, so it's easy to make.) Move the map to a quick access slot.

3 After you create a map, it will sync with any others and gradually fill in to show the landscape around you as well as structures such as villages (see Figure 11.10). However, you will need to wander around to complete the cartography because maps show only the territory you've explored. Move 🅰 to bring the map to eye level and back down again.

4 The map provides a key reference that you might find invaluable: the coordinates at the top. X refers to your east-west location, Y to your vertical level, and Z to your north-south position. If you're heading off on an explorative trek, take the time first to jot down the X and Z numbers before you begin, and as night begins to fall and you feel that tightening in the belly because navigation is about to become a shot in the dark, you now have the option to either dig a hole to wait it out or make a run for it back to base. It's a pleasant feeling to be able to find your way back home.

FIGURE 11.10 A map in the hand shows your position as a white arrow and the coordinates at the top. You can see a map placed in an item frame to the right, showing the current position as a green pin.

5 The arrow shows your current location. When you're in multiplayer mode, you'll also see all your buddies as different-colored arrows, making it easy to join up again after heading off in different directions. (Who doesn't want to explore?).

Crafting a Clock

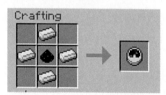

Clocks can help you keep track of time, so you know if it's safe to surface while exploring structures underground or working in your mine. Craft a clock with four gold ingots and one piece of redstone.

A clock works anywhere—in your inventory, in the Hotbar, or placed in an item frame. It even tells the time before you pick it up from the crafting table.

A clock works in a simple manner rotating clockwise (appropriately enough) between night and day phases represented by black and blue hemispheres. At midnight you see the moon located at the 12 o'clock position. The sun rotates to the same location by noon. Figure 11.11 shows a clock mounted in an item frame with sunrise on the approach, indicated by the border between the blue hemisphere starting to push the night disk aside.

FIGURE 11.11   Time to put down your tools and get back to the surface; morning has broken.

The Bottom Line

Minecraft's worlds are riddled with dungeons, abandoned mineshafts, and strongholds, as well as intricate, lengthy natural cave systems. You've probably seen some of this if you've done any flying around in Creative mode, where the landscape generates in real time starting from the bottom up, giving you the equivalent of x-ray goggles. Structures are much thinner, literally, on the ground, but villages do have their uses. One gameplay target you can set for yourself is to build the defensive systems that will protect the villages from zombie spawning and subsequent sieges. (A hint: Think of lots of walls and a lot of light!) Ready for more? Read on to learn about The Nether and The End.

Playing Through: The Nether and The End

In This Chapter

- Get kitted up and head to The Nether.
- Find your way through a region of plummeting lava falls, endless fiery lakes, and precipitous cliffs.
- Locate the Nether fortress, defeat its mobs, and take home its horde.
- Set course for a stronghold, and activate its portal.
- Travel to The End and defeat the dragon.

Pack your bags—we're off on another field trip: to Hell and back. In this chapter you explore Minecraft's other worlds: The Nether and The End. They're a little like Dante's vision of the seventh and ninth circles of Hell: flaming rivers in one, an icy core in the other. Defeating the Ender Dragon also completes your journey through the official game structure, earning your passage back to The Overworld. You'll bring home countless treasures, valuable experience, and the priceless achievement of having won the toughest battle in Minecraft. Think of it as going from Hell 9 to Cloud 9.

Alternate Dimensions

The Nether and End regions are not fun places to hang out (see Figures 12.1 and 12.2). You need to go in with specific goals and not dawdle too long. Both places are hazardous to your health, and any time you die, you respawn in The Overworld and lose anything you haven't been able to put away in a chest for safekeeping.

TIP

Nether Here and There

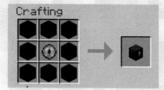

Ender chests transport the same items between all dimensions, so they are incredibly useful for stashing valuable finds when traveling in the more dangerous regions. Die in The Nether, and you can pick up anything you've already stored back in The Overworld when you respawn. Create an Ender chest with one Eye of Ender and eight obsidian blocks. (Of course, you need at least two—one at each end—to make this useful.) See "The End Game," later in the chapter, for more on creating those elusive eyes.

FIGURE 12.1   Seeing red? It's just The Nether: a cavernous, unforgiving place filled with more lava pools than a Krakatoan conference.

FIGURE 12.2 The End region is a dark dimension inhabited by a large dragon. He fires acid balls and continuously draws power from the end crystals that are perched atop high obsidian towers.

Getting through both dimensions and playing through to the end of the game takes a bit of work, but you can definitely get lucky. Although your experience will vary as much as it does in any unique Minecraft world, it will run something like this:

1 Take your time to build up your resources in The Overworld and become combat ready—you're heading into one heck of a fight, and it's going to take a lot more than just a couple of swords and some light armor to get through.

2 Build an obsidian portal to travel to The Nether.

3 Find a Nether fortress and defeat a dozen or so blaze mobs, collecting their dropped blaze rods.

4 Return to The Overworld and craft Eyes of Ender. Sound's easy, right? Well, first you'll need to defeat about 15 Endermen in The Overworld to gain the Ender pearls required for the recipe.

5 Use the eyes to find a stronghold and activate its end portal.

6 Defeat the Ender Dragon and travel through the exit portal back to The Overworld. In Minecraft's rather spare tradition, you won't see a fancy end game sequence, but you'll get to read the existential "End Poem" and see the credits roll, followed by a final score that is equal to your current experience points.

Try to be patient as you complete these six steps. This is not a first-person shooter that takes a day, some pizza, and a rack of energy drinks to finish off, although you certainly could finish it in one or two days. It also isn't an impossible challenge, and you'll see some great sights along the way.

Getting to The Nether

Most of a successful trip to The Nether is really about being prepared. Start by gathering the items on this survival checklist:

- **A full set of iron armor**—When it comes to armor, diamond is best, but given the scarcity of diamond blocks and accepting the fact that you'll almost certainly die and respawn without it, just stick with iron. If you can, apply an enchantment of feather falling to your boots so you can jump down cliffs, and any other protection enchantments you can summon up. Remember, though, that when you die your armor doesn't come back with you, so don't go overboard. Be utilitarian rather than trying to become invincible.

- **A couple of iron pickaxes and a few swords**—Make one of the swords diamond—it will help in a difficult fight.

- **Two iron shovels and a couple of stacks of dirt or gravel (64 blocks per stack)**—You'll need this stuff for pillar-jumping, getting across lava lakes, and the like. The Nether has a lot of crazy-tall cliffs you'll need to clamber up and down. Gravel is useful to get down cliffs as it drops to the floor and can quickly be built up into a column. You can also use sand for this if that's easier to find. In other cases, it's more useful to use a block such as dirt that sticks to wherever it's placed so you can create the equivalent of a set of steps down the side of a cliff. Digging steps directly out of the netherrack in a protected tunnel so you don't get hit by a ghast fireball blast is also a good option.

- **Two full stacks of cobblestone**—You'll need this to create temporary shelters, bridges, and barricades.

NOTE

Forget the Water

Don't worry about bringing water with you. There's no way to place it, so you can't convert any of the numerous, enormous lava lakes to cobblestone or obsidian for easier passage.

- **A bow and at least two dozen arrows**—Use these to shoot down ghasts, or use a bow with the infinity enchantment to save on arrows. Also consider bringing a fishing rod so you can pull them in, attack them with a sword, and collect their ghast tear drops for brewing potions.

- **Snow blocks**—Turn these into snowballs by placing them down and breaking them up with a shovel. Then toss them at blaze mobs to slow them down.

- **Ten obsidian blocks and a flint and steel**—Gather these in case you need to build another portal to return to The Overworld. See "Creating and Mining Obsidian" on page 189 if you need help finding obsidian.

- **Lots of torches!**—Bring as many as a full stack if you can. The torches are mostly useful for creating a trail of breadcrumbs so you can find your way back to your portal. (It's ridiculously easy to become lost down there.) Also consider bringing some jack-o'-lanterns because these are easily spotted across a longer distance.

- **A stack of wood blocks of any kind and 12 iron ingots**—You can use these to create a crafting table and additional weapons, tools, and ladders as needed.

- **An iron door and about six sets of iron bars**—Use these to create a temporary shelter for crafting, healing, taking a breather, and so on. Wooden doors can burn when hit by fireballs in The Nether, even though they are immune to fire in The Overworld. Don't forget to bring some stone or wooden buttons so you can open the doors. Use the bars to create windows in your shelter: they're impervious to ghast fireballs.

- **Food**—Bring bread and cooked meats, at least a dozen of each. You need to keep your hunger bar full so that your health continually regenerates.

- **A chest or two**—An Ender chest is fantastic, but you might not have been able to make one yet. Any other chest will do. It's far too easy to lose all your hard-won resources in The Nether. A chest provides safe storage while you tackle blaze mobs and the like, just in case you respawn. Plus, you can place most of your things in the chest when you first reach The Nether and go on short forays with fewer items while exploring.

- **A map**—The Nether is a confusing place, and bringing a map with you will let you use the displayed coordinate system to find your way around, even though the map itself won't update while in The Nether.

Arrange one of each weapon in the quick access slots, along with the torches, the shovel, the gravel, the cobblestone, and a couple of food stacks. You can leave the rest in the upper section of the inventory.

Ready? Let's go. The first order of business is to put up a portal.

Portal Magic

The Nether Portal acts as an interdimensional transport between The Overworld and The Nether. Follow these steps to create it:

1 Build an obsidian frame with an inner dimension that is three blocks high by two blocks wide (see Figure 12.3). The corner blocks can be made from any material. The frame must be vertical, either free-standing or built directly against any type of wall, including a natural cliff face.

FIGURE 12.3 Build your gateway to the underworld (I mean The Nether) with an obsidian frame.

CAUTION

Portals Are a Double-Edged Sword

After you've built a portal, a second appears in The Nether. Neither belongs to you exclusively, and they allow other mobs to travel back and forth, so expect to see a few more zombie pigmen in The Overworld in the near future. (They can even spawn near them in The Overworld without coming from The Nether.)

2 Use a flint and steel to light the top of either of the two bottom blocks. You see the interior spring to life with a shimmering blue and purple transparent texture, as shown in Figure 12.4.

3 Okay, take a last long look at The Overworld and hope that you won't see it for a while because that probably means you just respawned. Now, jump into that frame!

4 Wait until you see a wavy animation that covers the whole screen; then step through the portal to enter The Nether.

FIGURE 12.4   Once lit, the frame stays that way unless hit by a ghast's fireball, but you only need to worry about that with the companion frame in The Nether.

Now that you're here, you've got some work to do. Build a shelter first around the portal using cobblestone, the iron door, and the iron bars to create a window. You might need to do this while dodging ghast fireballs and burning netherrack. (Quick tip: Put out fires such as burning netherrack and nether brick with a pull of R2, as if you plan to mine it, so it doesn't keep setting you alight.) Remember, your main goal is to find a Nether fortress, but protect your portal and create a small safe-haven where you can set up a chest to store all your extraneous items and set up a crafting table and furnace. You also might want to take a look at your map and note down the current coordinates.

After you've done that, you're ready to set out.

TIP

Scared of the Dark?

It can be tricky seeing things in The Nether, and even more difficult in The End. Dial up the brightness by pressing ▶ and selecting **Help & Options**. Then go into **Settings** and then **Graphics**, and slide up the **Gamma**. You'll find a huge improvement in visibility as you push that slider toward the right.

The Nether has some very extreme terrain, so you might need to make use of any of the following techniques:

- Dig tunnels and stairs by mining the netherrack with your pickaxe to move up and down cliffs. Fortunately, netherrack breaks extremely quickly, so it's easy to get around.

■ Remember to place torches or jack-o'-lanterns as you go, always ensuring you can see the last one placed from the next position. If you do become hopelessly lost, consider building another portal to take you back to The Overworld. You might pop up a long distance away because every block traveled in The Nether is the equivalent of three blocks traveled in The Overworld.

■ Deal with mobs carefully, and don't attack zombie pigmen because this will bring an entire horde of them down on you. Your biggest risk as you explore comes from ghasts and their fireballs, but the fireballs are slow and you can knock them straight back at the ghast with a well-timed sword-swing or arrow. Zig-zag if you decide to retreat so they can't keep a bearing on you with the next volley. See "Nether Mobs," later in this chapter, for specific strategies.

■ Use Sneak mode when close to any cliffs and lava lakes to avoid taking a tumble.

■ Stop to pick up a few things as you go. The bright glowstone, red and brown mushrooms, soul sand, and nether quartz all exist in abundance and are all useful as crafting and brewing ingredients. You also might stumble across the red nether wart—a vital ingredient for brewing potions.

■ Pause every so often to take a good look for a Nether fortress. They're recognizable at a distance by their wide expanses of netherbrick, long exposed walkways and bridges, rows of windows, and (often) tall walls. You should look for any straight-geometric structure within the geological randomness of the cave system. Figure 12.5 shows the ramparts of a netherbrick wall signifying a fortress. How quickly you find one is where the luck comes in. It might take just a few minutes, in which case you can rush in, get things done, head back, and have almost all your possessions intact. Or it could take hours of hard slog. Nether fortresses generate along the north/south axis in long lines, so the easiest way to find one is to try to head east or west. A compass won't help because they spin randomly in The Nether, but you can use the coordinate system in a pinch. You'll find an exposed fortress in this book's world (created in Chapter 1, "Getting Started") at X: -33, Y: 63, Z: 112. Remember, Y is the actual level above the bottom of the world. You'll need to line up all three. The X-axis is aligned east/west, and the Z-axis north/south.

■ If you enter a fortress from below, use your pickaxe to dig out the netherbrick and ascend until you reach a corridor. If coming from above, just work your way down to a walkway and enter the fortress, or come in through a sidewall. You might need to navigate around broken walkways or cave-ins. However, fortresses are massive so if a viable entry isn't obvious at first, just look around until you can find a way in.

Now you're almost done. There is a bit of combat ahead, and then you can head back to The Overworld.

FIGURE 12.5   You can spot fortresses from below by the walls that extend down to the lowest levels of a cave. When looking down from above, you'll see long, straight walkways and rows of window spaces.

Surviving the Nether Fortress

Every fortress presents a similar experience: traipsing down long mazes of corridors before stumbling into a moment of extreme terror! Actually, it's not that bad. You will find long corridors and walkways. You also might find chests filled with some of the most valuable and rare items in the game. Then, once in a while, you'll probably find a small balcony containing a spawner churning out blaze mobs (see Figure 12.6). You'll also find magma cubes that behave similarly to slime in The Overworld and drop magma cream, a useful ingredient for crafting fireballs and potions.

Follow these tips to survive:

- Place torches on the ground as you pass intersections so you can find your way back to your original entry point and then back to the portal.

- Use blocks to create temporary barricades when attacking or being pursued by mobs. This is particularly useful in long corridors where it's impossible to dodge away from an arrow-wielding wither skeleton or when ducking out to attack the blazes springing from a spawner.

- Loot every chest you find. It's always worthwhile!

- Avoid spending too long on open walkways as you'll be vulnerable to ghast attacks.

- Look for the bright red nether wart growing around the base of wide stairways. It's the base of all potions, and a few potions will help you complete the final part of the game.

- When you find a blaze spawner, put up a two-block-high barricade nearby; then wait just behind the nearest corner to attack blazes as they approach from the other side. You can duck in and out, timing your attacks for when they've finished throwing their fireballs. If all goes south, retreat to the barricade and rebuild your health.

FIGURE 12.6 Create temporary barricades like the one shown on the left to provide protection from blaze fireballs. Wait until they get close; then duck out and smite!

- Remember, you're here mainly for the blaze rods. Collect them from each killed blaze until you have 10 or so, and grab any netherwart you see. Then head back to the portal and the bright, sunny, verdant Overworld.

- Place your spoils of victory in a chest near the fortress entry point now and then—or at least nearby—just in case you die. You can come back and pick up your loot later, or grab it on the way out after you've hit your quota.

That's all there is to it, really. It's not so difficult, and it becomes pretty easy after you've done it a few times.

Nether Mobs

You'll meet an interesting mix of mobs while exploring The Nether. If you're properly equipped, they won't present too much of a problem:

- **Zombie pigmen**—I first introduced these on page 90 ("Zombie Pigmen" in Chapter 5). Avoid fighting them because, as with zombies, you'll get rushed by a mob. Their drops aren't really worth the risk, and you'll find a lot more swag in a fortress.

- **Ghasts**—With a fittingly ghastly moan, these huge floating mobs attack you from a long distance (see Figure 12.7). They're slow moving but spit out dangerous fireballs that can cause as much damage with an indirect hit by setting the netherrack around you on fire as they do with a direct hit. Take care of them with two to three fully charged arrows, and dodge the fireballs by moving just a few blocks out of the line of fire. If you're brave enough, you can also haul in ghasts with a fishing rod and hack at them with a sword. Ghasts drop ghast tears which, like magma cream, are useful for brewing, but you'll need to find a ghast over land or pull it in with a fishing rod before it expires so the drops don't burn up in lava.

FIGURE 12.7   Ghasts typically float through The Nether's sulphurous air, but they can also sink into a lava lake and take pot-shots at you sniper-style.

- **Blazes**—You might find blazes floating down the corridors of a fortress, but they're usually near a spawner. They have a distinctive attack pattern, spinning up for a few seconds while emitting a fire effect and then shooting off three quick fireballs at you. They then go through a cool-down period, making them, albeit briefly, more vulnerable. Attack them while they're chilling down, or early on when they're spinning up. Swords work well if one of them separates from the pack; otherwise, use arrows and then make a dash to pick up the dropped blaze rods and glowstone dust.

- **Magma cubes**—These burning cubes split like slime mobs in The Overworld. They're slower but far more dangerous and harder to kill. Attack the large cubes and medium-sized cubes from a distance with arrows, and then finish off the small ones with your sword. You pick up a lot of experience points and the handy magma cream.

NOTE

Dante's Dimensions

It's probably all just coincidence, but there are some interesting parallels between Minecraft's other dimensions and Dante's own. Dante treated the levels of Hell as concentric spheres, each becoming smaller like the layers of an onion (with plenty of associated weeping and a lot of gnashing). The seventh level, the closest corresponding with the nature of The Nether, falls eight layers beneath the earth. In Minecraft on the PC, The Nether has a scale 1/8 that of The Overworld, so traveling 100 blocks in The Nether and then taking a portal back to the surface will have taken you 800 blocks in The Overworld. This is exactly how it would work if The Nether was a smaller sphere beneath The Overworld, and, of course, "nether" does mean *lower* or *under*. (Of course, on the PS3 it's actually just 1/3 that of the Overworld, but let's not let that get in the way of a good story.)

Dante's ninth and final circle is a small, frozen region protected by a winged Satan. Minecraft's End region is a similarly barren, tiny region protected by a winged dragon. While Dante's Satan was trapped in the ice and Dante and Virgil didn't have to defeat him, they nevertheless found their way back to the surface of the earth by climbing down through a hole in the center. In Minecraft you'll jump through a portal in the middle of The End to find your way back to the sunny side.

CAUTION

Chores Are Over: Don't Make Your Bed

Sleeping in a bed in either The Nether or The End regions is definitely not a good idea. Settle in for a quick nap, and the bed explodes faster than a creeper on final fuse.

With some blaze rods in hand, you have what you need for the final journey. The End, as they say, is nigh.

The End Game

Are you ready to start the final phase? Just as you prepared for The Nether, you'll need to gather a few items for The End. There are two parts to the conclusion. The first is finding a stronghold and finding The End portal; the second is defeating the Ender Dragon. You don't need to get everything on this list, but it will give you an idea of the level of preparation necessary:

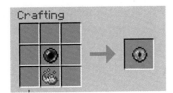

- **Eyes of Ender**—You'll need about 15. You might need up to 12 to activate the End portal (although this is unlikely) and the rest to find the stronghold. The only way to do that is to spend some time defeating 15 Endermen to collect 15 Ender pearls. Endermen are easiest to find at night. Place the blaze rods you collected from The Nether on the crafting grid (saving at least 1 for a brewing stand if you plan to concoct some potions), and collect the blaze powder. Combine that with the Ender pearls to create the Eyes of Ender.

- **Weapons**—Bring a diamond sword if you can, a couple of bows with infinity enchantments, or at least two stacks of arrows because it takes a lot of shooting to take down the dragon. Also bring some string in case you need to build additional bows.

- **Armor**—Diamond armor is ideal, including boots with a feather fall enchantment because you'll probably suffer a couple of long drops while fighting the dragon. However, given the scarcity of diamonds, at least ensure your iron armor is in good shape. Bring a helmet and a pumpkin, and consider using the latter at the expense of some visibility. It's best to not antagonize the numerous Endermen into a fight, and the pumpkin will be your saving grace. Bring iron ingots or diamonds to craft replacement armor and weapons.

- **Potions**—Brew up potions of regeneration and healing. Strength potions can help, but only when you can attack the dragon with a sword. You'll mostly use a bow and arrows for that. Refer to Chapter 10, "Enchanting, Anvils, and Brewing," if you aren't familiar with the brewing process.

- **Food**—Pack about half that recommended for The Nether expedition.

- **Tools**—Bring a couple of stacks of dirt, gravel, or sand and of course an iron shovel because there will be some pillar-jumping involved. Also bring two iron pickaxes because you'll need to dig down to the stronghold, and they'll help you in The End region.

- **Obsidian**—Twelve or so blocks should do, just in case you need to build a bridge that the Ender Dragon can't destroy.

- **Bed**—You can't use it in The End region, but you might need it while finding the stronghold. When you have a bed, you can set it up in the portal room of the stronghold to create a new spawn point.

- **The kitchen sink**—Bring anything else you can think of to set up a small shelter in the stronghold to act as your base, such as wood blocks and iron ingots for tools, additional diamonds, a crafting table, a furnace, a brewing stand, and so on. At least be prepared to make a small shelter in case you need to spend a night on your way to the stronghold.

Finding a Stronghold

Each Overworld generates with one stronghold located within a radius of 500 blocks of the world's original spawn point. You might be lucky enough to find a stronghold in just a few minutes, and in any case it shouldn't take any longer than 20. Strongholds can, on rare occasion, be exposed by natural terrain features such as ravines and valleys, but they are most often found deep underground.

Follow these steps to find your first stronghold:

1 Climb to a high spot, hopefully with some clear space around, look up, and throw an Eye of Ender. It will float into the air and zoom off in the direction of the nearest stronghold.

2 In four out of five cases the eye floats to the ground a short distance away. Pick it up to use again, and you're already on your way to the stronghold. In some cases the eye just explodes instead. Don't worry; just head in the same direction. (You'll find one in Elysium a short trek north of the village. The coordinates X:72, Y: 34, Z:-61 will place you right outside the end portal room. Dig down carefully because there are many caves down there and you'll also be landing in the midst of two spawners and, no doubt, some hostile mobs who are none too happy about your sudden invasion.)

3 Keep travelling for quite some way so you don't use too many eyes; then throw another. The eyes float high when the stronghold is distant and float quickly to the ground when you're close or over the top of the stronghold. The eyes will lead you to the center of the stronghold, and from there you'll need to find the portal room.

4 When you think you have its location zeroed in, start digging. Use normal mining techniques to create a staircase, turning every couple of steps so that you stay in the same general area. You'll know you're there when you start to dig up stone or mossy bricks. Keep going until you break through into a room or corridor, but don't dig straight down because you could fall into a lava pool (see Figure 12.8).

5 Build a safe room a little distance back up the tunnel between The Overworld and the stronghold, ensuring you've made it safe with temporary blocks or doors so no mobs can wander through. Set it up as a forward exploration base, placing anything you don't need for immediate short-term combat in a chest. Also place a bed and sleep in it at night to reset your spawn point to that room. This will become your home away from home while you explore the stronghold—a dangerous enough task in itself, so it's best to be prepared that you'll have to respawn at least once.

FIGURE 12.8 Eureka! Reaching the End portal room. Never dig straight down into a dungeon as, amongst the many dangers, there's also a lava pool directly under the portal.

Your task now is to locate the portal room shown in Figure 12.8. Each of these rooms contains a silverfish spawner. These mobs are best defeated in one blow (requires a diamond sword with at least a sharpness level 1 enchantment). Taking more than one blow alerts others, and you could end up with a swarm, but you can handle them even without an enchanted sword; if you're quick on your feet you can do so with an iron sword. Just try to dispatch them as quickly as possible, leading them back away from the spawner. Destroy the spawner as quickly as you can with a pickaxe.

After you've cleared the room, there are just a few more preparatory steps:

1 Move everything from your previous forward base into the portal room and secure it from mobs by blocking off any entrances.

2 Place a bed and sleep in it to reset your spawn. If you die in The End (which is very likely), you'll come straight back here.

3 Place torches around to prevent other mobs from spawning.

4 Place a chest and dump into it almost everything else you're carrying. You should take with you only the armor you're wearing (including the pumpkin, which you should place on your head), one of each weapon, about a dozen of the better food items such as cooked meat, a pickaxe, some potions, and a shovel—along with a couple of full stacks of sand, dirt, or gravel. You can also bring snowballs if you have them because these make an alternative to using arrows to knock out the ender crystals.

5 Check your tools and armor. I find that just exploring the stronghold and surviving a few close calls with creepers is usually enough to seriously degrade the armor, requiring replacement of at least some of the parts.

6 If you want to just take a look at The End region first, store everything you have in the chest except for a dozen or so dirt blocks and a pickaxe. This approach can help if you spawn in an awkward position and need to first build a bridge to the main island. If you get swept into the void by the Ender Dragon, you'll be able to come back and complete the job by bringing a complete set of tools and obsidian for the bridge to ensure a faster passage across next time. Any dropped items are not recoverable after respawning, although items placed in a chest in The End will survive. When you're ready to return, just die in some convenient way, pick up the main set of supplies stashed in the stronghold, and head back through the portal ready for battle.

CAUTION

Don't Destroy the Portal!

Be extra careful not to destroy any of The End portal blocks. There's no way to repair them, and this can spell the end of your journey.

Now, the final magic moment: activating the portal. (You might want to force a save of the game at this point and create a copy under Save Options in the launch screen, so that you can get back to where you were if all goes horribly awry before the Autosave kicks in.) Climb the steps and place Eyes of Ender into any of the empty slots on top of the stones surrounding the portal. You'll see it spring into deep black life, as shown in Figure 12.9.

FIGURE 12.9 The End portal, ready for action.

Ready for action? That dragon has no idea what's coming. Go ahead and jump in! Then feel free to press ▶ to pause the game, and read on.

> **TIP**
>
> **Pausing for Thought Not Working?**
>
> If you find time still passing even while the in-game menu is open, it could be because your world is running as an online game. Save and exit your current game, select it to reopen it, and choose **More Options**. Deselect **Online Game** and it should all go back to working as expected.

Defeating the Ender Dragon

The End region generates as a fairly small island floating in an endless void, dotted with obsidian towers and numerous Endermen. Your actual spawn point is probably located on this island, but it can also be underground (in which case you can use your pickaxe to dig out a staircase to the surface) or on an even smaller platform floating a small distance away from the mainland. If that's the case, you'll need to build a platform across using your dirt blocks or obsidian. Be sure you keep your bow handy so you can shoot the Ender Dragon if it attacks and tries to push you into the void. (This, fortunately, is quite unlikely as the Ender Dragon tends to flap around in circles near the center of the main island.)

The Ender Dragon is no quick kill. With 200 hit points and the ability to knock out up to half your health in a single blow, its wings are not easily clipped, and while it will spew acid at you if you spend too long standing still, it's also no Smaug. There's also nowhere to hide. When you get near the towers, even burrowing into the ground won't save you because the dragon can fly through the ground and any structures to reach you.

Defeat the dragon by following these steps. It's not impossibly difficult, but it can take a few attempts. Always keep your hunger bar topped up so your health can continually regenerate, and run to the edge of the main island if you need a breather to recuperate:

1 The dragon draws healing power from the Ender crystals located atop eight obsidian towers of varying height, arranged in a broad circle around the portal back to The Overworld (see Figure 12.10). You won't defeat the dragon without knocking out every one of those crystals, and the portal won't activate until you've knocked him out.

2 Put the pumpkin on your head so you don't annoy any Endermen. They'll needlessly sap your health if you glance their way, so it's worth having a reduced field of view for the time being (see Figure 12.11). Crank up the gamma as described earlier if you're having trouble seeing any detail. This can make a huge difference in the battle to come.

FIGURE 12.10 You'll probably first spot the Ender Dragon in the distance. Look for the line of shimmering power as it passes by an Ender crystal.

FIGURE 12.11 Wearing the pumpkin requires a bit more scanning to get the full picture, but it doesn't take too long to get used to it.

3 Head toward the nearest pillar. You'll be able to shoot out the Ender crystal on top with a single arrow shot or snowball toss if the pillar is low enough and not protected by an iron cage; otherwise, you need to pillar-jump to climb to the top. The fastest way to do that is to hold down **L2** and **X** with a stack of sand, dirt, or gravel selected in the Hotbar. Keep an eye out for the dragon. Wait until you can see it drawing energy from one of the pillars in the distance; then start your climb to the top. It will fire acid balls at you, and you can also get knocked off the pillar by its wing when it's flying by. That's

when armored boots with a feather falling enchantment are very handy. If it's on an attack run heading straight for you and you get the chance, fire an arrow into its head (its most sensitive part). You can also try whacking it with your sword. Otherwise, just keep on jumping up as fast as you can.

4 Try to hit the crystal with an arrow or a snowball when you're a block from the top, keeping as much distance as possible because the resulting explosion can cause substantial damage. (That explosion can also knock out other nearby crystals, so it can benefit you.)

5 Take a good look around from the top of the tower, and shoot out any other crystals that are within range.

6 Head back to the ground using your shovel to dig out the blocks you placed, and repeat until you've taken out every crystal. You should be able to spot any you've missed by looking for the beams that show up as the dragon draws healing power.

Now it's dragon time. Follow these steps to deal it a deathly blow:

1 Position yourself near the final portal in the middle of the circle of towers. The dragon will alight there now and then and turn to face you, spewing out acid. Just keep your distance and fire arrow after fully charged arrow into its head.

2 Keep your bow fully charged with the arrow ready to fly with a critical hit. You can also take off the pumpkin at this point to improve your vision because you really only need to look up at the dragon, so you're unlikely to antagonize any Endermen.

3 Don't waste arrows firing at the dragon until it turns to face you from its perch, but be ready to step sideways to dodge any acid balls it will throw your way when it's flying around. Figure 12.12 shows the moment you should unleash the arrow. Aim your crosshairs directly at the dragon's head.

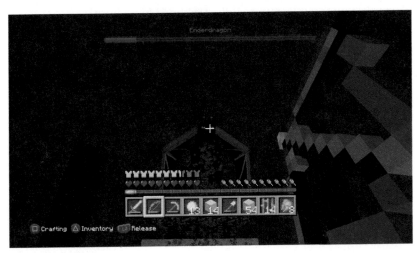

FIGURE 12.12 The Ender Dragon is at its most vulnerable when perched on the central pedestal.

4 A hit directly into the head causes maximum damage. You'll see the dragon flash red and its health bar take a hit. With correct timing, you should be able to fire off six or so shots without taking any damage.

5 Repeat until you've knocked the dragon's health down to zero. Then stand by for a striking purple-strobed explosion of splendid proportion (see Figure 12.13).

FIGURE 12.13 The final moments of the Ender Dragon.

Congratulations! Notch yourself up as a dragon slayer because you've just defeated the toughest mob in Minecraft! Enjoy the spectacle—it's probably been a long time coming and is over far too quickly.

Head over to the now activated portal. It will have a dragon egg perched atop—a shrine, if you like, to the dragon's defeat, or a celebration of your victory. Maybe both?

Before you take the fast route home by jumping into the portal, stop to pick up the numerous experience orbs dropped by the dragon. You'll collect up to 70–80 XP levels. You can also keep the pumpkin helmet on and start wailing on Endermen to gather experience, but you'll need to do so without the pumpkin for them to drop Ender pearls. You can always return through the stronghold portal to do that later.

TIP

Wanna Grab That Egg?

It's a little tricky and doesn't serve any purpose except as a trophy piece to put in an item frame back home, but why not? Build a small platform up to the egg, and hit it with any tool to knock it to the ground, hoping it doesn't just fall into the portal and disappear. There's only one way to crack this egg, and that's by digging two blocks under it, placing a torch on the lowest block, and then knocking out the one directly under the egg. Jump in to pick up the dropped egg and scramble out of there.

And that, as they say, is that. When you're ready, jump feet-first into the portal to view the "End Poem" (it's worth a read) and game credits—or press ● to skip. You'll return to your last spawn point in The Overworld.

Well done!

The Bottom Line

With The End game complete, you might be wondering what to do next. You've probably got a stronghold to explore, and at some point you might want to get home, but in any case, I have some good news. The end of Minecraft is actually just the beginning. Build, explore, survive, and thrive. The possibilities are as endless as the game itself.

INDEX

I

N

O

X

Y-Z

741.923

Old Master
Drawings from Chatsworth

101. RUBENS: Woman Churning

OLD MASTER DRAWINGS FROM CHATSWORTH

A Loan Exhibition

from the Devonshire Collection

5th July to 31st August

1969

DIPLOMA GALLERIES

ROYAL ACADEMY OF ARTS

LONDON

PRODUCED BY
THE MERIDEN GRAVURE COMPANY
AND
THE STINEHOUR PRESS

Foreword

by Sir Thomas Monnington, President of the Royal Academy

THIS EXHIBITION of Old Master Drawings from the Devonshire Collection at Chatsworth is substantially that which received so warm a reception when it was shown in seven major galleries in America and Canada in 1962-63. Van Dyck's portrait of Inigo Jones is not available for the present exhibition as it is included in the exhibition *Festival Designs by Inigo Jones*, only recently returned from an extended tour of America and to be seen at the Victoria and Albert Museum this summer. The four drawings by Inigo Jones included in the 1962-63 exhibition are not available, for the same reason, but it has been possible to omit these from this reprinting of the catalogue.

The 1962-63 exhibition was arranged and circulated by the Travelling Exhibitions Service of the Smithsonian Institution under the supervision of the Director of the Service at the time, Mrs. John A. Pope. We are indebted to the Smithsonian for the readily given permission to reprint this catalogue of the exhibition, the entries in which were prepared by Mr. A. E. Popham, who, with Miss Felice Stampfle of the Pierpont Morgan Library, and Miss Elizabeth Mongan, was also responsible for the final selection of drawings included. In the preparation of the catalogue notes Mr. Popham received assistance from Mr. Jacob Bean of the Metropolitan Museum of Art, New York, Professor Michael Jaffé, Mr. Philip Pouncey and Mr. Johannes Wild.

The Royal Academy is deeply grateful to His Grace The Duke of Devonshire and the Trustees of the Chatsworth Settlement for the privilege of showing this fine selection of drawings in London and wishes to acknowledge the most helpful co-operation of the Librarian and Keeper of the Devonshire Collections, Mr. T. S. Wragg, whose Introduction to the Catalogue gives a concise and interesting account of the whole collection.

W. T. MONNINGTON

[5]

Correction Catalogue No. 86: Since this catalogue was compiled it has been established that this drawing is a view of the North German town of Emmerich, on the Rhine. It is now attributed to Philips de Koninck, rather than Flinck.

Introduction

CHATSWORTH, the Derbyshire home of the Dukes of Devonshire, is known throughout the world as one of England's most splendid country houses. Year by year it is visited by hundreds of thousands of tourists, including many from America, who enjoy the magnificence of its surroundings, decoration and furnishings. They also get a glimpse of the great collections which it houses; but as Chatsworth is still a home and not a museum, the opportunity to display such treasures as books, manuscripts and drawings is of necessity limited. It is fortunate, therefore, that the present Duke and the Trustees set up by his father's will are (like His Grace's predecessors) extremely generous and co-operative in their support of exhibitions, both at home and abroad. Contributions from Chatsworth have figured in most of the great exhibitions of European art of the past, and this is especially true of the superb collection of drawings. However, only on two occasions in the past has an exhibition representative of the diverse riches of the Chatsworth drawings been attempted. The first was organized by the Arts Council of Great Britain and was shown in London and various provincial centers in 1949, while more recently (1961) a group of comparable number to the present exhibition was lent to the City Art Gallery in Manchester.

Now, through the generosity of His Grace and the Trustees, a similar representative exhibition has been made possible for America and Canada, under the auspices of the Smithsonian Institution. The present exhibition includes some forty examples which were among those shown in 1949, and there is a fortunate connection between the two events in that Mr. A. E. Popham, for many years Keeper of Prints and Drawings at the British Museum, who assisted with the selection of the drawings and the preparation of the catalogue in 1949, has willingly performed the same service for the present exhibition.

The present mansion at Chatsworth was built by William Cavendish, 4th Earl and later 1st Duke of Devonshire, in the twenty years between 1687 and 1707, replacing in a piecemeal fashion the Elizabethan House, built by the redoubtable Bess of Hardwick, which stood on the same site. It was his son, another William Cavendish, who succeeded as 2nd Duke in 1707, who was principally responsible for the formation of the collection of drawings. He appears to have displayed an interest in the arts long before he became Duke, and it is probable that it was he and not his father who figured as a buyer at the various sales such as those of the Lely and Lankrink collections which took place towards the end of the seventeenth century.

Although by 1723 he had already formed a considerable collection of drawings, it was in this year that he made his most important purchase, when he acquired the collection of Nicolaes Anthoni Flinck (1646–1723), son of Rembrandt's pupil Govaert Flinck (one of whose watercolor views is included in the present selection). The sloping capital F of Flinck is to be found on some 220 drawings in the Chatsworth Collection, and it was from this source that nearly all the splendid series by Rembrandt, Rubens and Van Dyck, a generous selection of which are now included, came. Often the F is accompanied by the D and coronet of the 2nd Duke. Shortly after it became known that the Duke had acquired this important collection, the French connoisseur Pierre Crozat wrote to him, saying:

"I take the liberty of complimenting you on the drawings of the late Mr. Flinck of Rotterdam, which you have just acquired. It is in my opinion the finest and best chosen collection I have ever seen and will materially enrich yours and make you the richest nobleman in Europe. All the drawings are admirable and worthy to find a place in your collection. I know the selection you had already made was no less choice."

Sometime between 1720 and 1728, the 2nd Duke bought the *Liber Veritatis* of Claude, a volume containing 200 drawings made by the artist to record his paintings, which Louis XIV himself had unsuccessfully tried to acquire. This, like the Sketchbook used by Van Dyck on his first visit to Italy in 1621 (another acquisition of the Duke's), has now left Chatsworth. Both were included among works of art handed over to the Treasury in part settlement of the huge death duties levied on the estate of the 10th Duke. Since 1957 they have been in the British Museum.

The remainder of the 2nd Duke's collection of drawings is still preserved intact, having suffered few losses or additions since his day. It therefore survives as representative of a 'cabinet of drawings' of a great nobleman of the first decades of the eighteenth century. One great change has, however, taken place. Originally all the drawings were contained in albums of various sizes (the extensive and important collection of engravings which the 2nd Duke formed at the same time as he acquired the drawings is still preserved in this way). They remained in their albums until 1835, when the 6th Duke (1790–1858) decided that their beauty should be more openly displayed. Many of the most important drawings were framed and glazed and hung in two galleries on the top floor at Chatsworth, still known as "The Sketch Galleries," which the Duke and his architect Wyatville built for the purpose. It was not until the early years of the present century that a beginning was made upon the task of properly mounting and protecting the individual drawings. The work was continued in the late 1920's, and today all the main series of drawings are separately mounted and stored in dustproof cases. This has made the whole of the resources of the collection available for exhibition purposes. It is regrettable that a number of the drawings framed for the 6th Duke suffered from the action of light and the atmosphere while they were hung in the Sketch Galleries, but fortunate that so many of the most important drawings (including the Rembrandts, Van Dycks and Rubenses) and especially those of the larger sizes, were allowed to remain in their albums by him. They survive in superb condition.

In addition to the 2nd Duke's collection, Chatsworth today houses another great group of drawings, the series of designs for costume and scenery for the Court Masques of James I and Charles I by Inigo Jones. These were originally in the possession of Richard Boyle, 3rd Earl of Burlington, patron of the arts and builder of Chiswick Villa and Burlington House, the present home of the Royal Academy in London. In 1748 the Marquess of Hartington, later to become the 4th Duke of Devonshire, married Burlington's daughter and eventual heiress, Charlotte Boyle. It was through this marriage that the vast Boyle properties and collections, including the Inigo Jones drawings and the celebrated series of architectural drawings by Palladio and others, now on permanent loan to the Library of the Royal Institute of British Architects, passed to the Dukes of Devonshire. The pencil portrait of Jones by Van Dyck in the present exhibition is a reminder of the connection between the two collections. Originally among the Flinck drawings acquired by the 2nd Duke, it was, as its inscription in Burlington's hand records, given to the 3rd Earl of Burlington by his good friend the 3rd Duke of Devonshire, to be placed with his series of theatrical drawings by the artist. Eventually, after Burlington's death, it returned to Chatsworth, bringing the Jones drawings with it! Four drawings from this group are now included, but as the costume drawings still remain in the two volumes into which they were placed by the 6th Duke, they are not available for individual exhibition.

As Mr. Popham said in his introduction to the catalogue of the Arts Council Exhibition of 1949:

"The contents of the collection as a whole provide a well-balanced illustration of the art of drawing in Europe from the time of the Renaissance to the end of the seventeenth century. There is no great period or phase of art, hardly a great name, except Michelangelo's, which is not represented. The Italian *quattrocento*, the High Renaissance, with its magnificent Raphaels and its extraordinarily rich representation of Raphael's school, Dürer and Holbein in Germany, Rubens and above all Van Dyck and Rembrandt in the Netherlands . . . the Hollars, the Inigo Jones drawings of masques and the mannerist and baroque painters of Italy, all are here. Though it is the Italian painters of the High Rennaissance, Raphael and his followers, who are most profusely represented, it is much to the credit of the second Duke that he did not neglect the then less fashionable countries and artists like Rembrandt. Indeed, the series of Rembrandt landscape drawings is perhaps the most outstanding feature of the collection."

The drawings by the mannerist and baroque painters include the important series of over seventy drawings by members of the Carracci family and the large group of Guercinos in which are the landscapes engraved by Pesne for the Duke of Modena. Despite the loss of the Claude *Liber*, his drawings are still well represented at Chatsworth. Owing to the richness of American collections in such drawings it was, however, decided not to include any in the present selection.

No catalogue of the drawings at Chatsworth is generally available. Volume XII of the Walpole Society's publications (1923/24) contains the descriptive catalogue of the Inigo Jones designs for masques, prepared by Mr. C. F. Bell and Mr. Percy Simpson, but the catalogue of the remainder of the drawings exists only in typescript. Prepared by Mr. Francis Thompson, my predecessor as Keeper of the Collections at Chatsworth, in 1929, it is based upon earlier attributions and lists made by Mrs. Eugenie Strong, early in the present century and is now augmented by the notes and comments of the many scholars of all nationalities who have been granted facilities to study the drawings since that date, through the liberality of the owners. This catalogue has formed the basis of the entries for the present one, and it is a hope for the future that some means will be found whereby its contents may be collated and edited and a complete catalogue made available to those interested. Such a project has already been mooted and has the approval of His Grace and the Trustees.

T. S. WRAGG

[11]

Collectors' Marks

Notes on collectors' marks which occur on more than one mount in the present exhibition.

WILLIAM CAVENDISH, 2ND DUKE OF DEVONSHIRE (1665–1729)   Lugt No. 718

The 2nd Duke of Devonshire succeeded in 1707 and was the founder of the Devonshire Collection (see introduction to this catalogue).

NICOLAES ANTHONI FLINCK   (1646–1723)   Lugt No. 959

A Director of the India Company of Rotterdam, the son of Govaert Flinck, a pupil of Rembrandt. From his father he inherited a considerable collection of works of art, which he later augmented by purchases. The major portion of his collection of drawings was purchased by the 2nd Duke of Devonshire in 1723. It is possible that other Flinck drawings were acquired by the 3rd Duke of Devonshire at a later date (1754). Two hundred and twenty-five drawings at Chatsworth bear the Flinck mark.

PROSPER HENRY LANKRINK   (1628–1692)   Lugt No. 2090

A German who studied at Antwerp and came to England where he was employed in the studio of Lely. He acted as auctioneer at the first Lely sale in 1688 and bought some of the drawings himself. He also acquired drawings from the collections of Charles I and Lord Arundel. His own collections were sold in London in 1693 and 1694. Forty-four drawings at Chatsworth bear his mark.

SIR PETER LELY   (1618–1680)   Lugt No. 2092

(Born Pieter van der Faes). Lely came to England in 1641 with William II, Prince of Orange. He reached the height of his fame as a portrait painter under Charles II. He bought largely at the sales following the dispersal of collections after the Civil Wars and also paintings and drawings by Van Dyck from his widow. After Lely's death his collections were sold to pay his debts in 1688 and 1694.

Catalogue

NOTE ON THE CATALOGUE: The entries for the drawings and, in most cases, the illustrations, have been arranged alphabetically under artists within the four schools. Where there is more than one drawing by the same artist, the drawings are arranged in the order of the Chatsworth inventory numbers. Height precedes width in the measurements. The drawings have been reproduced by permission of the Trustees of the Chatsworth Settlement.

BIBLIOGRAPHICAL REFERENCES
Publications Referred to in Abbreviated Form

BERENSON Bernard Berenson, *The Drawings of the Florentine Painters.* 3 vols., Chicago, 1938.

LUGT Frits Lugt, *Les marques de collections de dessins et d'estampes.* Amsterdam, 1921: Supplément, 1956.

STRONG S. Arthur Strong, *Reproductions of Drawings by Old Masters in the Collection of the Duke of Devonshire at Chatsworth.* London, 1902.

TIETZES Hans Tietze and E. Tietze-Conrat, *The Drawings of the Venetian Painters.* New York, 1944.

I have in most cases confined myself to quoting the latest authoritative work known to me in which a drawing is mentioned or catalogued. It can be assumed that this work will contain references to previous literature. I have, however, in every case given the number of the plate in Strong's volume of reproductions of Chatsworth drawings and also the catalogue numbers in Berenson and the Tietzes (see Bibliography). References are also given in shortened form to a number of exhibitions, the catalogues of which often provide valuable information. Of these the most significant are the following:

(A.E.P.)

Arts Council, London, 1949, *Old Master Drawings from Chatsworth* (first shown at the Arts Council Gallery in St. James's Square, London, and subsequently in other cities). Catalogue by A. E. Popham.

Bologna, 1956, *Mostra dei Carracci Disegni.* Catalogue by Denis Mahon.

Manchester, 1961, City Art Gallery, *Drawings from Chatsworth.*

Manchester (German Art), 1961, City Art Gallery, *German Art 1400–1800.* Catalogue by F. G. Grossmann.

Newcastle, 1961, King's College Newcastle upon Tyne Department of Fine Art, *The Carracci Drawings and Paintings.* Catalogue by Ralph Holland.

Royal Academy, London, 1927, *Exhibition of Flemish and Belgian Art 1450–1900.*

Royal Academy, London, 1929, *Dutch Art. 1450–1900.*

Royal Academy, London, 1930, *Italian Art 1200–1900.* (The numbers in brackets refer to A. E. Popham, *Italian Drawings exhibited at . . . Burlington House*, London, 1931.)

Royal Academy, London, 1938, *Exhibition of 17th-Century Art in Europe.*

Royal Academy, London, 1953, *Drawings by Old Masters* (Diploma Gallery). Catalogue by K. T. Parker and J. Byam Shaw.

Royal Academy, London, 1953–54, *Flemish Art 1300–1700.*

Royal Academy, London, 1960, *Italian Art and Britain.*

Wildenstein, London, 1950, *Peter Paul Rubens Sketches and Drawings.* Catalogue by Ludwig Burchard.

Catalogue

Italian

Anonymous Sienese School
early xvth century

1 THE BETRAYAL OF OUR LORD
(716)
Pen and brown ink and brown wash over black chalk, heightened with white.
8¾ × 7⅛ in.; 22.1 × 18.2 cm.
Literature: Philip Pouncey, *Burlington Magazine*, LXXXVIII (1946), p. 168; A. E. Popham and Philip Pouncey, *Italian Drawings . . . in the British Museum   The Fourteenth and Fifteenth* London, 1950, p. 169.

On the *verso* is a similar finished composition representing *Christ before the High Priest*. There is a companion sheet in the British Museum similarly drawn on both sides with representations of *Christ and the Woman of Samaria* and *Christ Healing the Man Born Blind*. This sheet was mounted by Vasari and bears his attribution to a certain Galante da Bologna of whom little but the name is known. The Chatsworth sheet on the other hand has an inscription in a sixteenth-century hand: *di m° Simone Memmi da Siena* (Simone Martini), which is much nearer the mark. The drawings in fact clearly show the characteristics and traditions of Sienese art in general and of Simone Martini in

particular and must be the work of some follower.

Niccolò dell' Abbate
c. 1506–1571

2 THE MARTYRDOM OF ST. CATHERINE (188)
Black chalk, brown wash and point of the brush, heightened with white.
21⅞ × 16½ in.; 55.7 × 41.7 cm.

Unmistakably from the hand of Niccolò dell' Abbate although the old attribution was to Francesco Primaticcio. The God the Father is practically identical with His figure as it appeared in a fresco by Abbate in the Palazzo Leoni in Bologna, representing the *Adoration of the Shepherds*.

Andrea del Sarto 1487–1531

3 TWO STUDIES OF A MAN SUSPENDED BY HIS LEG (710)
Red chalk.
8³⁄₁₆ × 7⁹⁄₁₆ in.; 20.6 × 19.2 cm.
Provenance: N. A. Flinck (Lugt 959). Exhibited at Manchester, 1961, No. 57.

Studies for paintings of three captains who had fled from Florence during the siege of 1529 and been declared traitors. Andrea del Sarto had undertaken to paint their effigies on a wall of the Mercatanzia Vecchia, as well as those of three civilian traitors on the

Palazzo Vecchio. They were to be represented according to Florentine custom suspended by one leg, as a warning, but the figures had been whitewashed over by the time Vasari (ed. Milanesi, Vol. v, pp. 53, 54) wrote in 1568, and only this and some other drawings in the Uffizi at Florence (Berenson 118a, 118b, 118c and 125) remain as a record of this gruesome commission. Although, according to Vasari, Andrea del Sarto painted the figures with his own hand, he preferred that his name should not be mentioned and that the commission should be in the name of a pupil, Bernardo del Buda. We are further informed by the same authority (Vasari, ed. Milanesi, Vol. vi, p. 63) that the sculptor Tribolo modeled the three figures in wax for his friend Andrea to draw from.

Federigo Barocci 1535?–1612

4   STUDY FOR THE HEAD OF CHRIST   (354)
Black chalk and pastel.
13³⁄₁₆ × 9¾ in.; 33.5 × 24.8 cm.
Provenance: Sir P. Lely (Lugt 2092); William, 2nd Duke of Devonshire (Lugt 718).
Literature: H. Olsen, *Federigo Barocci*, Uppsala, 1955, p. 158.
Exhibited at the Royal Academy, London, 1953, No. 99.

The features strongly resemble those of Francesco Maria della Rovere, Duke of Urbino, Barocci's patron. He used the study for the head of Our Lord in his painting of the *Last Supper*, dating from 1607, in the Duomo at Urbino. A similar but less finished study for the same head is in the British Museum (pp. 3–199).

5   STUDY FOR THE "MADONNA DEL POPOLO"   (357)
Pen and brown ink on brownish paper, heightened with white; the figures of the Virgin and Child in red and black chalk; squared.
21⅝ × 15⅛ in.; 55 × 38.3 cm.
Provenance: William, 2nd Duke of Devonshire (Lugt 718).
Literature: H. Olsen, *Federigo Barocci*, Uppsala, 1955, p. 130.

There are considerable differences between the painting, dated 1579, now in the Uffizi, Florence, and the drawing. The most striking of these is the substitution of a mother holding her child for the cleric seen leaning forward on the right of the drawing. The provenance given by Olsen for this drawing, Prince de Conti, Lempereur and Boileau, can hardly be correct: according to the mark on it, it must have been acquired by the 2nd Duke, who died in 1729. The Prince de Conti's sale was held in 1777 and that of Lempereur, whose mark does not appear on it, in 1773.

6   THE HOLY FAMILY   (363)
Red and black chalk, pen and brown ink and wash, heightened with white.
9⅛ × 9½ in.; 22.5 × 24 cm.
Provenance: Sir P. Lely (Lugt 2092).
Literature: H. Olsen, *Federigo Barocci*, Uppsala, 1955, p. 221.
Exhibited at the Royal Academy, London, 1953, No. 104.

Study for the painting of the *Rest on the Flight into Egypt* in the Vatican Gallery (No. 377), dating from 1573. The differences from the painting in its final shape are considerable. Olsen, for reasons which he does not explain, rejects the attribution to Barocci.

Domenico Beccafumi
c. 1486–1551

7 A STANDING AND A
RECLINING NUDE MAN (6)
Red chalk.
$8\frac{13}{16} \times 6\frac{1}{4}$ in.; 22.4 × 15.8 cm.
Provenance: N. Lanière (Lugt
2886); William, 2nd Duke of Devonshire (Lugt 718).

Inscribed in an old hand (that of Lanière?) *Meccarino*, Beccafumi's nick-
name. There is another closely related
study in the Uffizi, Florence (No. 1267^F;
photo. Gernsheim 2667) and an engraving signed *micarino F.* (Passavant Vol.
VI, p. 150, No. 4) apparently made from
the Chatsworth drawing.

Agnolo Bronzino 1503–1572

8 STUDY OF A SEATED YOUTH
(714)
Black chalk, squared in the same
medium. $10\frac{3}{8} \times 7\frac{3}{8}$ in.; 26.4 × 18.7
cm.
Provenance: N. A. Flinck (Lugt
959); William, 2nd Duke of Devonshire (Lugt 718).
Literature: Strong 16; Berenson
1957; J. A. Gere, *Burlington Magazine*, XCI (1949), pp. 169, 170.
Exhibited at the Royal Academy,
London, 1930, No. 538 (234); at the
Arts Council, London, 1949, No. 2.

Study for the painting by Bronzino of a
youth with a lute in the Uffizi Gallery,
Florence (No. 1575). The introduction
of the lute in the painting was obviously
an afterthought on the part of the artist,
as there is no indication of it in the present drawing.

Domenico Campagnola
1484?–1564

9 FOUR INFANTS, ONE
WINGED, IN FRONT OF A
TOWN; AN EAGLE ABOVE
THEM (247)
Pen and brown ink.
$6\frac{1}{8} \times 8\frac{3}{4}$ in.; 15.5 × 22.3 cm.
Provenance: William, 2nd Duke of
Devonshire (Lugt 718).
Literature: Tietzes 430.

A characteristic early work by this pro-
lific draughtsman, one of twelve or more
drawings by him at Chatsworth. The
subject is obscure.

Vittore Carpaccio working
1486 to c. 1525

10 UNIDENTIFIED SCENE (739)
Pen and brown ink over red chalk.
$6\frac{9}{16} \times 7\frac{3}{4}$ in.; 16.6 × 19.7 cm.
Literature: Strong 5; Tietzes, No.
591; Jan Lauts, *Carpaccio Paintings and Drawings*, London, 1962,
p. 266, No. 7.
Exhibited at the Arts Council, London, 1949, No. 3.

It has been suggested that the scene represents San Lorenzo Giustiniani bless-
ing Gian Galeazzo Sforza of Milan, but
there is no known painting related to
this drawing. Lauts on the other hand believes that the subject may be Cardinal
Bessarion presenting, in 1472, to three
representatives of the Scuola della Ca-
rità in Venice, the reliquary with a
fragment of the True Cross for transmis-
sion to that institution.

Attributed to Agostino
Carracci 1557–1602

11 STUDY OF TREES WITH A
GLIMPSE OF DISTANT
BUILDINGS ON THE RIGHT
(465)

Pen and brown ink.
$10^{15}/_{16} \times 7^{1}/_{2}$ in.; 27.9 × 19.1 cm.
Provenance: Sir P. Lely (Lugt 2092).

Annibale Carracci 1560–1609

12 VIRGIN AND CHILD ON CLOUDS ABOVE THE CITY OF BOLOGNA (428)
Pen and black ink and light brown wash.
$9^{5}/_{8} \times 7^{1}/_{4}$ in.; 24.5 × 18.5 cm.
Provenance: William, 2nd Duke of Devonshire, (Lugt 718).
Exhibited at Bologna, 1956, No. 99 and Fig. 34; at Newcastle, 1961, No. 148.

Study for the altarpiece painted by Annibale for the chapel of the Palazzo Caprari in Bologna, which is now in the collection of paintings at Christ Church, Oxford. It has been dated by Denis Mahon about 1593–1594 and is illustrated in the catalogue of the *Mostra dei Carracci* (paintings), Bologna, 1956, No. 74. There is a second study for the same altarpiece also at Chatsworth (No. 427) as well as two others in the Albertina at Vienna.

13 ST. GREGORY PRAYING FOR SOULS IN PURGATORY (435)
Pen and ink and wash, heightened with white.
$15^{1}/_{2} \times 10^{3}/_{8}$ in.; 39.3 × 26.3 cm.
Exhibited at the Royal Academy, London, 1938, No. 391; at Bologna, 1946, No. 120; at Newcastle, 1961, No. 153.

Study for the altarpiece formerly in San Gregorio Magno, Rome, and subse-quently in the Ellesmere collection at Bridgewater House, London. It was painted for Cardinal Antonio Maria Salviati, finished in 1603 and destroyed in the last war.

14 SHEPHERD BOY PIPING (446)
Black chalk.
$15^{1}/_{2} \times 10^{1}/_{2}$ in.; 39.3 × 26.6 cm.
Provenance: N. A. Flinck (Lugt 959).
Exhibited at Newcastle, 1961, No. 82.

Inscribed in an old hand: *Antonio da Correggio*, suggesting a period early in the career of Annibale, when he was particularly influenced by Correggio. The drawing is possibly a study for one of the musicians in the background of the *Fête Champêtre* in the Marseilles Gallery, which probably dates from about 1586 or 1587.

15 PORTRAIT OF A YOUTH (450)
Red chalk on grey paper, heightened with white.
$15^{1}/_{2} \times 10^{5}/_{8}$ in.; 39.7 × 27 cm.
Provenance: N. A. Flinck (Lugt 959); William, 2nd Duke of Devonshire (Lugt 718).
Literature: Adolfo Venturi, *Studi dal Vero*, Milan, 1927, pp. 398–399 and Fig. 274.
Exhibited at Bologna, 1956, No. 213; at Manchester, 1961, No. 20.

The drawing was attributed by the late Adolfo Venturi (*loc. cit.*) to the eighteenth-century Venetian G. B. Piazzetta, but the superficial resemblance is deceptive. The sheet had been in the Devonshire collection since 1723 and for some time previously in that of N. A. Flinck while Piazzetta was still alive. Moreover the costume of the boy seems, as far as it can be seen, to belong to the sixteenth century. There can in fact be little doubt that it is a youthful work by Annibale, to whom it was attributed when acquired by the 2nd Duke.

16   LANDSCAPE; SCENE ON A
     CANAL   (461)
     Pen and brown ink.
     4⅚₁₆ × 8 in.; 10.9 × 20.3 cm.
     Provenance: William, 2nd Duke of Devonshire (Lugt 718).
     Exhibited at Manchester, 1961, No. 21.

Lodovico Carracci 1555–1619

17   MAN PULLING ON A ROPE
     (410)
     Black chalk.
     13¾ × 10¼ in.; 35 × 26 cm.
     Provenance: Sir. P. Lely (Lugt 2092); William, 2nd Duke of Devonshire (Lugt 718).
     Literature: H. Bodmer, *Lodovico Carracci*, Burg bei Magdeburg, 1939, p. 140, n. 10.
     Exhibited at the Royal Academy, London, 1953, 153; at Bologna, 1956, No. 14; at Manchester, 1961, No. 22; at Newcastle, 1961, No. 3.

Inscribed in an old hand: *di lodovico Carazo*, an attribution which has been accepted by all authorities. The figure is obviously the study for an executioner in a scene of martyrdom or torture, perhaps for one tightening the bonds of Our Lord in a picture of the *Flagellation*.

Benedetto Castiglione 1616–1670

18   THE EXPULSION OF HAGAR
     (619)
     Pen and ink and colors.
     15⅜ × 10⅞ in.; 39 × 27.5 cm.
     Provenance: N. A. Flinck (Lugt 959), William, 2nd Duke of Devonshire (Lugt 718)

Correggio 1489?–1534

19   TWO PUTTI SUPPORTING A
     BLANK MEDALLION   (762)
     Red chalk on pinkish surface, heightened with white; squared in red chalk.
     8⅛ × 5⁷⁄₁₆ in.; 20.6 × 13.8 cm.
     Literature: A. E. Popham, *Correggio's Drawings*, London, 1957, p. 158, No. 45.

Study for the decoration of the same arch as Nos. 20 and 21.

20   TWO PUTTI SUPPORTING A
     MEDALLION IN WHICH THE
     VIRGIN IS REPRESENTED
     (763)
     Red chalk on pinkish surface, partly heightened with white; squared in red chalk.
     7½ × 5½ in.; 19.1 × 14 cm.
     Literature: A. E. Popham, *Correggio's Drawings*, London, 1957, p. 159, No. 46.
     Exhibited at the Arts Council, London, 1949, No. 4.

Study for the decoration of the same arch as Nos. 19 and 21 where, however, the Virgin in the medallion does not occur.

21 CHRIST IN GLORY IN A
CIRCLE (764)
Red chalk on pinkish surface,
heightened with white; squared in
red chalk.
Octagonal, width 5⅞ in.; 15 cm.
Literature: A. E. Popham, *Correggio's Drawings*, London, 1957, p.
158, No. 44.

Study for the figure of Christ painted in
a medallion on the underside of the arch,
opening into a chapel in S. Giovanni
Evangelista at Parma, formerly belonging to the Del Bono family. Opinions differ as to whether Correggio carried out
these frescoes himself or whether they
are the work of pupils. There can, however, be no doubt, on the evidence of this
and the two other drawings exhibited,
that he was responsible for the design of
the decoration.

Pietro da Cortona 1595–1669

22 AN ANGEL PRESENTING A
SOUL TO THE HOLY
TRINITY (590)
Pen and brown ink and brown
wash, heightened with white;
squared.
14⅞ × 11⁷⁄₁₆ in.; 37.7 × 29 cm.
Provenance: William, 2nd Duke of
Devonshire (Lugt 718).

According to Sir Anthony Blunt, this
drawing is a study for the altarpiece of
1628 in St. Peter's, Rome.

Domenichino 1581–1641

23 LANDSCAPE WITH A
CASCADE (506)

Pen and brown ink considerably
faded.
14³⁄₁₆ × 9⅝ in.; 36 × 24.5 cm.
Provenance: William, 2nd Duke of
Devonshire (Lugt 718).

Domenico Ghirlandaio 1449–1494

24 HEAD OF A WOMAN (885)
Black chalk or charcoal, the outlines
pricked.
14⁷⁄₁₆ × 8¹¹⁄₁₆ in.; 36.6 × 22.1 cm.
Literature: Strong 22; Berenson
866; J. A. Gere, *Burlington Magazine*, XCI (1949), p. 169.
Exhibited at the Royal Academy,
London, 1930, No. 37; at the Royal
Academy, London, 1953, No. 23
(*verso* of the sheet shown); at the
Arts Council, London, 1949, No. 5;
at Manchester, 1961, No. 29.

Cartoon for the head of a woman standing by the staircase on the left in the
fresco of the *Birth of the Virgin* in Sta.
Maria Novella, Florence. The whole
length figure of a woman on the *verso* of
the sheet is the study for one of the spectators in the same fresco. The commission for the extensive series of frescoes in
Sta. Maria Novella was given to Domenico and Davide Ghirlandaio in 1485.

Giulio Romano 1485–1546

25 DESIGN FOR THE DECORA-
TION OF A CEILING (93)
Pen and brown ink with corrections
in white, which has oxidized in
places.
9¾ × 12½ in.; 24.8 × 31.7 cm.
Provenance: Sir P. Lely (Lugt
2092); William, 2nd Duke of Devonshire (Lugt 718).
Literature: F. Hartt, *Giulio Ro-*

mano, New Haven, 1958, Catalogue No. 178 and Fig. 290. Exhibited at the Royal Academy, London, 1960, No. 571.

Design for the ceiling of a room in the Palazzo del Tè, Mantua, known as the "Sala d'Attilio Regolo." The fresco celebrates the virtues of Duke Federigo Gonzaga. There is an alternative design for the same fresco in the British Museum (Hartt, *op. cit.*, Catalogue No. 177).

26 DESIGN FOR A BOWL COMPOSED OF VINELEAVES (101)
Pen and brown ink and brown wash over black chalk.
8½ × 16 in.; 21.5 × 40.6 cm.
Provenance: William, 2nd Duke of Devonshire (Lugt 718).
Literature: F. Hartt, *Giulio Romano*, New Haven, 1958, Catalogue No. 102 and Fig. 138.

There is another drawing of the same bowl seen directly from above at Chatsworth (No. 100). They form part of a large series of designs for tableware made by Giulio Romano no doubt for the Dukes of Mantua.

27 A CUPID DRIVING A TEAM OF EAGLES WITH, ABOVE, THE COAT OF ARMS OF CARDINAL ERCOLE GONZAGA (105)
Pen and brown ink and brown wash.
16¾ × 11⅜ in.; 42.5 × 29 cm.
Provenance: Sir P. Lely (Lugt 2092); William, 2nd Duke of Devonshire (Lugt 718).
Literature: F. Hartt, *Giulio Romano*, New Haven, 1958, Catalogue

No. 362 and Fig. 518.
Exhibited at the Royal Academy, London, 1953, No. 59; at the Royal Academy, London, 1960, No. 571.

The design is for a tapestry probably dating from after the death of Federigo Gonzaga, Duke of Mantua, in 1540, when Cardinal Ercole Gonzaga took over the government of the state.

Guercino 1591–1666

28 SATIRICAL SUBJECT WITH CHARACTERS FROM THE "COMMEDIA DELL' ARTE" (513)
Pen and brown ink and brown wash.
7³⁄₁₆ × 10⅝ in.; 18.2 × 27 cm.

29 LANDSCAPE WITH A BROKEN COLUMN AND FIGURES ON THE RIGHT (533)
Pen and brown ink.
9⅞ × 16⅜ in.; 25 × 41.5 cm.

One of a series of fourteen landscapes at Chatsworth, all of which were engraved by J. Pesne and issued with a dedication by Guercino's nephews, Benedetto and Cesare Gennari, to the Duke of Modena. This is No. 12 of the series.

30 LANDSCAPE: A RIVER IN FLOOD AND PEASANTS WITH AXES AND OTHER TOOLS (544)
Pen and brown ink and some black chalk.
10⅜ × 16¹¹⁄₁₆ in.; 26.3 × 42.4 cm.

From the same series as No. 29 and also engraved by J. Pesne, No. 11.

31 VENUS SCOLDING CUPID (551)
Black and red chalk.
7½ × 10⁵⁄₁₆ in.; 19.2 × 26.2 cm.
Provenance: N. A. Flinck (Lugt 959).

Leonardo da Vinci 1452–1519

32 LEDA AND THE SWAN (717)
Pen and brown ink and brown wash over black chalk.
6⁵⁄₁₆ × 5½ in.; 16 × 13.9 cm.
Literature: Strong 35; Berenson 1013^{A}.
Exhibited at Milan (Leonardo Exhibition), 1939, No. 78; at the Arts Council, London, 1949, No. 7; at the Royal Academy, London (Leonardo Exhibition), 1952, No. 135.

Inscribed in ink in an old hand in the right-hand bottom corner: *Leonardo da Vinci.* One of a number of studies made by Leonardo for a composition representing Leda and the Swan with Castor and Pollux, and Helen and Clytemnestra being hatched from the eggs resulting from this union. There is a very similar study in the Boymans-van Beuningen Museum at Rotterdam (Berenson 1020^{A}) in which Leda is also kneeling, but in the final version she was represented in an upright position.

School of Leonardo da Vinci

33 STUDIES OF THE HEADS OF A WOMAN AND OF A CHILD (893)
Metal-point on green prepared surface.
11¾ × 8⅝ in.; 29.7 × 22 cm.
Provenance: William, 2nd Duke of Devonshire (Lugt 718).
Literature: Strong 37; Wilhelm Suida, *Leonardo und sein Kreis*, Munich, 1929, p. 55.
Exhibited at Manchester, 1961, No. 9.

The head of the child is copied from a drawing in the Louvre (Berenson 1067 and Fig. 487), which corresponds with the head of the infant St. John the Baptist in the painting of the *Virgin of the Rocks* and is probably by Leonardo himself. The head of the woman resembles that of the Virgin in a painting of the *Virgin and Child* published by Suida (*op. cit.*, Figs. 46 and 47) as a work by Leonardo, but which has not been generally accepted as his. There is, also according to Suida, another copy of the Virgin's head in the Ambrosiana at Milan. The present drawing has been generally attributed to Boltraffio, one of Leonardo's pupils, but there is no particular reason for this. It is, however, a typical and admirable example of the work of Leonardo's followers in Milan.

Filippino Lippi 1457–1504

34 HEAD OF A MAN WEARING A CHAPERON (704)
Metal-point on cream-colored prepared surface, heightened with white (oxidized in places).
8½ × 7⁵⁄₁₆ in.; 21.7 × 18.6 cm.
Provenance: William, 2nd Duke of Devonshire (Lugt 718).
Literature: Strong 2; Berenson 1277; A. Scharf, *Filippino Lippi*, Vienna, 1933, p. 129, No. 293. Ex-

hibited at the Royal Academy, London, 1930, No. 44; at the Arts Council, London, 1949, No. 8.

Formerly accepted as the work of Domenico Ghirlandaio, this fine head was assigned by Berenson to Filippino Lippi in view of its delicate and sensitive drawing, which is in contrast to Ghirlandaio's rather heavier touch. Berenson pointed to the resemblance which its style showed to that of the heads in Filippino's additions in the Brancacci Chapel dating from early in his career.

35   HEAD OF AN ELDERLY MAN
       IN AN OVAL   (705)
       Metal-point on slate-grey prepared surface, heightened with white.
       $7\frac{1}{2} \times 5\frac{1}{2}$ in.; 19 $\times$ 14 cm. (oval)
       Provenance: N. A. Flinck (Lugt 959).
       Literature: Strong 29; Berenson 1274[B].
       Exhibited at the Royal Academy, London, 1930, No. 466 (58); at Paris, 1935, No. 585; at the Arts Council, London, 1949, No. 9.

This drawing was apparently used by Vasari in the second edition of his *Lives of the Painters*, 1568, for the woodcut portrait of the sculptor Mino da Fiesole (died 1484). It seems therefore probable that it had formed part of Vasari's own collection of drawings. It was formerly attributed to Lorenzo di Credi, but its style rather indicates the hand of Filippino Lippi, to whom Berenson assigned it in the second edition of his *Drawings of the Florentine Painters*.

Filippino Lippi and Raffaellino del Garbo
c. 1470–1524

36   A PAGE FROM ONE OF
       GIORGIO VASARI'S BOOKS
       OF DRAWINGS   (960)
       (a). NUDE MALE FIGURE
       Metal-point on prepared grey surface, heightened with white.
       $7\frac{3}{4} \times 4\frac{1}{8}$ in.; 19.7 $\times$ 10.4 cm.
       Literature: Strong 34; Berenson 1276[B].
       (b). HEAD OF A YOUTH, AN
       ARM AND A HAND
       Metal-point on prepared mauve surface, heightened with white.
       $11\frac{3}{8} \times 7\frac{7}{8}$ in.; 28.8 $\times$ 20.1 cm.
       Literature: Strong 14; Berenson 760; A. Scharf, *Filippino Lippi*, Vienna, 1933, p. 129, No. 292.
       (c). BEARDED MAN LEANING
       ON A STAFF
       Metal-point on grey prepared surface, heightened with white.
       $7\frac{3}{4} \times 4\frac{3}{16}$ in.; 19.6 $\times$ 10.6 cm.
       Literature: Strong 34; Berenson 1276[A].
       (d). A KING SEATED ON A
       THRONE AND OTHER
       STUDIES
       Metal-point on prepared ochre surface, heightened with white.
       $8\frac{3}{4} \times 13$ in.; 22.1 $\times$ 33 cm.
       Literature: Berenson 1276; Scharf, *op. cit.*, p. 122, No. 207.
       Exhibited at the Royal Academy, London, 1930, No. 454 (50); and at the Arts Council, London, 1949, No. 10.

All four drawings are stuck on a leaf of one of the volumes into which Giorgio Vasari (1511–1574) pasted the drawings which he collected and to which he so often refers in the 1568 edition of his *Lives of the Painters* as his "Libro" in the singular, though it is certain that eventually it consisted of many volumes. The decorative borders and the inscription: *Filippo Lippi Pitt. Fior.* are his (Vasari did not use the diminutive when referring to the artist familiarly known as Filippino to distinguish him from his father Fra Filippo Lippi). The lowest drawing (d) is in fact certainly by Filippino and so perhaps are also the two single figures (a) and (c), but the large upper one is more probably by Raffaellino del Garbo. There are six other drawings pasted on the back of the sheet, of which the most important, a design for an altarpiece and its frame with St. Roch standing between St. Catherine and St. Anthony Abbot, was also attributed by Vasari to Filippo Lippi, but which is, according to Berenson, by Raffaellino del Garbo (Berenson 760).

Andrea Mantegna 1431–1506

37 BATTLE OF THE SEA-GODS
(897)
Pen and brown ink.
10¼ × 15 in.; 25.7 × 38 cm.
Provenance: N. A. Flinck (Lugt 959); William, 2nd Duke of Devonshire (Lugt 718).
Literature: Strong 4; P. Kristeller, *Andrea Mantegna* (English edition), London, 1901, p. 404; A. M. Hind, *Early Italian Engraving*, London, Vol. v, 1948, p. 15; E. Tietze-Conrat, *Mantegna*, London, 1955, p. 204.
Exhibited at the Arts Council, London, 1949, No. 11; at Mantua (Mantegna Exhibition), 1961, No. 125.

The drawing closely corresponds with the left-hand portion of the engraving of the *Battle of the Sea Gods* (Hind, *op. cit.*, Pl. 494) in the same direction. Its quality is so high and its appearance of originality so convincing that it has generally, and rightly I believe, been accepted as from Mantegna's own hand. Granted that this is the case, it is difficult to believe that the engraving which follows the drawing so exactly was also made by Mantegna himself, as has been almost universally believed.

38 STUDY OF FOUR SAINTS
(761)
Pen and brown ink.
7⅝ × 5³⁄₁₆ in.; 19.5 × 13.1 cm.
Provenance: William, 2nd Duke of Devonshire (Lugt 718).
Literature: Strong 32; Tietzes, No. A295.
Exhibited at the Royal Academy, London, 1953, No. 19; at Mantua (Mantegna Exhibition), 1961, No. 128.

Study for the left-hand panel of the polyptich in San Zeno, Verona, probably commissioned from Mantegna in 1456 and finished in 1459. The saints represented are, from left to right, Peter, Paul, John the Evangelist and Zeno. The attribution to Mantegna himself has been rejected by almost all critics from Morelli onwards as too obvious and most have favoured one to Giovanni Bellini.

Moretto da Brescia 1498–1554

39 STUDY OF A WOMAN'S HEAD
(743)
Black chalk on greenish paper, touched with white chalk.

10½ × 7½ in.; 26.6 × 19 cm.
Provenance: William, 2nd Duke of Devonshire (Lugt 718).
Literature: Strong 48; György Gombosi, *Moretto da Brescia*, Bâle, 1943, p. 116, No. 2.
Exhibited at the Royal Academy, London, 1930, No. 697 (261); at the same, 1953, No. 94.

Apparently the study for the head of St. Agnes, one of the five holy virgins in the lower part of the altarpiece by Moretto in S. Giorgio Maggiore, Verona, which is signed and dated 1540.

Lelio Orsi 1511–1587

40   DESIGN FOR THE FAÇADE OF HIS OWN HOUSE   (351)
Pen and brown ink and brown wash, heightened with white.
10⅝ × 13⅜ in.; 27 × 34 cm.
Provenance: Sir P. Lely (Lugt 2092); William, 2nd Duke of Devonshire (Lugt 718).
Exhibited at the Royal Academy, London, 1960, No. 594.
Inscribed: *al viso del vero f.*

The coat of arms with two confronted bears (orsi) is that of the artist. An almost identical but inferior version of the design is in the Estense Gallery at Modena (illustrated in the catalogue of the Lelio Orsi Exhibition held at Reggio Emilia in 1950, p. 113). There is also a separate study of the crossbowman shooting at the spectator in the Royal Library at Windsor.

Parmigianino 1503–1540

41   THE VIRGIN, HOLDING THE CHILD, SEATED ON THE

GROUND IN FRONT OF A CHAIR   (337)
Red chalk, heightened with white.
9⅝ × 6⅞ in.; 24.4 × 17.5 cm.
Literature: Strong 65.

To judge from its style this drawing dates from the early years of Parmigianino's career before his departure for Rome in 1523 or 1524.

42   THE MARRIAGE OF THE VIRGIN   (339)
Pen and brown ink and brown wash, heightened with white.
17⅞ × 9⅛ in.; 45.3 × 23.3 cm.
Provenance: Sir P. Lely (Lugt 2092); N. A. Flinck (Lugt 959); William, 2nd Duke of Devonshire (Lugt 718).
Literature: A. E. Popham, *The Drawings of Parmigianino*, London, 1953, Pl. XXVI.
Exhibited at the Arts Council, London, 1949, No. 12.

Finished design used by, and no doubt made for, Jacopo Caraglio to engrave (Bartsch XV, p. 66, No. 1). There is an old copy in the Louvre (No. d'ordre 6543) and studies for parts of the composition in the Pierpont Morgan Library. The drawing must date from the period of Parmigianino's stay in Rome between the end of 1523 or 1524 and 1527. Its composition shows some dependence on Rosso's painting of the same subject in San Lorenzo at Florence, which Parmigianino might have seen on his way from Parma to Rome.

43   DESIGN FOR PART OF THE VAULTING OF STA. MARIA DELLA STECCATA IN PARMA   (788)

Pen and ink and watercolor (damaged in parts).
9³⁄₁₆ × 6¹¹⁄₁₆ in.; 23.3 × 17 cm.
Provenance: unidentified armorial stamp on the *verso* of an eagle displayed with the initials P S (Lugt Supplement 2725ᵃ).
Literature: A. E. Popham, *The Drawings of Parmigianino*, London, 1953, Pl. LIV.

On the *verso* are two studies of a woman fondling a horse, a composition for which a number of other drawings are known.

One of the more elaborate among a large number of studies made for the decoration of the vaulting of this church, on which Parmigianino was engaged between 1531 and 1539, but which he never completed. The present drawing is the design for one half of the barrel vaulting leading to the eastern apse. The figures are much as they appear in the fresco except that there they do not join hands.

44   THE NATIVITY   (804)
Pen and brown ink and brown wash.
10 × 8½ in.; 25.3 × 21.6 cm.
Literature: A. E. Popham, *The Drawings of Parmigianino*, London, 1953, Pl. XL.

There is an unsigned engraving, possibly the work of a contemporary Bolognese, Girolamo Fagiuoli, mentioned by Vasari (ed. Milanesi, Vol. VII, p. 18), which reproduces this drawing. There is a copy (of the drawing) in the Louvre (No. d'ordre 6544).

45   THE VIRGIN AND CHILD,
ST. ELIZABETH AND
ST. JOSEPH   (805)

Pen and brown ink on green prepared surface, heightened with white.
6³⁄₈ × 4¹¹⁄₁₆ in.; 16.1 × 11.8 cm.
Provenance: Sir P. Lely (Lugt 2092); William, 2nd Duke of Devonshire (Lugt 718).
Exhibited at the Royal Academy, 1953, No. 72; at Manchester, 1961, No. 44.

The drawing probably dates from Parmigianino's Roman or Bolognese periods, 1523/24 to 1531, but is not connected with any existing work.

46   BEARDED FIGURE, SLEEPING
(806)
Red chalk.
7½ × 10¾ in.; 19.1 × 27.3 cm.
Provenance: Sir P. Lely (Lugt 2092); William, 2nd Duke of Devonshire (Lugt 718).

This is no doubt a study for a sleeping soldier in a composition of *Christ rising from the Tomb* and is possibly connected with the etching of this subject made by Parmigianino himself (Bartsch XVI, p. 9, No. 6).

Perino del Vaga 1500–1547

47   THE HUNTING OF THE
CALYDONIAN BOAR   (157)
Pen and brown ink and brown wash, heightened with white.
7¾ × 10¼ in.; 19.8 × 26 cm. (oval).
Provenance: Sir P. Lely (Lugt 2092); William, 2nd Duke of Devonshire (Lugt 718).

Design for one of the oval rock crystals decorating a casket in the Naples Museum. This was an elaborate silver-gilt casket by the Florentine goldsmith Manno di Bastiano Sbarri made for Cardinal Alessandro Farnese between 1548 and 1561, into which were set six crystal intaglios engraved by Giovanni Bernardi di Castelbolognese. Though there is, I believe, no contemporary record of Perino's having designed these, the old attributions of this and other drawings for the ovals to Perino are certainly trustworthy. There is another less finished design for the *Hunting of the Calydonian Boar* in the Museum at Besançon (No. 1398D).

Baldassare Peruzzi 1481–1536

48 DESIGN FOR THE FRAME OF AN ALTARPIECE (40)
Pen and brown ink and brown wash.
17⅞ × 14¾ in.; 45.3 × 37.4 cm.
Provenance: N. A. Flinck (Lugt 959); William, 2nd Duke of Devonshire (Lugt 718).

There is no indication of the church or chapel for which this design was made. The picture which it was presumably to contain measured 4⅚ by 3¾ *braccie* (about 9⅓ × 7¼ feet). Its style is very similar to that of the design for an organ in the Royal Library at Windsor Castle (Catalogue No. 1132).

49 PAN WITH NYMPH AND SATYRS (41)
Pen and brown ink and brown wash, heightened with white; squared in black chalk.

7 × 9½ in.; 17.7 × 24 cm. (oval)
Provenance: Sir P. Lely (Lugt 2092); William, 2nd Duke of Devonshire (Lugt 718).
Exhibited at the Royal Academy, London, 1960, No. 569.

Study for part of the ceiling decoration in a room in the Villa Madama, Rome, as observed by Philip Pouncey. Vasari makes no mention of Peruzzi as having collaborated in the work, but the style of this drawing and of a second one at Chatsworth corresponding with another oval in the villa, both anciently attributed to Peruzzi, make it certain that he had a hand in the design of this decoration, which Vasari (ed. Milanesi, Vol. v, p. 526) assigns to Giulio Romano and to Giovanni da Udine.

Pordenone 1484–1539

50 FIGURE OF TIME (234)
Pen and brown ink and brown wash on faded blue paper, heightened with white.
10⅞ × 16½ in.; 27.5 × 42 cm.
Provenance: William, 2nd Duke of Devonshire (Lugt 718).
Literature: Tietzes 1299.

Finished study for part of the decoration of the façade of the Palazzo d'Anna, Venice, which has perished, but the general appearance of which is known from a sketch of it in the Victoria and Albert Museum, London (Tietzes A1332).

Ugo da Carpi made a chiaroscuro woodcut of the figure, perhaps taken from the present drawing (Bartsch xii, p. 125, No. 27).

51 THE DEATH OF ST. PETER
MARTYR (746)
Red chalk.
9⅜ × 8 in.; 23.9 × 20.2 cm.
Provenance: William, 2nd Duke of
Devonshire (Lugt 718).
Literature: Strong 24; Tietzes 1301.
Exhibited at the Royal Academy,
London, 1930, No. 673 (273).

Study for the *modello* of the subject, now
in the Uffizi, Florence (Tietzes 1311),
prepared by Pordenone in a competition
for a painting for the church of SS. Giovanni e Paolo, Venice, in 1525. Titian,
one of the competitors, secured the commission, but his famous painting was destroyed by fire in 1867.

52 THE ALMIGHTY SUPPORTED
BY ANGELS (236)
Red chalk.
8½ × 8⅜ in.; 21.6 × 21.3 cm. (top
corners cut off).
Provenance: Sir P. Lely (Lugt
2092); William, 2nd Duke of Devonshire (Lugt 718).
Literature: Strong 38; Tietzes 1300;
G. Fiocco, *Pordenone*, Udine, 1939,
pp. 104, 155 and Pl. 140.
Exhibited at Manchester, 1961, No.
46.

Study for one or another of the very similar groups of the Almighty and Angels
in altarpieces in S. Rocco, Venice, and
in the Franciscan Church at Corte-
maggiore.

Giuseppe Porta (Salviati)
c. 1520–c. 1575

53 THE STORY OF THE SEVEN
KINGS (16)
Pen and brown ink and brown wash

on blue paper, heightened with
white; squared.
15⅜ × 19¾ in.; 39 × 50 cm.
Provenance: Sir P. Lely (Lugt
2092); William, 2nd Duke of Devonshire (Lugt 718).
Exhibited at the Royal Academy,
London, 1960, No. 559.

Probably the *modello* for a projected
fresco in the Sala Regia of the Vatican
Palace, for which Porta was paid 300
scudi in 1565 (cf. Carlo Ridolfi, *Le Maraviglie d'Arte*, ed. Hadeln, Vol. 1, Berlin, 1914, p. 243, n. 3), but which was
never even begun. This was no doubt due
to the death on December 9, 1565 of Pope
Pius IV, who had commissioned the
work and whose name is inscribed on the
pedestal of the statue on the left. The
probable connection of this drawing with
the commission for the Sala Regia was
discovered by Philip Pouncey. The seven
kings are obviously paying homage to a
pope, but who they were and when this
took place I have failed to ascertain.

Francesco Primaticcio
1504–1570

54 HERCULES SURPRISED WITH
OMPHALE (182)
Pen and brown ink and brown wash,
the outlines indented for transfer.
8⅞ × 15⅝ in.; 22.5 × 39.6 cm.
Provenance: N. A. Flinck (Lugt
959); William, 2nd Duke of Devonshire (Lugt 718).
Literature: L. Dimier, *Le Prima-
tice*, Paris, 1900, p. 471, No. 238.

Design for one of the frescoes decorating
the "Porte dorée" in the Palace at Fon-
tainebleau. The drawing was engraved
by the monogrammist "L. D." (Bartsch
XVI, p. 325, No. 50).

Raphael 1483–1520

55 THREE NUDE MEN IN
ATTITUDES OF TERROR (20)
Black chalk.
9¼ × 14½ in.; 23.7 × 36.8 cm.
Provenance: N. A. Flinck (Lugt
959).
Literature: Oskar Fischel, *Raphaels
Zeichnungen*, Part VIII, Berlin,
1942, No. 394.
Exhibited at the Arts Council, Lon-
don, 1949, No. 16; at Manchester,
1961, No. 48.

Study for a composition of *Christ rising
from the Tomb*, on which Raphael was
engaged at some time near the end of his
life, but which was never carried out as
a painting. Sketches for the whole composition are in the Ashmolean Museum,
Oxford (*Catalogue* by Sir Karl Parker,
1956, No. 558) and in the Bonnat Museum at Bayonne (*Catalogue* by Jacob
Bean, 1960, No. 132) and studies for individual figures at Oxford (*Catalogue*,
Nos. 559 and 560), in the Royal Library
at Windsor (*Catalogue* by A. E. Popham
and J. Wilde, 1949, No. 798) and in the
British Museum (1854–5–13–11).

56 STUDIES OF A MAN'S HEAD
AND OF A HAND (66)
Black chalk.
14⅜ × 13⅝ in.; 36.3 × 34.6 cm.
Provenance: William, 2nd Duke of
Devonshire (Lugt 718).
Literature: Oskar Fischel, *Burling-
ton Magazine*, LXXI (1937), p. 168;
F. Hartt, *The Art Bulletin*, XXVI
(1944), p. 87.
Exhibited at the Arts Council, Lon-
don, 1949, No. 18.

Study for the head and left hand of the
apostle pointing up at the Savior on the
left of the *Transfiguration* in the Vatican Gallery, which was left unfinished
at Raphael's death in 1520.

57 A WOMAN READING WITH
A CHILD STANDING BY
HER SIDE (728)
Metal-point on prepared grey sur-
face, heightened with white.
7½ × 5½ in.; 19 × 14 cm.
Provenance: Sir P. Lely (Lugt
2092); William, 2nd Duke of Dev-
onshire (Lugt 718).
Literature: Strong 49; Oskar Fi-
schel, *Raphaels Zeichnungen*, Part
VIII, Berlin, 1942, No. 375.
Exhibited at Paris (Italian Exhibi-
tion), 1935, No. 566; at the Arts
Council, London, 1949, No. 14; at
the Royal Academy, London, 1953,
No. 58.

Engraved by Marcantonio or one of his
pupils (Bartsch XIV, p. 54, No. 48). The
drawing seems to be a study from the
life, as the woman and child are dressed
in the costume of the period. Fischel suggested that it may have been drawn
about the period when Raphael was
working on the *Mass of Bolsena* in the
Stanza d'Eliodoro in the Vatican. A
drawing in the Ashmolean Museum at
Oxford (*Catalogue* by Sir Karl Parker,
1956, No. 561) is related in style, technique and subject to the Chatsworth
study.

58 STUDY FOR THE "SACRIFICE
AT LYSTRA" (730)

Metal-point on grey prepared surface, heightened with white.
9 × 4¹⁄₁₆ in.; 22.8 × 10.3 cm.
Provenance: Sir P. Lely (Lugt 2092); William, 2nd Duke of Devonshire (Lugt 718).
Literature: Strong 7; Oskar Fischel, *Raphael*, London, 1948, p. 365.
Exhibited at the Royal Academy, London, 1953, No. 62; at Manchester, 1961, No. 52.

Study for the figure of St. Paul rending his garments in the tapestry of the *Sacrifice at Lystra*, the cartoon for which is in the Victoria and Albert Museum in London.

59   VIRGIN AND CHILD   (902)
Black chalk.
16¼ × 8⅞ in.; 41.2 × 22.5 cm.
Provenance: N. A. Flinck (Lugt 959); William, 2nd Duke of Devonshire (Lugt 718).
Literature: Oskar Fischel, *Raphaels Zeichnungen*, Part VIII, Berlin, 1942, No. 369.
Exhibited at the Arts Council, London, 1949, No. 15; at Manchester, 1961, No. 54.

Probably made for the "Madonna di Foligno" now in the Vatican Gallery, though the Virgin and Child assumed a very different form in the picture when completed. It was painted for Sigismondo de' Conti, who died in 1512, and must have been commissioned before that date.

60   STUDY FOR THE "CONVERSION OF ST. PAUL"   (905)
Red chalk over a sketch with the stylus.

12⁵⁄₁₆ × 9½ in.; 31.3 × 24.1 cm.
Exhibited at the Royal Academy, London, 1953, No. 57; at Manchester, 1961, No. 50.

Study for running soldiers in the tapestry of the *Conversion of St. Paul*, the cartoon for which is lost.

Attributed to Raphael

61   VENUS ON CLOUDS POINTING DOWNWARDS   (53)
Red chalk.
13 × 9¹¹⁄₁₆ in.; 33 × 24.6 cm.
Provenance: Sir P. Lely (Lugt 2092); William, 2nd Duke of Devonshire (Lugt 718).
Literature: J. A. Gere, *Burlington Magazine*, XCI, (1949), p. 173.
Exhibited at the Arts Council, London, 1949, No. 17; at the Royal Academy, 1953, No. 61.

The strokes of the chalk running down diagonally from left to right as well as its slightly blurred effect indicate that the drawing is in the main an offset, that is an impression taken from another drawing by damping and pressure. It has, however, been extensively worked on, no doubt by the draughtsman of the original. The action of Venus pointing downwards suggests that it may have some connection with one of the spandrels painted with the story of Cupid and Psyche in the Farnesina in Rome. It remains a matter of controversy how much of this decoration and its design is due to Raphael himself and how much to his assistants, particularly Giulio Romano.

It has been observed that the present drawing was used by Cristofano Gherardi (1508–1556) on the vaulting of a room in the Villa Bufalini, near Borgo San Sepolcro, but the style and quality of the drawing preclude its being the work of this indifferent assistant of Giorgio Vasari, who borrowed extensively from other artists in this work.

62 NUDE WOMAN KNEELING IN PROFILE TO THE RIGHT (56)
Red chalk (with some later retouching).
10¹⁵⁄₁₆ × 7⁵⁄₁₆ in.; 27.8 × 18.6 cm.
Provenance: Sir P. Lely (Lugt 2092); William, 2nd Duke of Devonshire (Lugt 718).
Literature: Vasari Society, 2nd Series, VI (1925), No. 8; Oskar Fischel, *Raphael*, London, 1948, p. 104.
Exhibited at the Royal Academy, London, 1930, No. 469 (141); at Paris, 1935, No. 665; at Manchester, 1961, No. 49.

The drawing was regarded by Fischel (*loc. cit.*) as a study for one of the kneeling figures in the fresco of the *Mass of Bolsena* in the Vatican *Stanze*. The connection with the studies for the *Story of Cupid and Psyche* in the Farnesina seems to be a closer one. As already remarked the question of the attribution of these studies remains a controversial one. There is no unanimity of opinion as to which if any should be assigned to Giulio Romano and which to Raphael himself.

School of Raphael

63 THE HOLY FAMILY WITH THE CHILD ABOUT TO BE TAUGHT TO WALK (90)
Pen and brown ink and brown wash over black chalk.
8¹⁄₁₆ × 11⅜ in.; 20.6 × 28.8 cm.
Provenance: Sir P. Lely (Lugt 2092); William, 2nd Duke of Devonshire (Lugt 718).
Literature: Giles Robertson, *Vincenzo Catena*, London, 1954, p. 57.

This fine drawing, of which there was a replica at Wilton House (repr. S. A. Strong, *Wilton House Drawings*, London, 1900, Part II, No. 19), must have been made in the immediate *entourage* of Raphael, if not by the master himself. Giulio Romano, Perino del Vaga and Giovanni Francesco Penni have all been suggested as its possible authors. Vincenzo Catena copied it in a painting now in the Dresden Gallery.

Guido Reni 1575–1642

64 DESIGN FOR TWO HALF-LUNETTES WITH THE STORY OF HERACLIUS VICTOR OVER CHOSROES (481)
Pen and brown ink and brown wash.
12¼ × 7 in.; 31 × 17.8 cm. (each half)
Provenance: William, 2nd Duke of Devonshire (Lugt 718).

The left-hand section is inscribed: HERACHLIUS AUGUST. IMAGINEM VIRGINIS GESTANS COSRUEM PROFLIGAVIT, ET PERSIS DEVICTIS REGEM DEDIT; the right-hand section has the same inscription except that the words after "PROFLIGAVIT" have been omitted. This drawing is apparently an early project for two of the frescoes which Guido Reni was commissioned to paint in the Cappella Paolina, Sta. Maria Maggiore, Rome. They represent Narses victorious and the Emperor Heraclius so that their subjects must have been changed in part, and their presentation almost completely. Reni received payments for the frescoes between 1610 and 1612.

65   STUDY OF A WOMAN'S HEAD (485)
Red chalk.
11 13/16 × 8 11/16 in.; 30 × 22 cm.
Provenance: Sir P. Lely (Lugt 2092); William, 2nd Duke of Devonshire (Lugt 718).

Rosso Fiorentino 1495–1540

66   DRAPED FEMALE FIGURE WITH A BUNDLE ON HER HEAD   (712)
Red chalk.
10¾ × 5⅜ in.; 27.4 × 13.6 cm.
Provenance: N. A. Flinck (Lugt 959); William, 2nd Duke of Devonshire (Lugt 718).
Literature: K. Kusenberg, *Le Rosso*, Paris, 1931, p. 139, No. 5; Paola Barocchi, *Il Rosso Fiorentino*, Rome (1950), p. 200 and Fig. 161.

A characteristic early drawing by Rosso, dating according to Kusenberg, from before 1523. There is a copy of this drawing by Battista Franco in the Ashmolean Museum, Oxford (*Catalogue* by Sir Karl Parker, 1956, No. 236).

Bartolommeo Schedone 1560–1616

67   STUDY OF A BOY   (367)
Black chalk on grey paper, heightened with white; squared.
16⅞ × 9¼ in.; 42.8 × 23.5 cm.
Provenance: N. A. Flinck (Lugt 959); William, 2nd Duke of Devonshire (Lugt 718).
Literature: Strong 51.
Exhibited at the Royal Academy, London, 1930, No. 655 (292).

Study for the boy standing on the right in the painting of *Christian Charity* by Schedone in the Naples Gallery (No. 42).

Sebastiano del Piombo c. 1485–1547

68   RECLINING APOSTLE   (39)
Black chalk and brown wash on green paper, heightened with white; squared in black chalk.
9⅜ × 17½ in.; 23.7 × 44.4 cm.
Provenance: William, 2nd Duke of Devonshire (Lugt 718).
Literature: Strong 47; Berenson 2478; L. Dussler, *Sebastiano del Piombo*, Bâle, 1942, p. 167; R. Pallucchini, *Sebastian Viniziano*, Milan, 1944, p. 52 and Pl. 97.
Exhibited at the Arts Council, London, 1949, No. 21.

Study for the figure of the apostle on the right in the fresco of the *Transfiguration* in S. Pietro in Montorio, Rome. The fresco was commissioned by Pier Francesco Borgherini in 1517 and it has been suggested that the features of this apostle are those of the donor. They certainly resemble those of the donor in the National Gallery picture of the *Madonna and Child with St. Joseph and St. John the Baptist*, but there is no conclusive evidence that this represents Borgherini (see Cecil Gould, *National Gallery Catalogues   The sixteenth-century Venetian School*, London, 1959, No. 1450, pp. 81, 82).

Attributed to Sebastiano del Piombo c. 1485–1547

69 HEAD OF POPE LEO X   (38)
Black chalk.
18⅞ × 11¾ in.; 48 × 29.9 cm. (irregular)
Provenance: William, 2nd Duke of Devonshire (Lugt 718).
Literature: Strong 40; Berenson 2477; J. Hess, *Gazette des Beaux-Arts*, 6th Series, Vol. XXXII (1947), p. 84, n. 29; J. A. Gere, *Burlington Magazine*, XCI (1949), pp. 169–173; F. Hartt, *Giulio Romano*, New Haven, 1958, Vol. I, pp. 51 and 289, No. 39.
Exhibited at the Arts Council, London, 1949, No. 6.

Study used for the head of the pope named Clemens I in the Sala di Costantino in the Vatican. The features are undoubtedly those of Pope Leo X (died 1521), as indicated by the old inscription.

Though Vasari names Giulio Romano as the painter of the series of popes in the Sala di Costantino, the style of the present drawing points rather to Sebastiano del Piombo, to whom it was first attributed by Wickhoff. It is not as might at first appear the cartoon used for the head of Clement I, as it is smaller in size than the fresco. It is also known that after the death of Raphael, Sebastiano, with the backing of Michelangelo, had been trying to obtain the commission for the Sala di Costantino.

Pietro Testa 1607 or 1611–1650

70 DIANA AS HUNTRESS
(623)
Pen and brown ink.

12¼ × 11½ in.; 31 × 29.3 cm.
Provenance: N. A. Flinck (Lugt 959).

Attributed to Paolo Veronese c. 1530–1588

71 CHRIST AND THE DISCIPLES AT EMMAUS   (277)
Pen and brown ink and wash on greenish surface, heightened with white.
16⅝ × 22¾ in.; 42.1 × 57.6 cm.
Provenance: Sir P. Lely (Lugt 2092).
Literature: Tietzes 2055.

No doubt the *modello* for a picture. The Tietzes believed the present drawing to be a production of Paolo Veronese's shop rather than the work of his own hand. It is perhaps by Paolo Farinati.

Paolo Veronese c. 1530–1588

72 THE MARTYRDOM OF ST. JUSTINA   (279)
Pen and ink and point of the brush and wash on greyish-blue prepared surface; squared.
18½ × 9½ in.; 47 × 24 cm.
Literature: Tietzes 2056.
Provenance: P. H. Lankrink (Lugt 2090); William, 2nd Duke of Devonshire (Lugt 718)

Modello for the altarpiece in S. Justina at Padua, commissioned from Veronese in 1575. The Tietzes believe it to be a drawing mentioned by Carlo Ridolfi (*Le Maraviglie d'Arte*, Venice, 1648, Vol. I, p. 304) as kept in his day in the rooms of the Abbot of S. Justina.

Follower of Andrea Verrocchio c. 1435–1488

73 DESIGN FOR AN ALTAR WITH A TABERNACLE FOR THE EUCHARIST (889)
Pen and brown ink and brown wash.
15⅞ × 9⅞ in.; 41.2 × 25 cm.
Literature: Strong 17; Berenson 2780ᴮ; Otto Kurz, *Journal of the Warburg and Courtauld Institutes*, XVIII (1955), pp. 35ff.

Connected with a series of no less than seven designs for an altar and tabernacle, which are discussed in detail by Kurz in the article cited above. All are certainly Florentine, dating from the last quarter of the fifteenth century. Three of them in the Victoria and Albert Museum, London, three in the Uffizi, Florence, and one in the Louvre, Paris, are apparently designs for the same altar and tabernacle and the work of the same artist. The Chatsworth design seems to be by a different and slightly superior hand and differs in its general design from the others in that there is no altar table and that the tabernacle rests on a sarcophagus. Nevertheless figures and motifs occurring in some of the other designs are to be found here and it seems probable that it also represents an alternative design by a different artist for the same commission.

Neither the artist of the Chatsworth drawing nor that of the other designs can be certainly identified. Berenson believed the former to be the work of a certain G. B. Utili (who is more probably to be identified as Biagio di Antonio). Of the other drawings in the series, one in the Victoria and Albert Museum, which belonged to Vasari, was attributed by him to Desiderio da Settignano; another in the Uffizi to Lorenzo di Credi, but the name of Francesco di Simone has been the one most generally favored. He has been plausibly identified as the author of the drawings in a sketch-book now broken up and widely dispersed, which was formerly attributed to Verrocchio himself. But, as Kurz has pointed out, though motives from more than one of the designs occur on leaves of the sketchbook, they are certainly copies from and not studies for the altarpiece under discussion.

Federigo Zuccaro 1542/43–1609

74 SCENE OF FALCONRY (202)
Pen and brown ink and brown wash over black chalk with occasional touches of red chalk.
14⅛ × 15⅞ in.; 35.8 × 40.3 cm.
Provenance: N. A. Flinck (Lugt 959); William, 2nd Duke of Devonshire (Lugt 718).

Design for a stage hanging prepared by Federigo for the festivities on the occasion of the marriage of Francesco de' Medici and Joanna of Austria in Florence in 1565 (cf. Vasari, ed. Milanesi, Vol. VII, p. 100). Studies for the same scenery are in the British Museum and elsewhere. The actual hanging, in the Uffizi in Florence, is illustrated by Giuliano Briganti, *Il Manierismo e Pellegrino Tibaldi*, Rome, 1945, Fig. 101.

75 PORTRAIT OF A MAN (908)
Black, red and yellow chalk.
11¼ × 8¹⁄₁₆ in.; 28.5 × 20.5 cm.
Provenance: N. A. Flinck (Lugt 959).

A characteristic portrait drawing by Federigo.

Taddeo Zuccaro 1529–1566

76 THE ADORATION OF THE
SHEPHERDS (194)
Pen and brown ink and brown wash,
heightened with white.
15½ × 20⅛ in.; 39.4 × 51 cm.
Provenance: Sir P. Lely (Lugt
2092); P. H. Lankrink (Lugt
2090); N. F. Haym (Lugt 1971).
Literature: A. E. Popham and J.
Wilde, *Italian Drawings at Wind-
sor Castle*, London, 1949, p. 355,
No. 1071 note.
Exhibited at the Royal Academy,
London, 1960, No. 597.

There are variants of the composition in
the Uffizi, Florence and a preparatory
study at Stockholm. A drawing at Windsor (No. 1071 of the catalogue cited
above and Pl. 89) may be a study for the
right-hand half of the same composition.

Dutch and Flemish

Pieter Bruegel the Elder
1525/30–1569

77 VIEW OF THE "RIPA
GRANDE," ROME (841)
Pen and two shades of brown ink.
8³⁄₁₆ × 11⅛ in.; 20.8 × 28.3 cm.
Literature: C. de Tolnay, *The
Drawings of Pieter Bruegel the El-
der*, London, 1952, No. 4; L. Münz,
Bruegel The Drawings, London,
1961, No. A24.
Exhibited at the Royal Academy,
London, 1927, No. 527; at the Arts
Council, London, 1949, No. 23; at
Manchester, 1961, No. 67; at the
Los Angeles County Museum, 1961,
No. 99.

Inscribed by the artist "a rypa." The so-
called Ripa Grande was the main harbor
of Rome. Bruegel is known to have been
in the city some time between 1552 and
1553. The present drawing has been accepted by all authorities as the work of
the elder Pieter Bruegel. Only the late
Ludwig Münz in his recently published
book assigns it to Jan Bruegel, to whom
in fact it had originally been attributed.

Sir Anthony van Dyck
1599–1641

78 THE ENTOMBMENT (856)
Some pen and ink and point of the
brush, brown wash, red chalk and a
little faint green.
10 × 8⅝ in.; 25.3 × 21.8 cm.
Provenance: N. A. Flinck (Lugt
959).
Literature: Vasari Society, 1st Series, Part VI (1910), No. 19.
Exhibited at the Royal Academy,
London, 1938, No. 585.

On the *verso* is a partial study for the
same composition.

79 CASTOR AND POLLUX
CARRYING OFF THE DAUGH-
TERS OF LEUCIPPUS (993)
Pen and brown ink and brown wash
and black chalk on blue paper,
heightened with white.
9¹¹⁄₁₆ × 11⅜ in.; 24.5 × 29 cm.
Provenance: N. A. Flinck (Lugt
959).
Exhibited at Genoa, 1955, No. 993;
at Nottingham, 1960, No. 47; at
Manchester, 1961, No. 75.

Though Rubens treated the same subject
in a painting now in the Alte Pinakothek
at Munich, the present sketch does not

show any dependence on the older master's composition. There is a very slight sketch on the *verso* of the same subject.

80   PIETER BRUEGEL THE
      YOUNGER   (995)
Black chalk.
9⁹⁄₁₆ × 7¾ in.; 24.2 × 19.7 cm.
Provenance: N. A. Flinck (Lugt 959).
Literature: Vasari Society, 1st Series, Part III (1907–08), No. 17.
Exhibited at the Royal Academy, London, 1938, No. 586; at Rotterdam, 1948–1949, No. 84; at Nottingham, 1960, No. 49; at Antwerp and Rotterdam, 1960, No. 79.

Preparatory study in reverse for the etching by Van Dyck himself in the "Iconography" (M. Mauquoy-Hendrickz, *L'Iconographie d'Antoine Van Dyck, Catalogue raisonné*, Brussels, 1956, p. 154, No. 2).

81   CAROLUS DE MALLERY
      (1001)
Black chalk.
9¾ × 7¹¹⁄₁₆ in.; 24.8 × 19.5 cm.
Provenance: N. A. Flinck (Lugt 959).
Literature: Vasari Society, 1st Series, VIII (1912–1913), No. 24.
Exhibited at the Royal Academy, London, 1938, No. 577; at the Arts Council, London, 1949, No. 26.

Preparatory study for the portrait engraved by Lucas Vorsterman in the "Iconography". (M. Mauquoy-Hendrickz, *L'Iconographie d'Antoine Van Dyck, Catalogue raisonné*, Brussels, 1956, p. 250, No. 86). There is a copy or replica in the Ecole des Beaux-Arts, Paris.

82   INIGO JONES   (1002ᴬ)
Black chalk.
9½ × 7¾ in.; 24.1 × 19.7 cm.
Provenance: N. A. Flinck (Lugt 959).
Literature: M. Delacre, *Le Dessin dans l'oeuvre de Van Dyck*, Brussels, 1934, pp. 92, 93 and Pl. 24.
Exhibited at Antwerp and Rotterdam, 1960, No. 87; at Manchester, 1961, No. 77.

Inscribed on the mount: *Van Dyck's original drawing, from which the Print by van Voerst was taken in the book of Van Dyck's Heads. Given me by the Duke of Devonshire.*
                    Burlington.
It returned to the Devonshire collection through the marriage of the Earl of Burlington's daughter to the 4th Duke, at the same time as the designs for masques by Inigo Jones (see Nos. 110, 111, 112, 113). Engraved by V. van Voerst in Van Dyck's "Iconography" (M. Mauquoy-Hendrickz, *L'Iconographie d'Antoine Van Dyck, Catalogue raisonné*, Brussels, 1956, p. 235, No. 72).

83   UNFINISHED LANDSCAPE
      WITH MEADOWS, TREES
      AND A SQUARE TOWER IN
      THE DISTANCE   (1003)
Pen and brown ink and watercolor.
10¾ × 13⅜ in.; 22.4 × 34 cm.
Literature: A. P. Oppé, *Burlington Magazine*, LXXIX (1941), p. 190 and Pl. IIa.
Exhibited at the Royal Academy, London, 1938, No. 584; at Rotterdam, 1948–49, No. 94; at the Arts Council, London, 1949, No. 27; at Antwerp and Rotterdam, 1960, No. 120; at Manchester, 1961, No. 78.

The present drawing and No. 84 probably represent English landscapes sketched during Van Dyck's residence in the country after 1632.

84 LANDSCAPE WITH A HOUSE AMONG TREES (1005)
Watercolor.
7½ × 14¼ in.; 19 × 36.2 cm.
Provenance: N. A. Flinck (Lugt 959).
Exhibited at the Arts Council, London, 1949, No. 29; at Antwerp and Rotterdam, 1960, No. 121.

85 HEAD AND FOREQUARTERS OF A HORSE (1009)
Black and white chalk.
13¼ × 12⅜ in.; 33.7 × 31.4 cm.
Exhibited at the Royal Academy, London, 1953, No. 271; at the same, 1953–54, No. 524; at Nottingham, 1960, No. 59; at Manchester, 1961, No. 80; at Antwerp and Rotterdam, 1960, No. 12.

Study for Van Dyck's early painting of *St. Martin Dividing his Cloak with a Beggar*, particularly with the version in the church at Saventhem (*Van Dyck Klassiker der Kunst* 24).

Govaert Flinck 1615–1660

86 VIEW OF THE TOWN OF CLEVES (1160)
Pen and ink and watercolor.
7¹³⁄₁₆ × 12½ in.; 19.3 × 31.7 cm.
Exhibited at Manchester, 1961, No. 81.

Govaert Flinck, the draughtsman of this view, was a pupil of Rembrandt and the father of N. A. Flinck, whose collection was bought *en bloc* by the 2nd Duke of Devonshire in 1723. Though the present drawing is not stamped with the initial "F" found on so many of the finest drawings at Chatsworth and which establishes their provenance from N. A. Flinck, there can be little doubt of its having come from this source.

Jan Gossaert (Mabuse) c. 1478–1533/36

87 ADAM AND EVE (935)
Pen and black ink on grey prepared surface, heightened with white.
13¾ × 9⅜ in.; 34.8 × 23.9 cm.
Provenance: N. A. Flinck (Lugt 959).
Literature: Strong 54; Max J. Friedländer, *Die Altniederländische Malerei*, Vol. VIII, Berlin, 1930, p. 64, No. 1; H. Schwarz, *Gazette des Beaux-Arts*, 1953, pp. 155–156.
Exhibited at the Arts Council, London, 1949, No. 31; at Manchester, 1961, No. 82.

One of a series of drawings of the subject, of which others are in the Albertina, Vienna, in the Staedelsches Kunstinstitut at Frankfurt and in the Rhode Island School of Design.

Rembrandt van Rijn 1606–1669

88 ST. AUGUSTINE IN HIS STUDY (1018)
Pen and brown ink.
7¼ × 5⅞ in.; 18.3 × 15 cm.
Provenance: N. A. Flinck (Lugt 959).

Literature: O. Benesch, *Rembrandt's Drawings*, Vol. I, London, 1954, No. 120 and Fig. 132.
Exhibited at the Royal Academy, London, 1953, No. 316; at Manchester, 1961, No. 89.

Dated by Benesch about 1636. The subject was formerly believed to be St. Gregory in his study, but in view of other drawings representing St. Augustine made by Rembrandt about this time (e.g., Benesch, Nos. 121 and 122) Benesch believes that this saint is represented. To the authors of the catalogue of the Exhibition at the Royal Academy in 1953 "the pose suggests a study of an actor or studio model, rather than of any particular religious subject."

89   VIEW ON THE AMSTEL AT THE OMVAL; ON THE LEFT THE RINGVAART OF THE DIEMERMEER   (1026)
Pen and brown and grey wash on greyish-brown prepared surface.
4¼ × 7¾ in.; 10.8 × 19.7 cm.
Provenance: N. A. Flinck (Lugt 959).
Literature: O. Benesch, *Rembrandt's Drawings*, Vol. VI, London, 1957, No. 1321 and Fig. 1555.
Exhibited at the Royal Academy, London, 1929, No. 602; at the Royal Academy, 1938, No. 547; at the Arts Council, London, 1949, No. 34.

On the *verso* is the study of a man seen from behind walking towards the left (ill. Benesch, Fig. 1556). Another view of the same locality is introduced into the background of Rembrandt's etching, *The Omval*, dated 1645 (Hind 210), but Benesch dates the present drawing later, about 1653.

90   A ROAD LEADING THROUGH A WOOD   (1029)
Pen and brown ink and wash on grey tinted paper.
6³⁄₁₆ × 7¹⁵⁄₁₆ in.; 15.6 × 20 cm.
Provenance: N. A. Flinck (Lugt 959).
Literature: O. Benesch, *Rembrandt's Drawings*, Vol. VI, London, 1957, No. 1253 and Fig. 1478.
Exhibited at the Royal Academy, London, 1929, No. 611; at Amsterdam, 1935, No. 73.

Dated by Benesch about 1650–1651. Another drawing of the same road through a wood is illustrated by him, Fig. 1480.

91   VIEW OVER THE RIVER Y FROM THE DIEMERDIJK   (1030)
Pen and ink and brown wash on greyish paper, with some white body-color.
3¹⁄₁₆ × 9⅝ in.; 7.6 × 24.4 cm.
Provenance: N. A. Flinck (Lugt 959).
Literature: O. Benesch, *Rembrandt's Drawings*, Vol. VI, London, 1957, No. 1239 and Fig. 1465.
Exhibited at the Royal Academy, London, 1929, No. 609; at the same, 1938, No. 587; at the Arts Council, London, 1949, No. 35.

Dated by Benesch about 1650–1651.

92   VIEW NEAR THE RAMPOORTJE, AMSTERDAM   (1031)
Pen and brown ink and brown wash on yellowish-brown paper.
5¼ × 8⅝ in.; 13.2 × 21.8 cm.

Provenance: N. A. Flinck (Lugt 959).

Literature: O. Benesch, *Rembrandt's Drawings*, Vol. VI, London, 1957, No. 1263 and Fig. 1490.

Exhibited at the Royal Academy, London, 1929, No. 605; at Manchester, 1961, No. 92.

Dated by Benesch about 1651. The buildings have been more precisely identified by Lugt as the bulwark called "De Rose" and the windmill called "De Smeerpot."

93 FARM WITH A DOVECOTE AND A HAYRICK (1037)

Pen and brown ink and brown wash. 5⅛ × 7⅞ in.; 13 × 19.9 cm.

Provenance: N. A. Flinck (Lugt 959).

Literature: O. Benesch, *Rembrandt's Drawings*, Vol. VI, London, 1957, No. 1233 and Fig. 1460.

Exhibited at Amsterdam, 1935, No. 70; at the Arts Council, London, 1949, No. 39.

Dated by Benesch about 1650. Inscribed on the *verso Rembrandt van Rijn* in a hand of the seventeenth century.

94 A FARMSTEAD BESIDE A STREAM (1042)

Pen and brown ink and brown wash. 4¼ × 8¹¹⁄₁₆ in.; 10.8 × 22 cm.

Provenance: N. A. Flinck (Lugt 959).

Literature: O. Benesch, *Rembrandt's Drawings*, *Vol.* VI, London, 1957, No. 1295 and Fig. 1525.

Exhibited at Amsterdam, 1935, No. 77; at the Arts Council, London, 1949, No. 41.

Dated by Benesch about 1652–1653. The same farmstead seen from the opposite side occurs in a second drawing at Chatsworth (Benesch, No. 1294); and in others belonging to Mr. Frits Lugt in Paris (Benesch, No. 1296) and in the Art Institute at Chicago (Benesch, No. 1297).

95 THE RIJNPOORT AT RHENEN (1043)

Pen and blackish-brown ink and some wash, rubbed with the finger. 4¾ × 6⅞ in.; 12 × 17.6 cm.

Provenance: N. A. Flinck (Lugt 959).

Literature: O. Benesch, *Rembrandt's Drawings*, Vol. VI, London, 1957, No. 1301 and Fig. 1531.

Dated by Benesch about 1652–1653. There is another view of the same gate from a slightly different point of view in the Louvre (Benesch, No. 1300).

96 A THATCHED COTTAGE BY A LARGE TREE (1046)

Pen and two shades of brown ink. 6⅞ × 10½ in.; 17.5 × 26.7 cm.

Provenance: N. A. Flinck (Lugt 959).

Literature: O. Benesch, *Rembrandt's Drawings*, Vol. VI, London, 1957, No. 1282 and Fig. 1510.

Exhibited at the Royal Academy, London, 1929, No. 612; at the same, 1938, No. 555; at the Arts Council, London, 1949, No. 42.

Dated by Benesch about 1652. The same cottage and tree are the subject of another drawing in the Lubomirski Museum at Lwów (Benesch, No. 1283).

97 A WINDMILL AND A GROUP OF HOUSES (1047)
Pen and brown ink on rough greyish paper.
4⅜ × 7¼ in.; 11.2 × 18.4 cm.
Provenance: N. A. Flinck (Lugt 959).
Literature: O. Benesch, *Rembrandt's Drawings*, Vol. vi, London, 1957, No. 1308 and Fig. 1538.

Dated by Benesch about 1652–1653. Rather tentatively identified by Lugt (*Wandelingen met Rembrandt in en om Amsterdam*, Amsterdam, 1915, Fig. 61) as "Het Molentje."

Sir Peter Paul Rubens 1577–1640

98 A GARLAND OF FRUIT AND CORN (679ᴬ)
Pen and brown ink.
6⅝ × 16½ in.; 16.7 × 41.9 cm.
Exhibited at the Royal Academy, London, 1927, No. 569.

Inscribed at the top: *Questo si fara di tutto Rilevo* and at the bottom on the right: *B. Cris*. The first inscription implies that the design was to be carved or molded in relief and it has been suggested by Michael Jaffé that it may have been intended for the decoration of the Jesuit church at Antwerp in which Rubens was largely concerned. The church was destroyed by fire in 1718. The significance of "B. Cris" has not been explained.

99 TWO FRANCISCAN FRIARS (964ᴬ)

Black and white chalk with some red chalk on the faces.
22 × 15⅞ in.; 56 × 40.3 cm.
Literature: Julius Held, *Rubens Selected Drawings*, London, 1959, No. 93 and Pl. 108.
Exhibited at the Arts Council, London, 1949, No. 43; at Manchester, 1961, No. 95.

Study for the *Last Communion of St. Francis* in the Antwerp Gallery (No. 305). This was painted by Rubens in 1619 for the altar of the saint in the church of the Recollets at Antwerp. The figure stretching out his arms is for the monk supporting St. Francis; the cowled monk lower down on the sheet for a head in the background on the left edge of the painting.

100 A MAN THRESHING AND A HAY WAGON (983)
Black chalk with some red chalk and touches of blue, yellow and green; parts of the cart reinforced in pen and ink.
10 × 16⅜ in.; 25.5 × 41.5 cm.
Literature: Julius Held, *Rubens Selected Drawings*, London, 1959, No. 129 and Pl. 141.
Exhibited at the Royal Academy, London, 1938, No. 614; at the Arts Council, London, 1949, No. 45; at Manchester, 1961, No. 96.

The drawing is dated by Held about 1615–1617. Though the man threshing does not occur anywhere in Rubens' paintings the wagon was used by him on three occasions: in the *Prodigal Son* in the Antwerp Gallery (*P. P. Rubens, Klassiker der Kunst*, 1921, 182), in the *Winter* at Windsor Castle (Klassiker der

Kunst 238) and finally in the *Landscape with a Country Cart* at Leningrad (Klassiker der Kunst 185).

101   WOMAN CHURNING (984)
Black chalk with red chalk on the woman's face and bodice.
13⅛ × 10 in.; 33.3 × 25.5 cm.
Literature: Julius Held, *Rubens Selected Drawings*, London, 1959, No. 95 and Pl. 103.
Exhibited at the Royal Academy, London, 1938, No. 605; at the Arts Council, London, 1949, No. 46; at Wildenstein's, London, 1950, No. 54.

The figure does not occur in any existing painting by Rubens and there is no agreement about its exact dating. Held would place it about 1619–1620, Ludwig Burchard (Wildenstein Exhibition Catalogue) about 1631 and Glück and Haberditzl about 1635.

102   TREE TRUNK AND BRAMBLES (1008)
Red and black chalk, pen and brown ink and some color.
13¾ × 11¾ in.; 35.2 × 29.8 cm.
Literature: Julius Held, *Rubens Selected Drawings*, London, 1959, p. 145 and Fig. 17.
Exhibited at the Arts Council, London, 1949, No. 48.

The drawing is inscribed in Rubens' hand: *afgevallen bladern ende op sommighe plaetsen schoon gruen grase door kyken* ("fallen leaves and in some places green grasses peep through"). It is related to a drawing in the Louvre (Held, No. 131) which was used by Rubens in the painting of a *Boar Hunt* at Dresden (Klassiker der Kunst 184) which dates from about 1615–1620.

German

Hans Burgkmair 1473–1531

103   PORTRAIT OF A MAN, DATED 1518. (933)
Black chalk.
13¾ × 10⅝ in.; 35.2 × 27.2 cm.
Literature: Strong 9; Vasari Society, 1st Ser., IV (1908–09), No. 29; L. Kaemmerer, *Mitteilungen des Osterr. Vereins für Bibliothekswesen*, Vienna, IX (1905), p. 42.
Exhibited at the Arts Council, London, 1949, No. 50; at Manchester (German Art), 1961, No. 147.

Kaemmerer identified the personage as Wolfgang von Maen, who was chaplain to the Emperor Maximilian and is likely to have accompanied him to the Diet at Augsburg in 1518, where Burgkmair was then working. Though only small woodcuts record the features of Wolfgang von Maen their resemblance to those of the present drawing are striking.

Albrecht Dürer 1472–1528

104   WOMEN'S PUBLIC BATH (931)
Pen and light brown ink, the profile of the man on the right in darker ink.

11¼ × 8½ in.; 28.5 × 21.5 cm.
Provenance: William, 2nd Duke of Devonshire (Lugt 718).
Literature: Charles Ephrussi, *Les Bains de Femmes d'Albert Dürer*, Paris, 1881, p. 10; Friedrich Winkler, *Die Zeichnungen Albrecht Dürers*, Vol. III, Berlin, 1938, No. 622.

There is an old copy of this drawing in the Berlin Kupferstichkabinett according to Winkler (No. 4973). Dürer had already many years earlier in 1496 made a drawing of a women's bath (Winkler, *op. cit.*, Vol. I, No. 152). It was presumably his only opportunity of drawing from the nude.

Hans Holbein the Younger
1497–1543

105   PROFILE OF A SCHOLAR OR CLERIC   (835)
Drawn with the point of the brush and black ink over black chalk, on a pink prepared surface.
8½ × 7¼ in.; 21.7 × 18.4 cm.
Provenance: William, 2nd Duke of Devonshire (Lugt 718).
Literature: Strong 26.
Exhibited at the Arts Council, London, 1949, No. 52; at the Royal Academy, London, 1950–51, No. 125.
Inscribed in upper left-hand corner: *HH*.

106   HEAD OF A YOUTH IN A BROAD-BRIMMED HAT (836)
Black and red chalk.
9⅝ × 8 in.; 24.5 × 20.2 cm.

Provenance: William, 2nd Duke of Devonshire (Lugt 718).
Literature: Strong 55.
Exhibited at the Arts Council, London, 1949, No. 54; at the Royal Academy, London, 1950–51, No. 133.

107   SIX DESIGNS FOR MEDALLIONS AND ONE OTHER
(mounted together)   (837)
Pen and ink and wash or watercolor.
Literature: Strong 18; Paul Ganz, *Drawings by Hans Holbein II*, Vol. V, Nos. 257–261 and 281.
Exhibited at the Arts Council, London, 1949, No. 53; at Manchester (German Art), 1961, No. 151.
(a). THE FALL OF ICARUS circular diam. 2 in.; 5.1 cm.
(b). THE LAST JUDGMENT circular diam. 1¹³⁄₁₆ in.; 4.7 cm.
(c). CUPID STUNG BY BEES, with inscription *"Nocet empta dolore voluptas."* circular diam. 2³⁄₁₆ in.; 5.6 cm.
(d). HAGAR AND ISHMAEL circular diam. 2⅛ in.; 5.4 cm.
(e). DIANA AND ACTAEON circular diam. 2 in.; 5 cm.
(f). ALLEGORY OF TIME, with inscription *"Aspetto la Hora."* circular diam. 2⅛ in.; 5.5 cm.
(g). THE RAPE OF HELEN OF TROY (?). 2¹⁵⁄₁₆ × 2⅛ in.; 7.5 × 5.4 cm.

The six drawings (a) to (f) are probably designs for pendants or hat badges and date from the period of Holbein's second residence in England, between 1532 and 1543. The seventh drawing (g) may have been for the decoration of a dagger sheath. Though it is not included in Ganz's Corpus of Holbein Drawings and an attribution to Etienne Delaune had been suggested by the compiler of the present catalogue in 1949, he now believes that it is in fact also by Holbein, as apparently does Dr. F. G. Grossmann, the compiler of the catalogue of the Manchester German Exhibition in 1961.

Wenceslaus Hollar 1607–1677

108 THE RHINE, WITH THE TOWN AND FORTRESS OF ENGERS; LORD ARUNDEL'S BARGES IN THE FORE-GROUND. (H.2)
Pen and ink and watercolor.
$4^{15}/_{16} \times 10^{1}/_{2}$ in.; 11 × 27.1 cm.
Literature: F. Sprinzels, *Wenceslaus Hollar and his Drawings*, Vienna, 1938, No. 185 and Fig. 170.

Inscribed by the artist in the sky *Engers;* below, in the river *Rhenus fluvius* and signed *WH 10M* in the bottom left-hand corner. This and the following number record a journey made by Hollar in the suite of Henry Howard, Earl of Arundel, in 1636. Another member of Arundel's staff, William Crowne, kept a diary of the journey which was printed in 1637, from which we learn that the Earl was at Engers on April 30 and at Frankfurt from May 5 to May 7. A number of other drawings made on the same journey are preserved at Chatsworth.

109 VIEW OF FRANKFURT-AM-MAIN (H. 8)
Pen and ink and watercolor.
$4^{3}/_{8} \times 10^{3}/_{4}$ in.; 11.1 × 27 cm.
Literature: F. Sprinzels, *Wences-*

laus Hollar and his Drawings, Vienna, 1938, No. 214 and Fig. 172. Exhibited at the Arts Council, London, 1949, No. 55.

Inscribed by the artist, in the sky, *Francofurtum ad Moenum* and below in the river *Moenus fluvius* and signed in the bottom left-hand corner *W. Hollart delineavit 1636.* There is an outline sketch, from which the present drawing was elaborated, in the Staedel Institut at Frankfurt (ill. Sprinzels, *op. cit.*, Fig. 175).

English

Sir Peter Lely 1618–1680

114 A KNIGHT BOWING (958)
Black chalk on grey-blue paper.
$18^{7}/_{8} \times 14^{11}/_{16}$ in.; 46.8 × 37.3 cm.
Provenance: Earl of Warwick (Lugt 2600).
Literature: John Woodward, *Tudor and Stuart Drawings*, London, 1951, p. 49; E. Croft-Murray and Paul Hulton, *British Museum Catalogue of British Drawings*, Vol. I, London, 1960, p. 409.
Exhibited at the Royal Academy, London, 1953, No. 436.

One of a series of drawings by Lely, numbering at least thirty, of figures taking part in some ceremony of the Order of the Garter on St. George's Day, April 23. They must date from between 1663 and 1671, but the exact purpose for which they were prepared is not known. One of the few drawings added to the collection since the eighteenth century. It was sold in the Warwick Sale in 1896 and subsequently purchased.

Illustrations

1.   ANONYMOUS SIENESE OF THE 15TH CENTURY: (*recto*) The Betrayal

(*verso*) Christ before the High Priest

2.   ABBATE: The Martyrdom of St. Catherine

5. BAROCCI: Study for "Madonna del Popolo"

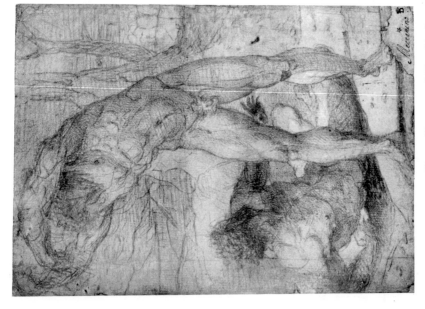

7. BECCAFUMI: Standing and Reclining
Nude Man

3. ANDREA DEL SARTO: Studies of a Man Suspended

4. BAROCCI: Head of Christ

8. BRONZINO: Study of a Seated Youth

6. BAROCCI: The Holy Family

9. CAMPAGNOLA: Four Infants

11.   AGOSTINO CARRACCI: Study of Trees

10.   CARPACCIO: Unidentified Scene

12.   ANNIBALE CARRACCI: Virgin and Child above Bologna

13.　ANNIBALE CARRACCI:　St. Gregory Praying

14. **ANNIBALE CARRACCI:** Shepherd Boy Piping

15.　ANNIBALE CARRACCI:　Portrait of a Youth

18. CASTIGLIONE: Expulsion of Hagar

16. ANNIBALE CARRACCI: Landscape on a Canal

17.   LODOVICO CARRACCI: Man Pulling a Rope

19.   CORREGGIO: Two Putti Supporting
       a Blank Medallion

20.   CORREGGIO: Two Putti Supporting a Medallion

21.   CORREGGIO: Christ in Glory

24.   GHIRLANDAIO: Head of a Woman

22.　CORTONA:　Angel Presenting a Soul to the Holy Trinity

25.   GIULIO ROMANO: Design for a Ceiling Decoration

27. **GIULIO ROMANO:**
Cupid Driving a Team of Eagles

26.   **GIULIO ROMANO:**   Design for a Bowl

23. DOMENICHINO: Landscape with Cascade

29. GUERCINO: Landscape with Broken Column

30.   GUERCINO: Landscape with River in Flood

28.   GUERCINO: Characters from the "Commedia dell' Arte"

31.   GUERCINO: Venus Scolding Cupid

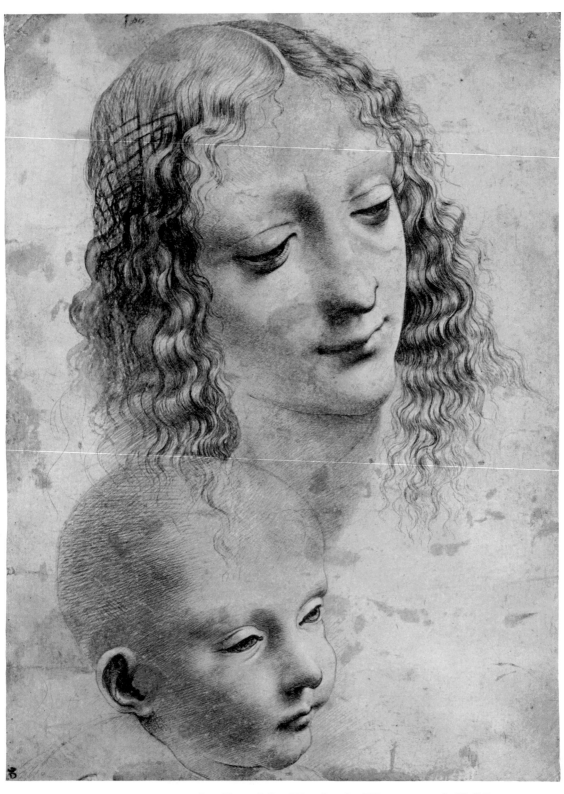

33.　SCHOOL OF LEONARDO:　Studies of the Heads of a Woman and Child

32. LEONARDO: Leda and the Swan

34.　**FILIPPINO LIPPI:**　Head of a Man

35. FILIPPINO LIPPI: Head of an Elderly Man

36. FILIPPINO LIPPI and RAFFAELLINO DEL GARBO: (*recto*) Page from Vasari, Notebook

(*verso*) Page from Vasari, Notebook

38.   MANTEGNA: Study of Four Saints

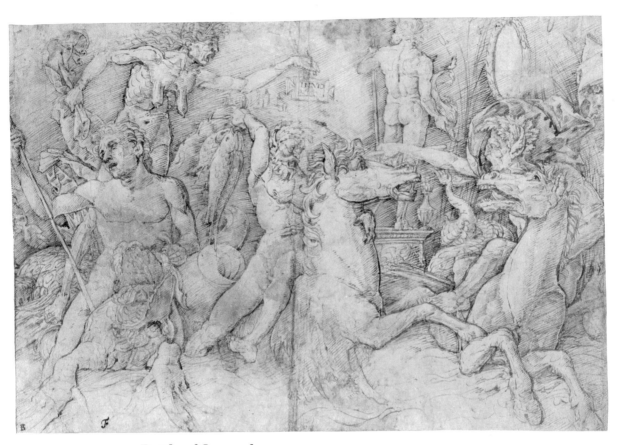

37.   MANTEGNA: Battle of Sea-gods

39. MORETTO: Study for Head of a Woman

40. ORSI: Design for Façade of the Artist's House

43. PARMIGIANINO: Design for Vaulting

41.　PARMIGIANINO:　The Virgin and Child

45. PARMIGIANINO: The Virgin and Child, St. Elizabeth and
St. Joseph

44.   PARMIGIANINO: The Nativity

46.   PARMIGIANINO: Bearded Figure, Sleeping

42.   PARMIGIANINO: The Marriage of the Virgin

47. PERINO: Hunting of the Calydonian Boar

48. PERUZZI: Design for an Altarpiece Frame

49.   PERUZZI: Pan with Nymph and Satyrs

51.   PORDENONE: Death of St. Peter Martyr

50.   PORDENONE: Figure of Time

52.   PORDENONE: The Almighty Supported by Angels

53.   PORTA, called SALVIATI: The Story of the Seven Kings

54.   PRIMATICCIO: Hercules Surprised with Omphale

56.   RAPHAEL: Studies of a Man's Head and Hand

55. RAPHAEL: Three Nude Men in Attitudes of Terror

57.　RAPHAEL:　Woman Reading with a Child

59.   RAPHAEL: Virgin and Child

58.   RAPHAEL: Study for the "Sacrifice at Lystra"

60. RAPHAEL: Study for the "Conversion of St. Paul"

61. ATTRIBUTED TO RAPHAEL: Venus on Clouds

62. ATTRIBUTED TO RAPHAEL: Nude Woman Kneeling

63.   SCHOOL OF RAPHAEL: The Holy Family

Heraclius August. imaginem Virginis gestans Cosdruem profligauit et persis deuictis Regem dedit.

Heraclius Auguse. imaginem Virginis gestans Cosdruem profligauit.

64. GUIDO RENI: Design for Two Half-Lunettes

65.   GUIDO RENI: Study of a Woman's Head

67.   SCHEDONE: Study of a Boy

66.   ROSSO: Draped Female Figure

68.   SEBASTIANO: Reclining Apostle

Ritratto di Leon.e x.°

69.   ATTRIBUTED TO SEBASTIANO: Head of Pope Leo X

73. *Follower of* VERROCCHIO: Design for an Altar

72.   VERONESE: The Martyrdom of St. Justina

71.   ATTRIBUTED TO VERONESE: Christ and the Disciples at Emmaus

75. FEDERIGO ZUCCARO: Portrait of a Man

70. TESTA: Diana as Huntress

74.   FEDERIGO ZUCCARO: Scene of Falconry

76.   TADDEO ZUCCARO: The Adoration of the Shepherds

77.   PIETER BRUEGEL THE ELDER: View of the "Ripa Grande," Rome

85.   VAN DYCK: Head and Forequarters of a Horse

79.   VAN DYCK: Castor and Pollux Carrying off the
Daughters of Leucippus

80.   VAN DYCK: Pieter Bruegel the Younger

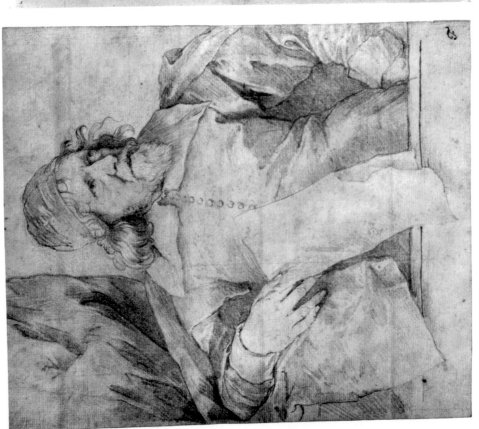

82.   VAN DYCK: Inigo Jones

81.   VAN DYCK: Carolus de Mallery

84. VAN DYCK: Landscape with a House

83. VAN DYCK: Unfinished Landscape

78. VAN DYCK: The Entombment

87.   GOSSAERT, called MABUSE: Adam and Eve

88.　REMBRANDT:　St. Augustine in his Study

89. REMBRANDT: View on the Amstel

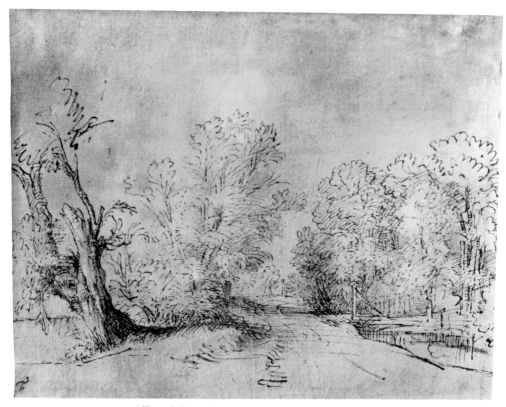

90. REMBRANDT: Road Leading through a Wood

91.   REMBRANDT: View over the River Y

92.   REMBRANDT: View near the Rampoortje, Amsterdam

94. REMBRANDT: A Farmstead by a Stream

96.   REMBRANDT: A Thatched Cottage

95. **REMBRANDT**: The Rijnpoort at Rhenen

97. **REMBRANDT**: A Windmill and a Group of Houses

93. **REMBRANDT:** Farm with a Dovecote and a Hayrick

86. **FLINCK:** View of the Town of Cleves

98.   RUBENS: A Garland of Fruit and Corn

102. RUBENS: Tree Trunk and Brambles

100.   RUBENS: A Man Threshing

99.   RUBENS: Two Franciscan Friars

104.   DÜRER: Women's Public Bath

103. BURGKMAIR: Portrait of a Man

105.   HANS HOLBEIN THE YOUNGER: Profile of a Scholar or Cleric

106. HANS HOLBEIN THE YOUNGER: Head of a Youth

107.   HANS HOLBEIN THE YOUNGER: Six Designs for Medallions
and One Other

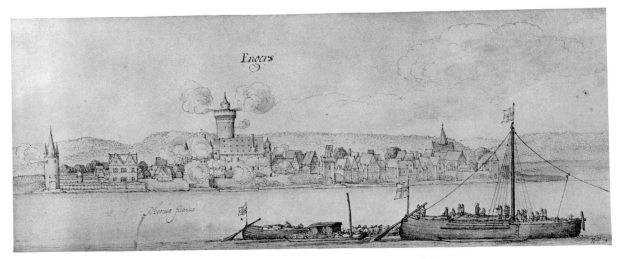

108. HOLLAR: The Rhine, with the Town and Fortress of Engers

109. HOLLAR: View of Frankfurt-am-Main

114.   LELY: A Knight Bowing